Community Services for Retarded Children

Community Services for Retarded Children
The Consumer Provider Relationship

Edited with Introductions by

John J. Dempsey, Dr.P.H.
Consultant on Handicapped Children
United States Department of Health,
Education, and Welfare

University Park Press
Baltimore • London • Tokyo

UNIVERSITY PARK PRESS
International Publishers in Science and Medicine
Chamber of Commerce Building
Baltimore, Maryland 21202

Copyright © 1975 by University Park Press

Typeset by The Composing Room of Michigan, Inc.
Printed in the United States of America by Universal Lithographers, Inc.

Library of Congress Cataloging in Publication Data
Main entry under title:

Community services for retarded children.

  Bibliography: p.
  Includes index.
  1. Mentally handicapped children—United States—Addresses, essays, lectures. 2. Mentally handi-capped children—Family relationships—Addresses, essays, lectures. 3. Social work with mentally handicapped children—United States—Addresses, essays, lectures. I. Dempsey, John J., 1935-
HV894.C57   362.7'8'30973   75-11699
ISBN 0—8391—0812—5

To all my former students,
from whom I have learned so much

Contents

Part III. **Role of the Professions**

Part IV. **Detection and Diagnosis**

Preface

Since World War II there has been a progressive de-emphasis of the need to institutionalize retarded children, so that more and more of them are being reared in their own homes. How well this turns out is principally a function of three factors: the quality of parental care, the quality of community services, and the quality of the relationship between parents and community services, i.e., the consumer–provider relationship. This book focuses mainly on the third factor, the quality of the consumer–provider relationship.

Any chronic condition such as mental retardation implies a long-term relationship between the consumer and the provider. Unfortunately, the full nature of the relationship has not been systematically studied to date; consequently, the service system is somewhat limited in its ability to improve its contribution to the relationship on the basis of findings from systematic inquiry.

This book is intended to serve three purposes. First, it offers a very simple conceptualization of the consumer–provider relationship in regard to chronic conditions among children. Second, and in reference solely to the chronic condition of retarded children and their parents, it provides readings from the literature for selected aspects of the conceptualization. Third, it offers an assessment of the adequacy of the literature for the needs of the conceptualization of the consumer–provider relationship.

It is my hope that this book will be of use to professionals in the field who serve families with retarded children, to policy makers who design service systems, to students who are preparing themselves for a service or research career in mental retardation, and to teachers who train the professional manpower of the future.

John J. Dempsey

Acknowledgments

Special thanks are due those who reviewed an early draft of this work: Michael Begab, Head, Mental Retardation Research Centers, National Institute of Child Health and Human Development; Florence Burnett, Nursing Consultant, Maryland State Health Department; William Hersey, Director of Social Work, The John F. Kennedy Institute; Paul Lemkau, Chairman, Department of Mental Hygiene, The Johns Hopkins School of Hygiene and Public Health; and Ruben Meyer, Chairman, Department of Maternal and Child Health, University of Michigan School of Public Health.

Much of this work is a derivative of research sponsored by the MCHS, Department of Health, Education, and Welfare, over the years, and this support is herewith acknowledged.

Celia Feierstein provided invaluable assistance with parts of the literature search, and the following helped at various times with the typing: Mrs. Iris Shriner, Miss Lucy Smith, Miss Tisha Fleming, and Mrs. Brenda Lawson.

Twelve years of professional and personal contacts with parents of handicapped children have continuously reinforced the need to develop this work.

Many thanks are due my wife, Judy, and my three children, Judy, Kathy and Paul, for tolerating my weekends away from them and my grumpy mood during periods of limited progress.

Credits

Material for this book is reprinted from the following sources by permission of the original publishers.

Chapter 2. "Restoring the Balance" by William J. Hershey, Jr., M.S.W. and Karin R. Lapidus, M.S.W. *Pediatric Clinics of North America,* 20 (February): 221–231, 1973. (W. B. Saunders Co., Philadelphia)

Chapter 3. "Legal Implications of Parental Prerogatives for Special Class Placements of the Mentally Retarded" by Joseph Rodriquez and Thomas P. Lombardi. *Mental Retardation,* 11(October): 29–31, 1973.

Chapter 4. "The Two Camps in Child Psychiatry: A Report from a Psychiatrist-Father of an Autistic and Retarded Child" by John Kysar. *American Journal of Psychiatry,* 1968, Vol. 125, pp. 103–109. Copyright 1968, The American Psychiatric Association.

Chapter 6. "Unmet Needs of the Mentally Retarded in the Community" by Michael J. Begab. *American Journal of Mental Deficiency,* 62 (January): 712–723, 1958.

Chapter 7. "Parents' Feelings About Retarded Children" by Leo Kanner. *American Journal of Mental Deficiency,* 75(May): 685–691, 1971.

Chapter 8. "Modeling and Shaping by Parents to Develop Chewing Behavior in Their Retarded Child" by William H. Butterfield. *Journal of Behavior Therapy and Experimental Psychiatry,* 4(September): 285–287, 1973.

Chapter 9. "Health Insurance: A Dilemma for Parents of the Mentally Retarded" by Frank Warner, Thomas Golden, and Maureen Henteleff. Reprinted from *Exceptional Children,* Vol. 39, September 1972, pp. 57–58 by permission of The Council for Exceptional Children. Copyright 1972 by The Council for Exceptional Children.

Chapter 10. "Foster Family Care for the Retarded: Management Concerns of the Caretaker" by Robert S. Justice, Janice Bradley, and Gail O'Connor. *Mental Retardation,* 9(August): 12–15, 1971.

Chapter 11. "Home Care of Severely Retarded Children" by K. S. Holt. *Pediatrics,* 22(October): 744–755, 1958.

Chapter 12. "Parents of the Mentally Retarded Child: Emotionally Overwhelmed or Informationally Deprived?" by Adam P. Matheny and Joel Vernick. Reproduced with permission from the *Journal of Pediatrics* 74: 953–959, 1968. Copyrighted by the C. V. Mosby Company, St. Louis, Missouri.

Chapter 13. "Shopping Parents: Patient Problem or Professional Problem?" by William C. Keirn. *Mental Retardation,* 9:(August): 6–7, 1971.

Chapter 15. "Clinical Management of the Mentally Retarded Child and the Parents" by Reynold A. Jensen. *American Journal of Psychiatry,* 1950, Vol. 106, pp. 830–833. Copyright 1950, The American Psychiatric Association.

Chapter 16. "Role of Physician in Maintaining Continuity of Care and Guidance" by Robert W. Deisher. Reproduced with permission from *Journal of Pediatrics* 50: 231–235, 1957. Copyrighted by the C. V. Mosby Company, St. Louis, Missouri.

Chapter 17. "Interpreting Mental Retardation to Parents" by Harriet L. Rheingold. *Journal of Consulting Psychiatry,* 9(May): 142–148, 1945.

Chapter 18. "Counseling with Parents of Retarded Children Living at Home" by Sylvia Schild. Reprinted with permission of the National Association of Social Workers, from *Social Work,* Vol. 9, No. 1 (January 1964), pp. 86–91.

Chapter 19. "Nursing's Concern for the Mentally Retarded is Overdue" by Mary Anne Noble. *Nursing Forum,* 9(2): 192–201, 1970.

Chapter 20. "The Teacher Works with the Parent of the Exceptional Child" by Frances A. Mullen. *Education,* 80(February): 329–332, 1970.

Chapter 21. "The Ministry and Mental Retardation" by Harold W. Stubblefield. Reproduced with permission from *Journal of Health and Religion,* 3(2): 136–147, 1964. Institutes of Religion and Health, New York, New York 10001.

Chapter 23. "Selected Aspects in the Development of the Mother's Understanding of Her Mentally Retarded Child" by Leonard Rosen. *American Journal of Mental Deficiency,* 59(January): 522–528, 1955.

Chapter 24. "A First Survey of the Effects of a Subnormal Child on the Family Unit" by Fred J. Schonell and B. H. Watts. *American Journal of Mental Deficiency,* 61(July): 210–219, 1956.

Chapter 25. "Early Identification of Mildly Retarded Children" by Sonya Oppenheimer. *American Journal of Orthopsychiatry,* 35(October): 845–851, 1965.

Chapter 26. "Parents' Estimates of the Intelligence of Retarded Children" by Jerome L. Schulman and Sheila Stern. *American Journal of Mental Deficiency,* 63(January): 696–698, 1959.

Chapter 27. "Recoil from the Diagnosis of Mental Retardation" by Barbara Keogh and Camille Legeay. Copyright, The American Journal of Nursing Company. Reproduced with permission from *The American Journal of Nursing,* April 1966, pp. 778–780.

Chapter 28. "Parents of the Mentally Retarded: An Operational Approach to Diagnosis and Management" by Frank J. Menolascino. *Journal of the American Academy of Child Psychiatry,* 7(October): 589–602, 1968. Copyright, the American Academy of Child Psychiatry.

Chapter 29. "Embarrassment in the Diagnostic Process" by Wolf Wolfensberger. *Mental Retardation,* 3(June): 29–31, 1965.

Chapter 31. "Counseling with Parents of Mentally Retarded Children" by Helen L. Beck. *Children,* 6(November–December): 225–230, 1959.

Chapter 32. "Group Therapy with Parents of Mentally Deficient Children" by James C. Coleman. *American Journal of Mental Deficiency,* 57 (April): 700–704, 1953.

Chapter 33. "Parent Education in Managing Retarded Children with Behavior Deficits and Inappropriate Behaviors" by Leif Terdal and Joan Buell. *Mental Retardation,* 7(June): 10–13, 1969.

Chapter 34. "Homemaker Services to Families with Young Retarded Children" by Irene Arnold and Lawrence Goodman. *Children,* 13(July–August): 149–152, 1966.

Chapter 35. "A State Program of Day Care Centers for Severely Retarded" by Charles P. Jubenville. *American Journal of Mental Deficiency,* 66(May): 829–837, 1962.

Chapter 36. "The Family of the Child in an Institution" by Laura L. Dittmann. *American Journal of Mental Deficiency,* 66(March): 759–765, 1962.

Chapter 37. "Foster Family Services for Mentally Retarded Children" by Beatrice L. Garrett. *Children,* 17(November–December): 228–233, 1970.

Chapter 38. "A Comprehensive Care Program for Children with Handicaps" by John E. Allen and Louis Lelchuck. *American Journal of Diseases of Children,* 111(March): 229–235, 1966.

Chapter 39. "Generic Services for the Mentally Retarded and Their Families" by R. C. Scheerenberger. *Mental Retardation,* 8(December): 10–16, 1970.

Chapter 41. "Some Approaches and Problems in the Study of the Use of Services – An Overview" by John B. McKinlay. *Journal of Health and Social Behavior,* 13(June): 115–152, 1972.

Introduction

This is really two books in one. It is, of course, a book of readings dealing with parents of retarded children. But it is also a discourse on how to conceptualize the division of labor between parents and professionals for the care of handicapped children. The book originates from my efforts to develop a mode of conceptualizing service systems for handicapped children. No existing mode seems adequate for the changing times in which program evaluation and accountability are dominating much of professional thought. The process of developing and testing a new mode led to a serendipitous encounter with the literature on parents of retarded children, and the book is the by-product of this encounter.

CONCEPTUALIZATION

At its simplest level, the conceptualization of the service system for handicapped children consists of eight concepts. The first is *time.* By definition, handicapping conditions have an element of duration to them, so that the consumer (the handicapped child and his parents) and the provider (all relevant elements of the service system) are in contact over a period of time.

The next four concepts are concerned with the four types of encounters consumers have with the service system over time: *detection, diagnosis, treatment,* and *surveillance.* Detection refers to the initial recognition that "something appears to be wrong." Diagnosis refers to the full examination of the child which yields a judgment as to whether the child is or is not retarded. Treatment, for instance for a child with a club foot, consists of surgery, various services to reduce the extent of residual disability, counseling the parents on child care, etc. Surveillance is "keeping in touch" to ensure that things are progressing according to plan. Each of these four concepts is discussed in more detail in various sections to follow.

The last three concepts refer to the divisions of labor during the four encounters described above. First, there is a *multidisciplinary division of labor.* No handicap comes to mind which demands professional services which all lie within the purview of one profession. Second, there is an *interorganizational division of labor.* A teacher who suspects that a child has hearing loss may refer the child to a hospital for diagnosis; this interorganizational division of labor between school and hospital is also the link between detection and diagnosis.

The final concept is the *division of labor between parents and professionals* to carry out the detection, diagnosis, treatment, and surveillance. This book emphasizes that division of labor.

Such an eight-concept model is quite simple and straightforward, but it will become apparent in sections to follow that each of the concepts breaks down into more and more detailed components, so that it may become as complex as one cares to make it. At its simplest eight-concept level, however, it is a very clear mode of conceptualizing the service system for handicapped children.

(The focus of the model is confined here to the clinical interface between the consumer and provider. The roles of higher levels of administration and government relative to the interface are not germane to the sections to follow and are not considered in the model in this book.)

CONCEPTUALIZATION LIMITED TO PARENTS OF RETARDED CHILDREN

For handicapping conditions such as cleft lips and palates, there simply is too meager a literature on parents to warrant a book such as this. For other handicapping conditions there is an enormous literature, and none is larger than the literature on parents and families of retarded children. Since the mode of conceptualization discussed above requires much information, it was decided to tap this largest of literatures.

There is one liability to the use of the literature on parents of retarded children: it really is two literatures. First, there is the literature which resembles that dealing with parents of children with physical handicaps such as blindness, orthopedic problems, and diabetes. The focus of such literature is on the problems parents face in *rearing* the children. Second, there is the literature which resembles that dealing with parents of emotionally disturbed children. The focus is on the ways parents *contribute* to the development of the handicaps. Clearly, the nature of the mode of conceptualizing the service system described above is focused more on the first than on the second literature. Consequently, the readings that follow are oriented to child care problems rather than to the role of parents in the etiology of mental retardation.

It is not entirely possible to separate the two literatures. They both originate from an earlier literature which stressed the familial nature of retardation. The study of the Kallikak family (Goddard, 1912) described not only several generations of retardates but also the concomitant squalor, criminality, prostitution, and assorted character problems. Added to such an orientation is the documentation on many "retarded" children who were ultimately found to be really emotionally disturbed as a consequence of destructive parental upbringing. We also have a literature on deprivation in which reduced intellectual functioning of children is seen as a partial result of environmental deprivation, most importantly, deprivation of parental stimulation.

Such a variety of orientations makes it difficult to separate the two literatures. Diagnostic personnel must be especially alert to the possibility of parental contribution to subnormal mental functioning, and papers which emanate from service programs frequently refelct this awareness. For about twenty years, however, various authors have tended to champion the parents, since many parents have not contributed to their children's retardation and need more than a probing, investigative attitude from the service system. (This attitude is apparent in many of the selected readings, and is found to a lesser degree in parts of my narrative.)

With all this in mind, the book focuses on those parents who have not contributed to the retardation of their children any more than parents contribute to club feet, cleft lips, or diabetes. Such an organic orientation is not intended to denigrate the importance of parental contributions to functional subnormality, but is designed to stay within the confines of the conceptualization described above. A more obvious limitation of the book is its focus on retarded children cared for at home. This excludes from formal consideration the large numbers of children who are cared for in institutions.

Furthermore, the book has been prepared more for professionals than for parents. Consequently, the stress is on the division of labor between parents and professionals in the service system, *from the point of view of the professionals.* It would seem somewhat obvious that professionals should submit to systematic inquiry the relationship they collectively form with parents so that the relationship may be progressively improved.

The last limitation is the book's focus on the parent as a consumer for the child; this is out of tune with much of the recent literature on consumer involvement which generally implies that the consumer is a representative of his fellow consumers, that he sits on advisory committees or is even employed by the service system in a position such as "out-reach worker."

NOMENCLATURE

Reflecting the lack of precise terminology in the literature, that used in this book is also somewhat imprecise. On the one hand "professionals" and the "service system" are terms which are used interchangeably, although they clearly have different meanings. On the other hand, "parents" and "consumers" are also used interchangeably. This requires a comment. Unlike children with other handicaps, retarded children—especially severely retarded children—will always be dependent upon their parents for the consumption of professional services. Therefore, the term "consumer" has two meanings; it refers to the parent who consumes something like counseling on his own behalf, and it refers to the parent who is the necessary agent for the retarded child or adult to consume services. It is hoped that variations in the meaning of parent–professional, parent–service system, or consumer–provider relationship are clear from the context in which the terms are used.

Furthermore, the terms used to describe the child's condition are used somewhat in the popular sense. Various groups at various times have urged a standard vocabulary for more precise communication. For instance, the World Health Organization attempted to gain acceptance for standard terms such as mental subnormality, mental deficiency, and mental retardation. Mental subnormality was intended to describe the general condition with mental deficiency referring to biologically determined cases and mental retardation to socially determined cases. However, such distinctions have not been made consistently in the literature and will not be made in the text to follow.

In summary, then, the book focuses on parents of "organically" retarded children who care for their children at home, and stresses the division of labor they form with the service system for child care.

SOURCE MATERIALS

The major source of material for this book is the professional journal. More than 700 articles were examined. When the hundreds of articles were separated by subject, it was found that the earliest works on a subject tended to give the best overviews of it and that the most recent works tended to reflect the best research. The selected readings, therefore, span several decades for most subjects. The inclusion of "old" articles to ensure a complete picture may be one of the most important contributions of the book. An analysis of the references in current articles reveals that most authors do not cite many works more than seven or eight years old. Consequently, some of the finest treatises on subjects are in danger of being lost merely because of their dates of publication.

ORGANIZATION OF THE BOOK

The book is divided into several Parts. The introductions to the Parts amplify the mode of conceptualization to which a Part is devoted, and they also introduce the readings which have been selected for the Part.

The readings should obviously provide the detail for each Part, but do so with less than perfect efficiency. None of the authors set out to write an article according to the conceptualization I have in mind. Consequently, each article touches on many subjects beyond the purview of the Part within which it appears. In a few articles, when the "relevant" material comprises less than half of the article, only the relevant material is printed in excerpt form; but most of the articles are presented in their entirety and thus may contain some material that does not fit the conceptualization. (Since the reader's main interest will be in what the authors themselves have to say, most lists of references have not been reprinted. However, statements of the number of references in the original articles have been included.)

Although this requires the reader to concentrate more on the relevant aspects of each article, it does have a redeeming feature. The nonrelevant components of the articles in the early sections tend to prepare the reader for the subjects of the later sections; and the nonrelevant components of the articles in the later sections tend to review the topics considered in the earlier sections and to integrate the subjects of all the Parts. Also, those who read only one Part of the book will gain a larger perspective from the "irrelevant" components of the readings.

Part I considers the extent of the subject, and Part II explores the definition of the problem. That is, what is it about having a retarded child that warrants consumption of professional services in the first place? Part III covers professional roles; various professionals discuss their perceptions of problems in families with retarded children in terms of what their professions can appropriately respond to. The next three Parts are devoted to the concepts of detection, diagnosis, treatment, and surveillance. The final Part gives the author's conclusions and offers guidelines for additional reading.

Community Services for Retarded Children

Part I

THE DIMENSIONS OF THE SUBJECT

1 Introduction to Part I

It is unfortunate but true that the consumer-provider relationship has received little formal consideration in the mental retardation literature. In more than 400 articles, the relationship is always implied, generally in the context of a specific profession or service activity, but rarely discussed as a subject unto itself. To provide an introduction to the general topic of the consumer-provider relationship, three articles are presented in Part I.

First, there is an excerpt from a 1973 article by Hersey and Lapidus which provides one of the few formal statements about the relationship to be found in the literature. The authors focus on the parent-pediatrician relationship by considering it to be essentially contractual in nature; the two parties explicitly assume a mutually agreed set of complementary roles. Such an orientation may be generalized regarding all consumer-provider divisions of labor.

Second, there is an article by Rodriquez and Lombardi (1973) on legal implications of parental prerogatives for special class placements of mentally retarded children. In recent years consumers generally have take to the courts and legislatures for redress of grievances about their relationships with providers, and this is true of the field of mental retardation as well. The extent to which this has led to formalized relationships is reflected in the Rodriquez and Lombardi article which reports findings from a national survey on the degree to which parents are or must be involved in the decision to place a child in a special class.

The third article is by Kysar (1968), and the reason for its selection requires some background information. Naturally everyone is interested in the parents' view of the relationship betweeen consumer and provider, and articles by parents occur by the dozens in the professional and the lay literature. A careful reading of these articles and of those by the professionals yields an interesting finding: the two sets of readings are mirror images of each other. The professionals suggest what the parents are concerned about, what their problems are, and what services they want. The parents' literature, sure enough, conforms to the predictions (expectations?), even using the same language as the professionals. Editorial policies and procedures may well operate in a selective way and make professionals' predictions self-fulfilling prophecies.

A serious consequence of this editorial selection is a dearth of useful works by parents. Kysar's is one of the few exceptions. A psychiatrist and the father of an autistic and retarded child, he encountered considerable difficulty in his relationship with the service system. Unlike most parents, however, he was a member of one of the professions that serves families with retarded children and was able to publish this article in one of his profession's own journals.

It is not the intention of this book to dwell solely on problems in the consumer-provider relationship. Problems do identify critical dimensions of the relationship, and the Kysar article suggests several such dimensions. The following principle should be kept in mind while reading this article: to the extent that elements of the service system operate in harmony, they also provide positive benefits. Put another way, the quality of the interorganizational and/or interdisciplinary division of labor determines whether the service system does more harm than good.

The three articles above serve only to introduce some of the general dimensions of the consumer-provider relationship. Specific dimensions will be considered in sections to follow, and a general integration of dimensions will be attempted in Part VII.

2 Restoring the Balance

*William J. Hersey, Jr.,
and Karin R. Lapidus*

The birth of a retarded child, or child with a developmental handicap, threatens and disturbs the existing balance in the family to which he is born. . . . Professionals outside the field of pediatric medicine and obstetrics—teachers, social workers, nurses, and other doctors—frequently criticize the pediatrician. He is blamed for not setting the stage from the beginning for a proper resolution of this problem within the family. After all, it is he who has the first opportunity to deal with the child and the disbelieving, shocked parents. In the following years, when counsellors have an opportunity to let parents ventilate what their first diagnostic counselling session entailed, it is easy to see why the parents are still bewildered and floundering. . . .

Within hours after the birth of a child, or more frequently beforehand, a pediatrician has been selected by the family and a contract for care has been initiated. The use of the word "contract" at this point is important. Perhaps most families and physicians do not consider the contractual aspects of the beginning relationship. "It is not like building a house or having the lawn resodded"; as a matter of fact, the situation is one in which an implied contract is set up. Some spelling out of expectations between family and pediatrician can only lead to better relationships between the two. For example, if the pediatrician makes it clear that he is not available at a particular time, that an alternate has agreed to take his place, and the family has a chance to agree to this arrangement, then his absence will be less problematic in such a situation.

The selection of a pediatrician, the agreements, and resultant relationship between the family and the pediatrician are eased if there have been previous contracts for care of other children in the family. When the new patient is a handicapped child, however, it might be wise for both the pediatrician and the parents to review past relationships and renegotiate agreements.

The phrase "assumption of responsibility for care" has been used. The pediatrician must consider the medical as well as other needs of the child in determining whether he is willing to assume the responsibility for care of this newborn handicapped child. Certainly he can discuss his willingness to be in the hospital long nights caring for a child with pneumonia or other routine pediatric management cases. But how does he feel about assuming years of responsibility for crises for which no cure is available? It is recommended that the pediatrician consider whether the present demands of his practice will allow him to handle this new case, and whether he is personally willing to endure its additional demands.

During a period of assessment, the pediatrician takes a supportive role in helping the parents become aware of the contract and the part they will play. Without frightening the parents, he promotes a candid discussion of both sides of the contract as well as other alternatives. This discussion is factual, relevant, and anticipatory; it is also timely and educative, frank and supportive. As a leader, he can help the parents conceptualize their side of the contract and formulate questions and fears. Counsellors frequently hear that the pediatrician did not tell parents the facts. It would seem that if he frankly admitted a lack of knowledge and candidly spoke of withholding information until parents were ready to hear such information, or until time had proven facts, such complaints would not be heard.

Together, parents and pediatrician discuss alternatives, such as referral to a pediatric specialist in the developmental disabilities, or to an established team of professionals dealing with handicapped children. Such a discussion leads to free choice by both parents and pediatrician, and to a firm sense of what each can expect from the other.

3 Legal Implications of Parental Prerogatives for Special Class Placements of the Mentally Retarded

Joseph Rodriquez and
Thomas P. Lombardi

Recently the legality and advantages of special class placement have been under attack by the courts and prominent educators. An example is the court case of Diana vs. State Board of Education (1970) in Northern California. Nine Mexican-American public school students charged that they were improperly placed in classes for the mentally retarded on the basis of tests which discriminated against them. Each of the students came from homes in which Spanish was the predominant or only spoken language. They were placed in classes for the mentally retarded on the basis of I.Q. scores derived from Stanford-Binet and Wechsler intelligence tests. The plaintiffs argued that the tests relied basically on verbal aptitude in English and were standardized on white, native Americans. They contended then, that the tests related, in subject matter, to the white, middle class culture and discriminated against the Mexican-American.

The case was settled in February 1970 by a stipulated agreement which set forth the following practices to be observed in the future:

1. All children whose primary home language is other than English must be tested in both their primary language and English.

2. Such children must be tested only with tests or sections of tests that do not depend on such things as vocabulary, general information, and other similar unfair verbal questions.

3. Mexican-American and Chinese-American children already in classes for the mentally retarded must be retarded in their primary language and must be reevaluated only as to their achievement on nonverbal tests or sections of tests.

4. Each school district is to submit to the state in time for the next school year a summary of retesting and re-evaluation and a plan listing special supplemental individual training which will be provided to help each child back into the regular school class.

5. State psychologists are to work on norms for a new or revised I.Q. test to reflect the abilities of Mexican-Americans so that in the future Mexican-American children will be judged only by how they compare to the performance of their peers, not the population as a whole.

6. Any school district which has a significant disparity between the percentage of Mexican-American students in its regular classes and in its classes for the retarded must submit an explanation setting out the reasons for this disparity.

7

The classic controversy concerning the validity of inclusion or exclusion of trainable mentally retarded children in public school programs can finally be considered moot. A recent complaint, filed in the United States District Court for the Eastern District of Pennsylvania, asked for "preliminary and permanent injunctive relief and declaratory judgment to prevent the denial to plaintiff retarded children, aged six to 21 years, of their equal right to education" (Complaint, Civil Action No. 71–42, p. 1). This court action was filed by the Pennsylvania Association for Retarded Children and the parents of the 13 retarded children excluded from public school, against the Commonwealth of Pennsylvania, David H. Kurtzman, Secretary of Education for Pennsylvania et al.

The Pennsylvania Association for Retarded Children is challenging certain sections of the Pennsylvania Public School Code which:

1. Establish standards for temporary or permanent exclusion from the public schools of children who are found to be uneducable and untrainable in the public schools (Pa. Public School Code, 24 Purd. Stat., Sec. 13–1375).
2. Give the board of school directors the right to refuse to accept or retain beginners who have not attained a mental age of five years (Pa. Public School Code, 25 Purd. Stat., Sec. 13–1304).
3. Provide exemptions regarding the compulsory attendance laws to any child who has been examined by an approved mental clinic or school psychologist and found unable to profit from further public school attendance (Complaint, Civil Action No. 71–42).

4. Violate the equal protection guaranteed under the Fourteenth Amendment to the United States Constitution (Complaint, Civil Action No. 71–42).

On June 18, 1971, Judges T. A. Masterson, R. J. Broderick, and A. M. Adams of the U.S. District Court for the Eastern District of Pennsylvania ruled on the P.A.R.C. v. Commonwealth of Pennsylvania case. As a result of this decision, due process hearings are mandatory, upon request of the parent or guardian, for any child 5 years, 6 months through 21 years, who is mentally retarded or suspected of being mentally retarded prior to a change in "educational status" as described in the stipulation. Stipulation means postponement, exclusion, placed on a waiting list, excused, shifted from regular class to special class, etc., and also those who have never had an educational assignment (Order, Civil Action No. 71–42).

Under this court order the parents also have the right to inspect the child's school records before the hearing, cross-examine school officials, and are entitled to the services of a local center for an independent medical, psychological, and educational evaluation of the child. The independent evaluation may be used as evidence at the hearing.

This growing activity, by parents and other interested parties, in the legality of inclusion and exclusion of pupils into special education classes, along with the increased questioning of the worth of special class placement, supported a search for legal implications of special class placements as they pertain to parental prerogatives. A review of the research regarding parents of exceptional children offered no information on this legal matter. A written inquiry to the Bureau of Education for the Handicapped, Health, Education and Welfare Department had similar results. On August 4, 1971, the Director of the Division of Training Programs for the Bureau of Education for the Handicapped suggested a survey for this information be conducted by the authors.

SURVEY PROCEDURE AND RESULTS

A questionnaire was developed and sent to the State Department of Education in each of the 50 states. It contained five statements which require a "yes" or "no" answer and one question which invited comment, under certain circumstances. The statements were:

1. Parental permission is required to legally place pupils in special class.

2. Parents may assume the responsibility of providing their children's education as an alternative to special class placement. Example: private school, home tutoring, etc.

3. Parental permission is not required; however, children are not placed if the parent objects to the placement.

4. Parental permission is required; however, a child may be placed without permission, under certain circumstances.

5. If the answer to question four was "yes," briefly explain the circumstances necessary.

6. Children may be excluded from school by the Boards of Education upon the recommendation of a school

Table 1

	Yes	No	N/A*
Parental permission is required to legally place pupils in special class.	8 16.32%	37 75.48%	4 8.16%
Parents may assume the responsibility of providing their children's education as an alternative to special class placement.	41 83.64%	4 8.16%	4 8.16%
Parental permission is not required; however, children are not placed if the parent objects to the placement.	28 57.12%	12 24.48%	9 18.36%
Parental permission is required; however, a child may be placed without permission, under certain circumstances.	7 14.28%	35 71.40%	7 14.28%
Children may be excluded from school by the Boards of Education upon the recommendation of a school psychologist or other personnel certified to conduct individual psychological tests, in your state.	26 53.04%	18 36.72%	5 10.20%

*N/A indicates no state law pertaining to the statement or no response to the statement.

Table 2. Responses to Questionnaire Listed by State

Question	1	2	3	4	6
Alabama	NO	YES	YES	NO	NO
Alaska	NO	YES	YES	YES	NO
Arizona	YES	YES	N/R	NO	YES
Arkansas	NO	YES	YES	NO	YES
California	NO	YES	YES	NO	YES
Colorado	NO	YES	YES	NO	YES
Delaware	YES	YES	N/R	NO	N/R
Florida	NO	YES	NO	YES	NO
Georgia	NO	YES	YES	NO	NO
Hawaii	NAL	NAL	NAL	NAL	NAL
Idaho	NO	YES	YES	NO	YES
Illinois	NO	YES	NO	NO	NO
Indiana	NO	YES	YES	NO	YES
Iowa	NO	YES	NO	NO	NO
Kansas	NO	YES	YES	N/R	YES
Kentucky	L/P	L/P	L/P	L/P	L/P
Louisiana	YES	NO	NO	NO	NO
Maine	N/R	N/R	N/R	YES	YES
Maryland	NO	YES	YES	NO	YES
Massachusetts	NO	NO	NO	N/A	NO
Michigan	NO	YES	YES	NO	YES
Minnesota	NO	YES	YES	NO	NO
Mississippi	NO	YES	YES	NO	NO
Missouri	NO	YES	NO	NO	YES
Montana	NO	YES	NO	NO	YES
Nebraska	NO	YES	YES	NO	NO
Nevada	NO	YES	YES	NO	YES
New Hampshire	YES	YES	NO	YES	YES
New Jersey	NO	YES	L/P	N/R	NO
New Mexico	NO	YES	YES	NO	NO
New York	NO	YES	NO	NO	YES
North Carolina	NO	YES	NO	NO	YES
North Dakota	NO	YES	YES	NO	NO
Ohio	NO	NO	YES	YES	YES
Oklahoma	NO	YES	YES	NO	NO
Oregon	YES	YES	NO	NO	YES
Pennsylvania	NO	YES	YES	NO	NO
Rhode Island	YES	NO	N/A	NO	NO
South Carolina	NO	YES	YES	YES	YES
South Dakota	NO	YES	YES	NO	YES
Tennessee	NO	YES	YES	NO	NO
Texas	L/P	L/P	L/P	L/P	L/P
Utah	NO	YES	YES	NO	YES
Vermont	NO	YES	YES	NO	NO
Virginia	YES	YES	N/A	NO	YES
Washington	YES	YES	NO	NO	YES
West Virginia	NO	YES	L/P	NO	YES
Wisconsin	NO	YES	YES	N/A	YES
Wyoming	NO	YES	NO	NO	YES

L/P—Local Prerogative   N/R—No Response
N/A—Not Applicable   NAL—No Applicable Law

psychologist or other personnel certified in conducting individual psychological tests, in your state.

Forty-nine or 98% of the questionnaires were returned. Table 1 shows the combined responses of all the states and Table 2 shows the individual responses of each state.

REFERENCES

[Nineteen references not reprinted.]

4 The Two Camps in Child Psychiatry: A Report from a Psychiatrist-Father of an Autistic and Retarded Child

John E. Kysar

It probably has rarely happened (particularly in psychiatry) that a physician would report on the diagnosis or therapy of a member of his own family. For obvious reasons, such as lack of objectivity, this should be avoided. However, it is a longstanding tradition in the medical profession that physicians should report to their colleagues on cases which may advance some aspect of medical theory or practice.

Because it is unlikely that the experiences recounted in this paper would otherwise be reported in similar perspective, it seemed justified to break with the customary reticence about therapy in one's own family. It is the author's opinion, verified in numerous discussions with mental health professionals and with parents, that the observations included here are not unique. Apparently such sequences are commonplace because there are two camps in child psychiatry.

Inevitably, this paper will be discounted by some as the biased account of an angry father. The latter adjective is entirely accurate, but this does not reduce the need to examine the events which are described. Even if the reader makes allowances for some bias on the part of the writer, the implications should be clear enough.

TOM: EARLY DEVELOPMENT

Tom, our diagnostic-problem child, is the second of three sons. The gestation and childbirth were unremarkable except for some questionably significant troubles in the last trimester and at delivery. The first two years of his development seemed normal, although in retrospect we can recall some signs of lack of affective response and relatedness. His feeding, walking, and general motor activity were within the normal range. Like most parents of such children, for some time we minimized and denied the seriousness of the deviations.

Between the second and third years the difficulties became evident. Toilet training was slow but was largely accomplished, except for nighttime bed-wetting, by age three. Language development at first seemed only moderately delayed. By two and one-half years of age, Tom could easily recite nursery rhymes, sing songs, and use a fairly wide vocabulary of single words and short phrases. However, his development in many areas did not progress; in particular, his use of language remained static at the two-and-one-half- to three-year-old level. His ability to play with and relate to other children was limited not only by his language deficiency but also by his generally low capacity for learning the patterns of play.

Most disturbing of all were the gradually more prominent remoteness and aloneness in Tom. His inattentiveness to verbal and other stimuli and his self-isolation and self-absorption became marked between three and four years of age. He played obsessively and repetitively with a few favorite toys while ignoring all others; certain compulsions (e.g., to turn light switches on and off endlessly) also developed. His hyperactivity, aimless running about, and inability to sit still even for meals became very disruptive to the household. He insisted on sameness in the environment, and there were catastrophic reactions when he was frustrated. His distractibility, poor eye contact, and short attention span, in addition to other factors, made it an arduous task to attempt to get Tom to learn or share anything. Meanwhile, although the number of words in his vocabulary slowly expanded, Tom rarely spoke more than a word or two for any communicative purpose. These were simple requests for food, toys, or activities (e.g., "ride bike"). He did not employ pronouns at all, and the names or designations for people generally eluded him. Frequently he showed the signs of difficulty in word-finding that are characteristic of expressive aphasia. Echolalia was also present.

INITIAL DIAGNOSIS

Early in his fourth year Tom was evaluated in a clinic headed by a child psychiatrist of excellent reputation. After he was carefully examined by members of the several disciplines and interviews with my wife and myself took place, a diagnosis of brain damage with retardation and autism was made. It was not possible to specify the exact cause, location, or extent of the brain damage. Several "soft" neurological signs were present (e.g., absence of handedness, general muscular atonia, poorly coordinated fine movements, an aphasic quality to the language impairment, toe walking, foot drop, etc.). The autistic withdrawal was believed to be due in part to parental expectations and pressures too high for Tom's very limited capacities, but the major part was ascribed to the direct effects of the brain damage. The developments over the next two years, as Tom's self-isolation continued in spite of reduced parental demands, tended to confirm the hypothesis that the organic impairment and marked retardation were the basic causes of his autistic barrier.

From Tom's fourth to sixth year, constant efforts were made by my wife and myself to provide the best possible therapeutic milieu for him in our home. Countless hours were devoted to giving him personal attention, trying with specially adapted techniques to help him to learn and develop (but with minimal pressure and with expectations adjusted to his limited capacities). There were reevaluations at the clinic with counseling about our management of the many problems associated with the rearing of such a difficult child. Suitable nursery schools and day camps were found to give Tom socializing experiences and relationships outside the family. Several medications were given a trial, but with little beneficial result. Play therapy was considered, but it was decided that this would not be significantly helpful at this stage. Residential treatment also was not recommended. In short, everything was done that could be done.

All this produced very little change, i.e., Tom's development was relatively static. There was a slow reduction in some of the compulsions. Gross motor activity continued to develop, but capacity for skilled, purposeful movements remained very limited. Speech and communication remained at about the three-year level. Hyperactivity, self-isolation, and all the other characteristics enumerated continued—with some variations, but essentially unchanged.

Earlier it had been impossible to predict accurately what level of functioning, intellectual and otherwise, could be anticipated. By his sixth year it was apparent that Tom was operating at a retarded level with an IQ of not more than 50. Up to this time, life had been stressful in the family with the daily strain of coping with this very disturbed and retarded child. But at least the situation was managed fairly realistically. The autism and the other emotional and behavioral abnormalities were regarded as derivatives of the brain damage which might improve a little with a favorable family, social, and educational milieu.

NEW DIAGNOSIS

Near his sixth birthday, in order to secure appropriate placement for schooling the following year, we had Tom evaluated by the special educa-tion center of the local public school district. The special education team arrived at a different conception of the problem and launched us into a series of events which were ultimately so destructive that they prompted the writing of this report. After one testing session with the psychologist and only one play-interview with Tom by the consultant in child psychiatry, they came forth with a diagnosis of childhood schizophrenia (by this they meant a completely functional illness with no organic component). This diagnosis was made after minimal history-taking and with no real effort to know and understand Tom's parents. The clinical signs of brain damage syndrome, the neurological findings, and the retardation were brushed aside as equivocal and of no real significance. The previous diagnosis was ignored.

At the same time the special education team told us of this new diagnosis of schizophrenia, they offered to place Tom in a special class for emotionally disturbed children. Although I disagreed with the diagnosis and said so, I did not immediately make an issue of it. We badly needed a school placement for Tom and it seemed at the time that the diagnosis would make relatively little difference in the kind of educational program prescribed, so I decided not to dispute the label.

TRANSFERENCE AND THE "OMNISCIENT" THERAPIST

Within a few weeks, however, it became clear that the diagnosis could not be treated so lightly. As part of the special education program, my wife was to see the psychiatric social worker. She willingly entered into a detailed exploration of Tom's development and the entire family history. Through her comments and her repeated reviewing of the family movies and events in Tom's early years, I realized that the interviews with the social worker were proceeding headlong on the basis of the following premises: Tom was diagnosed as schizophrenic with an entirely functional, reversible disorder without any organic basis and with no permanent retardation. Therefore this disorder was environmentally induced, and the causes were to be found in the family. My wife was propelled by her own irrational, unjustified guilt about Tom's autistic withdrawal and by the social worker's attitude (backed by the consulting child psychiatrist) to search out "the sickness" in herself and in our family.

Sensing the dangers in this and the vulnerability of my wife to suggestions along these lines, I tried to intervene. Discussions with my wife about the issue at this time proved futile because she had seized upon the illusory hope that at last someone had the remedy for Tom's behavior. Her transference to the social worker and the consulting child psychiatrist as potential saviors of her sick child was very intense. She had never been able to completely accept the initial diagnosis of extensive brain damage and mental deficiency. The feeling of helplessness and the rather gloomy prognosis had been intolerable to her. Now her denial of the organic impairment was reinforced, and the schism between her attitude and my own toward Tom's disturbed behavior was magnified.

Therefore I took Tom for another

evaluation by a prominent neurologist who was experienced with this type of problem. He unequivocally confirmed the previous diagnosis of brain damage. One might think that this should have been sufficient to make the consulting psychiatrist reconsider his diagnosis of Tom as schizophrenic (with his definition of schizophrenia as nonorganic in origin). Instead, I was regarded as "defensive" and "neurotically competing" with the child psychiatrist, and in an interview with him I was told that there should be no more evaluations of Tom by others! Furthermore, when I questioned why Tom was regarded with such certainty as being non-brain-damaged and not retarded, I received such inadequate replies as: "He's not as apathetic and passive as a retarded child; he has more drive."

Although I was alarmed about this situation, there was little that I could do for the time being. My wife's dogged determination to do everything possible to help Tom led her to place absolute trust in those who seemed to know the cure. Furthermore, there was the powerful drive to become a successful mother, to overcome the overwhelming, irrational feelings that she had failed with Tom. With the encouragement of her therapist, she was constantly overinterpreting in psychodynamic terms every aspect of Tom's activities. It appeared that I would only be viewed as the villain in this plot if I adamantly removed Tom and my wife from this misguided therapy. So instead, I went back into analytic therapy myself for a period to work through my distress about the situation.

Several months later Tom's condition was essentially unchanged. The "therapeutic classroom," plus my wife's efforts to understand Tom's behavior psychodynamically and to apply her own motherly "therapy" with the encouragement of the social worker, were to no avail. Once again one might suppose that the consulting child psychiatrist would reevaluate the initial premises. Instead, play therapy was recommended as the next panacea; after much delay while arrangements were made, this was undertaken. The play therapist, being of a persuasion similar to that of the consulting child psychiatrist, was convinced that Tom would improve with prolonged play therapy, although no one could explain in any sensible terms how this could work with a hyperactive, autistic, nonverbal, and retarded boy like Tom.

A period of play therapy also failed to bring any significant improvement, and Tom was becoming much more of a management problem at home. The consulting child psychiatrist proceeded to the next step following from the premise that Tom's disorder was entirely functional: He should be placed for a period of two to five years in a psychotherapeutically oriented residential treatment center. Once again the mystique of the "miracle workers" in this field and my wife's desperate hope that someone would at last save our son led her to press ardently to accomplish this placement.

Although I had grave misgivings, I went along with negotiations for such a placement because it was so crucial to my wife. To summarize: we eventually were led through a series of evaluations of Tom by directors and staff members of three different residential centers. Each of them in turn confirmed the diagnosis of schizophrenia and made statements such as: "Tom is potentially a very bright boy" and "Tom may not turn out to be entirely normal, but great improvement can be achieved with long-term residential therapy." However, it was noteworthy that each of these institutions for various reasons would *not* consider Tom for admission, even in the future when an opening would be available. The reasons they gave for rejecting him always had to do with the operation of their particular residential center and did not help to clarify my wife's confusion.

My own views on this can be succinctly stated: it is quite possible that the diagnosis of schizophrenia by the referring child psychiatrist was accepted too unquestioningly. Still, some reservations must have lurked in the minds of the residential center psychiatrists about the severity of the case and its amenability to their therapy; otherwise, they would have accepted Tom for admission. Yet they did not hesitate to perpetuate the myth of the indications for residential treatment in this case; none of them said that treatment in a psychotherapeutic residential center was not indicated.

OUTCOME

The impact on my wife, who had pinned her faith on Tom's treatment in one of the residential centers, was thoroughly demoralizing. The rejections of our son for admission resulted, for her, in a depressive reaction which was not of long duration but was severe. This created such a pressure on the family situation that it became necessary to hospitalize Tom temporarily. During Tom's hospitalization opinions were rendered by two additional child psychiatrists that his illness was non-organic. Remarks such as "The home is where he got sick, so he should be removed from there and have residential therapy" continued the powerful current of opinion that we were schizophrenogenic parents. Signs of my wife's distress (which had been generated by having to rear an autistic, hyperactive, retarded child and were compounded by the misguided therapy with the social worker) were taken as prima facie evidence that Tom's disturbed behavior was parentally induced. Fortunately, there were a few colleagues who staunchly held to their position in the other camp; this greatly aided us in keeping our bearings through all the conflict of opinion.

Finally my wife became disenchanted with the social worker, the consulting psychiatrist, and ultimately with the others in the string of authorities who insisted that Tom's illness was functional. First she expressed her motherly wrath that they claimed our son could respond to therapy but actually did very little about it (rejected him for residential treatment, terminated the play therapy, and later even dropped him from the "therapeutic classroom"). Gradually she became able to assess more skeptically the insinuations that Tom's disorder was family induced. A process (very painful to her) ensued of recognizing the

extent of the brain damage and accepting the limited possibilities for Tom's improvement without giving up all hope.

We severed all connections with the social worker and the child psychiatrist who had misled us. My wife began sessions with an analyst based on a different set of premises, and we searched for a more appropriate day school for Tom. This search proved to be fruitless and discouraging, since in our area there is a paucity of adequate schools or day care centers for seriously disturbed school-age children. After several months we mobilized to face the task of establishing a private school for ourselves and for other parents who also were searching in vain for a suitable program for their children.

One of the principles on which the new school was founded is that it is a debatable proposition that residential treatment is superior. The supposed superiority of residential treatment is unproven; it is based on the assumption that these serious disturbances of early childhood are nonorganic and parentally caused. We believe that these seriously handicapped children will have a chance to develop under more optimal conditions in a day school, where they are not separated from their homes.

In the process of selecting children with serious learning and behavior problems of various types for enrollment in our day school, we have repeatedly encountered comments by other professionals who seemed to ignore the organic factors and fix blame on either the child or his parents. For example: (1) with a very hyperactive, nonverbal, retarded boy, "The real problem here is the parents"; (2) with a boy having severe problems in perception, integration, and communication with abnormal EEG and other clinical signs of organicity, "The boy is not learning because he is covertly angry and withholding. He is a real provocateur." Such pejorative remarks seem nonscientific and antitherapeutic.

DISCUSSION

The theory that serious learning and behavior disorders of early childhood may often have an organic basis is not new to eclectic child psychiatrists. But our experience has demonstrated that there are quite a few persons in the field who dogmatically look at only behavior and psychopathology while ignoring the impairment of the nervous system. To child psychiatrists in that camp, autism and childhood schizophrenia are invariably psychologically caused. Some mention of constitutional factors may be made, but this is quickly ignored. Real investigation of the psychoneurological aspects of the problem is not even considered. Treatment of the parents and prolonged play therapy or residential treatment for the child are unquestioningly indicated. Where does this misconception arise? Perhaps it stems from inadequate training programs which lack the breadth, depth, and balance provided by different points of view.

Especially lacking are the necessary training and experience in evaluating neurologically impaired and retarded children with their wide variety of learning handicaps and behavioral abnormalities. The denial by some child psychiatrists of organicity and mental deficiency is truly astonishing. One of the reasons behind this denial seems to be an overriding need to explain all deviations solely in psychodynamic terms. Particularly, autistic manifestations are seen by that camp of child psychiatry as purely functional; this assumption is accompanied by the dubious notion that all other psychopathology in a child with autistic tendencies is also completely functional.

Schulman in an article in this journal in 1963 spoke of the sustained interest in the syndrome of infantile autism. This interest derives from the baffling behavior and early onset of the disorder. There has been considerable speculation about the etiology of autism, much of which may be summarized as a version of the nature-nurture controversy. Schulman's experience has led him to the belief that there is an innate biologic disturbance of brain function in autistic children. He deplores the tendency to view as inadequate anything less than long-term, intensive, psychotherapeutically oriented residential treatment. He reviews other follow-up studies and reports his own, all of which fail to support the position that infantile autism is a psychogenic illness and that psychotherapeutic residential treatment is imperative.

There have been a number of other excellent publications which take the position that although parent-child interaction may contribute to the psychopathology in the serious disorders of early childhood, biologic factors are of great importance in a major number of cases. As one of these authors said to me: "There probably are some children with psychoses of early childhood with no organic impairment, but you would have to really brutalize a child to produce that degree of disturbance." We believe that our experience would tend to confirm the importance of the organic aspects and to raise serious question about the theory and practice of the other camp.

In spite of the questionable value of psychotherapy for the child, psychotherapy or casework with parents of disturbed and retarded children can be very helpful. The therapist or caseworker should bear in mind the possibility that *in some cases* the parent-child interaction may have been a major causative factor in the production of the psychopathology and impaired intellectual functioning in the child. But the therapist should also consider the vulnerability of these parents to irrational guilt which may lead to morbid self-accusations. The therapist should also be sufficiently aware of the organic causes of such childhood disorders and be alert to the possibility of counter-transference which might bias his perspective.

In discussing casework with parents of autistic children, L. Wing states that the worker should not have the preconceived notion that any disturbance in the home environment has *necessarily* caused the original abnormality, even though the home environment does obviously influence the behavior of the child. She points out that it may be hard for some therapists to accept that sadness and suffering strike without moral reason because it brings home one's own vulnerability. It may be easier to believe that the victims in some way deserve their fate.

The fact that our misfortunes were compounded by the involvement with the special education program should be noted. New state and federal funds are being made available for education of all types of handicapped children, including those with the broad category of "learning disabilities." The possibility that a considerable number of other children and their parents may undergo similar trials has been part of the reason for this report. The training of child psychiatrists and other mental health personnel who may be employed as consultants to special education departments and school systems is a matter of crucial importance for the welfare of the seriously disturbed child and his entire family.

A few words should be said about the role of the new community mental health centers in relation to children with severe learning and behavior disorders (not all of whom are psychotic in any sense, of course). The community mental health centers are intended to provide a broad range of services for children (including retarded children) as well as adults. In any metropolitan area there are likely to be hundreds of these children whose parents are unable to find any suitable care or school placement. Most of the day schools for retarded children offer little to children with combinations of learning disability and disturbed behavior.

Many parents do not want to institutionalize their children. We have found in the course of establishing our new school that there are many parents, especially those with some stability and warmth, who struggle for years with little help with the daily ordeals of a seriously disturbed child. We have also heard over and over again the stories of sincerely cooperative parents being bounced back and forth between the two camps in child psychiatry, i.e., being told "there's no evidence of organicity; it's entirely emotional" by one group and then the opposite by another group. It is small wonder that these parents go shopping around for repeated evaluations.

But it appears that even the new community mental health services will offer them little. Most of these centers are not interested in the long-term day care necessary for these youngsters. It may be that our society is temperamentally ill-suited to cope with chronic illness, particularly chronic mental illness in children. On the other hand, the interest of individuals and organizations making contributions and the eagerness of college youth and housewives to offer volunteer services to our school attest to the fact that there is a reservoir of human concern to be tapped in lay people in general as well as in the parents of such disturbed children. Perhaps this is an area that should be given more attention by the community mental health centers.

CONCLUSION

The author's experience with his own son and with other children having serious learning and behavior disorders beginning in early childhood has led to the observation that there are two camps in child psychiatry. One group tends to regard all psychopathology as psychogenic and to overlook or deny organic factors; the second group attempts to integrate the organic with the psychologic aspects in understanding the etiology and prescribing treatment for these multi-handicapped children.

The inability of the first group to synthesize the genetic-biologic-constitutional-organic elements with the psychological is typified in the following common statement: "This child is not retarded; he is an autistic child." Members of this camp seem unable to say (even when it seems most accurate and appropriate): "This child is autistic *and* retarded." The effects of this limited viewpoint on the child, his family, and the schools and agencies who work with them can be very destructive.

FOLLOW-UP NOTE

In regard to the author's own son, a follow-up note should be added about his present condition. At eight and one-half years of age he has lost nearly all the earlier hyperactivity and autistic characteristics. What remain are clear signs of retardation and expressive aphasia, but nonverbal relatedness and willingness to try to learn within his capacity are evident.

REFERENCES

Schulman, J. L. 1963. *Amer. J. Psychiat.* 120:250–54.

Wing, L. 1966. In Wing, J. K., ed. *Early Childhood Autism—Clinical, Educational, and Social Aspects.* Toronto: Pergamon Press, pp. 258–59. [Six references not reprinted.]

Part II

DEFINITION
OF THE PROBLEM

5 Introduction to Part II

The consumer-provider relationship forms around the family's problems in caring for the child at home, so that there is need to specify some of these problems at the outset. Since parents of retarded children and professionals in the service system derive their orientations to mental retardation from the same culture, it would be expected that their responses to it would be somewhat similar. Barsch (1964, not reprinted) found such a similarity in his most unique study. He identified ten conditions: cerebral palsy, mental retardation, mental illness, brain injury, blindness, epilepsy, deafness, polio, heart disorders, and diabetes. The severity of these conditions was ranked by parents of children with cerebral palsy, brain damage, mongolism, deafness, and blindness. The severity of these conditions was also ranked by 22 comparison groups (2,375 respondents) which were composed of nursing students, parents of non-handicapped children, catholic nuns, optometrists, etc. Overall, cerebral palsy and mental retardation were ranked as most serious. Furthermore, the rankings differed little from group to group with only a few notable exceptions.

In a society which uniformly deems mental retardation as most serious, it is expected that parents would be motivated to consume helping services and that professions in the service system would be motivated to provide helping services. The article by Begab (1958) is selected to illustrate this. For various stages in the life of the retardate, family problems are identified and responsive services are described.

The all-pervasive concern of the service system is with the emotional disequilibrium a retarded child may cause in a family, especially shortly after the diagnosis. This may be due partly to a feeling of empathy on the part of individuals and partly out of concern for the devastating effect the emotional disequilibrium may have on all members of the family if time alone does not restore normal emotional functioning. The article by Kanner (1953) is selected to illustrate this concern. His case examples describe children who were diagnosed as retarded in the early school years, and he stresses the relationship between parental adjustments and the social and emotional circumstances of families.

Aside from the emotional dimension, families at any given time may face very real and very practical problems and the articles by Butterfield (1973) and Warner (1972) are selected to illustrate these. Butterfield shows how demanding one isolated child-care problem may be: an eight-year-old mongoloid child could not chew solid foods, so the parents were taught operant conditioning techniques to use at home. After forty-two weeks, the child had made considerable progress, but the parents reported some lingering eating problems which required reactivation of the case.

Warner illustrates how families may be incurring unnecessary economic burdens. Of twenty health insurance companies studied in San Francisco, only two offered usual-cost coverage for mentally retarded dependents. One wonders what proportion of families with retarded children in the area knew this, and what proportion were paying inflated premiums or doing without hospitalization insurance altogether.

Problems in child care have been the subject of many types of investigations, and the articles by Justice et al. (1971) and Holt (1958) are given as examples. Justice et al. report on 59 foster families who had cared for 195 retardates. Since these are highly motivated people who had not experienced the trauma of having a retarded child of their own, the difficulties they reported in caring for retarded children might indicate the real problems biological parents face, emotionally overwhelmed or not. Fewer than a third of the foster parents reported no problems; the remainder reported public misconceptions and lack of acceptance in the community, school problems, behavior problems, lack of necessary supportive services, etc. Recreation programs were most frequently cited as needed community service, both to help the child and to provide relief for the foster parent.

Holt studies a broad spectrum of problems in 201 families with a retarded child. Their practical problems in rank-order of frequency were: (1) parents never out together, (2) constant supervision of child, (3) additional expenses, (4) exhaustion of mother. All of these overlap and seem to add up to the finding of Justice above about the caretaker's need to get relief. Care of a retarded child can be quite demanding for biological and foster parents alike. Collectively the problems identified in the articles by Begab, Kanner, Butterfield, Warner, Justice et al., and Holt constitute some of the situations which incline parents to seek professional service for themselves and/or their children.

However, as suggested by Kysar in Part I, the service system itself may be a source of problems for the parent. Matheny and Vernick (1969) consider information-giving to be one of the principal functions of the service system. They respond most negatively to many authors who are concerned solely with the emotional dimension of the family.

"What the parents require most from diagnostic or informative counseling is specific, clearly transmitted, honest information about the child, implications for his future, and knowledge of what concrete steps they can take to deal with the problems."

At times parents may be both emotionally distraught and in need of much information. A provider who responds solely to the emotional disequilibrium may aggravate rather than improve it; he is certain to aggravate the questioning parent at the very least. On the other hand, as Kanner implies, a question is frequently more than a question. After exploring the problem of the parents' emotions, he identifies twenty-three types of questions parents ask and stresses the importance of simple, clear answers. At the same time he adds: "They ask seemingly specific or insignificant questions, and are most appreciative if such hints are understood and they are given an opportunity to talk themselves out before an experienced and sympathetic listener."

Those who are deemed to be preoccupied solely with the emotional dimension have also been taken to task recently regarding "shopping behavior," an ill-defined term used to describe parents who go to more than one program for diagnostic and/or therapeutic services. This practice is cited in so many articles that there is no question that it occurs widely.

Until recently, the practice has been attributed to some basic parental denial of the fact their child is retarded or to a frantic need to gain a more favorable diagnosis or to some other neurotic mechanism. Like all forms of behavior, there is no one cause, and authors in recent years have begun to blame other than parental factors. Anderson (1971, not reprinted), for example, maintains "that it takes two to shop," and that "the diagnostic and therapeutic shopping of parents of retarded children is . . . a learned response to unsatisfactory contacts with professional people." There is indirect support for Anderson's position in the many articles in which various professionals exhort their colleagues not to be so brusque with parents and not to be evasive about sharing information; certainly, one could argue, a parent who is quoted a huge estimate for car repairs by a brusque and evasive mechanic would be well advised to seek a second opinion.

The basic question is this: Does shopping behavior indicate parental maladjustment or poor service? Indeed, what *is* the extent of shopping behavior? Keirn (last article in Part II) found a remarkably low incidence. He is also reluctant to attribute the behavior solely to the parent or solely to the service system.

The information-giving issue and the shopping-behavior issue may have several things in common. First, together they may represent a growing disenchantment among providers with too much stress on the emotional dimension of family life with a retardate. Second, and more important, they may reflect the need for a different classification of parent problems and a changing perception of the role of the service system. Obviously there are the problems that the literature cites so voluminously—the disruption of an entire life pattern by virtue of the realization that "you" have a retarded child and the problems in the child's care. And there are problems when the community has no service, problems when the parents want to consume one thing (information) and the service system offers something else (a catharsis for one's feelings), and problems when elements in the service system are simply incompetent.

Such a diversity of problems is itself a problem: A given family may not be incapacitated by a mild eating problem or by an intolerant neighbor or by a school psychologist who never gives a straight answer. However, the weight of several concomitant problems may well be incapacitating.

At the same time, such diversity suggests a second role for the service system. The first role, of course, is provision of service to families. The second role would be monitoring the service to minimize any damage. For example, if shopping behavior is defined solely in terms of parental maladjustment, there is little chance that the service system will ever isolate its own contribution to the phenomenon.

6 Unmet Needs of the Mentally Retarded in the Community

Michael J. Begab

Changing concepts and new insights into the problems of the mentally retarded have greatly affected pre-existing attitudes and policies in the care, training and treatment of this group. As with every process involving public education and social reform, however, there is seldom universal agreement as to the methods best designed to accomplish stated objectives.

In approaching the social problems presented by our mentally retarded population there is fairly wide acceptance of the notion that these persons, like other handicapped people, should be rehabilitated wherever possible to become productive members of the community. Though few would argue with this stated goal, there are nevertheless many segments in society who give "lip service" to this ideal but are not really convinced of the potentialities of retarded persons.

It is quite understandable that a problem of such magnitude would give rise to a great deal of skepticism. Even those who have been intimately involved with retarded children and their parents for many years are not altogether agreed on the nature of the problems or the most suitable solutions. Professional persons in the field as well are not in total agreement as to the basic factors constituting mental deficiency per se.

Undoubtedly, this lack of a well understood and universally accepted concept underlies the extremely varied approach of different communities to the needs of the retarded child. Laws governing the adjudication and commitment of mentally deficient persons vary between the states, and even within a given jurisdiction one court may differ from another in its interpretation and application of the statutes. Recognizing that these variations do exist and that many practical considerations such as available local and state resources must also be taken into account, it is not at all remarkable that programs for the mentally retarded have frequently been characterized by an erratic and unintegrated development.

The purpose of this paper is to determine how the unique skills and training of the social worker can fulfill some of the unmet needs of retarded persons and their families. Further, how can we assist in the integration of services so vital to their general adjustment? In developing this theme, it should be understood that mental deficiency is not a specifically medical, psychological, social, or legal concept but rather a combination of factors as defined by these disciplines.

A person's mental capacities can probably be measured with some degree of validity, but his ability to adapt to his social environment is exceedingly more difficult to evaluate. One cannot say how much intelligence (as measured by objective tests) is needed adequately to incorporate acceptable social values, form satisfactory interpersonal relationships, or know "right from wrong." Social adequacy or deficiency involves the person's total personality and its interaction with his environment, and it is this component in mental deficiency that the social worker is best equipped to evaluate and sometimes modify.

The specific service offered by the caseworker is generally influenced by the nature of the setting and the function of the agency by whom he is employed as well as the particular needs of the client. Although certain basic needs are common to all retarded persons, regardless of age, for purposes of clarity and understanding, they shall be considered according to various levels of development.

THE PRE-SCHOOL-AGE CHILD

For the many parents whose child's mental retardation is the result of prenatal factors, birth trauma, or postnatal injury or disease, etc., early assistance with their problem is of utmost important. In some clinical types, medical diagnosis is a relatively simple matter; however, this is more complex in instances where normal physical and mental growth is disrupted by illness or disease. In such cases, parents are not always able or willing to recognize that a deficiency exists and may accept reality only after repeated disillusionment.

The importance of early and competent clinical diagnosis of the patient is self-evident, yet paradoxically the needs of parents during this initial period of distress often go unfulfilled. The heartache and frustration that accompany the knowledge that one's child is mentally retarded and beyond medical cure is frequently a debilitating force, and yet the panic and confusion encountered are sometimes unwittingly intensified rather than alleviated.

The principle that every child needs the emotional nurture of an accepting home environment is widely accepted in dealing with the problems of the emotionally disturbed, the delinquent, or the physically handicapped child. The parents of these children are frequently able to seek help with their problems from a variety of community resources, or where the child's home environment is not subject to modification, foster homes may be utilized in meeting his needs.

It is common knowledge that these resources are not as readily available to the parents of retarded children, despite the urgency of their needs. Though many agencies and clinics will provide diagnostic services for these children and interpret to the parents the child's prognosis and limitations, in most areas there is little planned effort to help the parents with their conflicts or anxieties or to offer them concrete guidance in administering to the daily needs of the child.

Perhaps underlying this common policy of social agencies is the attitude that little can be done for this group through casework services and that the limited financial and personnel resources of the agency should be applied to persons with greater potential to profit by them. It may also be that many social workers feel ill-equipped by training or experience to cope with the unique problems of the retarded and are reluctant to assume responsibility for these cases. Whatever the explanation, it is apparent that the needs of parents and relatives of retarded children are often unfulfilled.

For the pre-school-age child, casework services obviously must be directed toward helping the parents understand and adjust to the child's condition. We all recognize that the emotional atmosphere and stability of the home are extremely important in personality development, yet this basic concept is frequently minimized in evaluating the retardate's behavior and level of social functioning.

Retarded children, by the very nature of their condition and its many social implications, will often produce instability in a previously stable family unit. Parents may be ego threatened and blame each other for the child's deficiency; they may disagree in matters of training or discipline or they may make the child a scapegoat for personality conflicts of their own. Where these attitudes exist there is obviously a need for professional help. Realistic interpretation of etiological factors in the child's mental condition,

accurate appraisal of the child's abilities and limitations, and exploration of inter-family relationships may readily serve to ameliorate parental attitudes.

Let us examine the reasons offered by parents for institutionalizing children of pre-school age. Some of the most common are (1) hyperactive, aggressive, destructive or generally uncontrollable behavior, (2) negative influence on other siblings in the home, (3) effect on mother's physical and mental health.

Excluding the familial defective or clinical types of pre-natal origin, such as mongolism, microcephaly, etc., the large majority of other classifiable types of retarded children can be considered as brain-damaged. The behavior of these children, often described as in (1) above, is considered primarily as organically induced and is realistically extremely difficult to modify by ordinary methods of training. We can well understand the frustration of parents faced with this kind of chronic behavior pattern. Under these trying circumstances even the most stable parent is likely to react with anger, hostility, and rejection or attempt to assuage intolerable guilt feelings through overprotection or overindulgence. The effect on parent-child relationships needs no elaboration. We cannot determine the extent to which emotional factors may contribute to the disturbed behavior of brain-damaged children, yet they unquestionably play an important role. This is well supported by empirical observation of children who demonstrate better controlled behavior following institutionalization or placement outside of the home. Though tranquillizing medicines may be a factor in some instances, others have shown marked improvement without benefit of medication.

Recognizing how parental attitudes may perpetuate aggressive and destructive behavior, the question arises as to whether the cyclical affect so produced can be interrupted by professional services. The techniques for the training and discipline of brain-damaged children are beyond the scope of this paper, yet it would seem that helping the parents understand their child's behavior, enabling them to relieve guilt and anxiety feelings and making possible more positive attitudes would do much toward maintaining more stable and wholesome parent-child relationships.

The casework approach, like any other unilateral approach, can achieve only limited success with a problem of this magnitude, unless it is closely coordinated with other services. A valuable adjunct to casework therapy would be the establishment of day nurseries and summer day camps for the retarded child of pre-school age. Facilities of this kind could supplement the social habit training provided in the home and contribute to the child's socialization through the advantages of a controlled group living experience.

As with normal children, the benefits of a nursery school experience for the retarded cannot be measured altogether by the positive habits learned or degree of socialization achieved. The secondary gains, namely temporary relief of the mother from the demands of constant supervision and emotional stress, can in many instances by the primary factor in guilding the child's future growth and development. Homemaker services permitting the mother to be gainfully employed or to develop outside social interests could have similar beneficial effects. The stabilizing effect of programs of this nature may frequently enable parents to care for their children in the home and preclude the trauma that often results from separation and institutional care. Even in the absence of financial assistance from public agencies to establish such resources, organized parents' groups can do much to alleviate their common problems by setting up small informal groups within their own homes under the shared leadership of emotionally mature parents. With the reduction of tension and anxiety thus made possible, parents are in a better position to develop insight and understanding into their own problems and establish a more wholesome atmosphere in the home.

The notion that the retarded child has a negative effect on other siblings in the home has received considerable support by various professions as well as by parents faced with realistic evidence of disturbed behavior in their "normal" children. Some have even concluded that a deteriorating influence is inevitable and that institutionalization of the retarded child is the only possible solution. The validity of this observation is subject to serious question, even though conflict situations in these families undoubtedly exist. We must not content ourselves merely with the empirical evidence that siblings of retarded children sometimes demonstrate disturbed behavior, but must instead investigate the *why* and *wherefore* of such behavior.

It would appear that in this regard we might well borrow from experience and research in fields concerning other handicapped children. Historically speaking, blind and deaf children were also formerly regarded (and still are to a great extent) as the cause of maladjusted behavior in their brothers and sisters. Research studies have demonstrated, however, that it is not the handicap per se which is the major disabling force, but rather the attitudes toward the handicapped person by those with whom he has intimate contact—primarily the parents. In those families characterized by parental maturity, understanding, acceptance and realistic planning, the handicapped child has a better opportunity to adjust satisfactorily to the demands of daily living, and inter-personal family relationships are more likely to remain on a constructive level.

The handicaps referred to are, of course, somewhat different in nature from mental retardation, yet the effects on parental attitudes and other family members are not too dissimilar. Feelings of trauma, despair and helplessness, frustration, anxiety, and guilt are emotional reactions common to parents of most handicapped children, whether the defect be physical or mental. Because of social attitudes and pressures the task of habilitating retarded children may be somewhat more complicated, yet in this respect the blind, too, were at one time in history literally "cast out of society."

Though the attitudes and comments of peers may sometimes instill in siblings of retarded children feelings of shame and stigma, primary causation in their emotionally disturbed behavior may be traced to parent-child relationships. Confused and anxious parents will frequently pour all their energies into the care of their retarded child. There is a natural tendency toward overprotectiveness and disciplinary laxness which causes other children to feel neglected or to be dealt with unfairly. In their efforts to compete with the retardate, siblings may resort to imitative behavior or temper tantrums or to various forms of negative attention-getting behavior.

These few comments are not intended to reflect the full complexity of the retarded child's effect on intra-family relationships but it is suggested that this specific problem may be ameliorated through professional casework or psychiatric services. It is conceivable in fact that a retarded child may have a positive and maturing effect on other siblings if the latter are encouraged to participate in the former's care and training. Intimate contact with handicapped persons can help to develop attitudes of patience and tolerance, a sense of respect for the needs of others and a feeling of emotional satisfaction in contributing to the happiness and well-being of others.

There will, of course, always be situations that even the most intensive and competent services cannot alleviate. The severity of the child's condition, limitations in the natural and emotional resources of the family, or the external pressures of society are some of the circumstances which may make institutional care of the patient the most logical remedy. Yet, even in these cases, professional services to the parents, enabling them to feel comfortable with this plan, can do much to preserve their mental health and sense of integrity.

SCHOOL AGE AND ADOLESCENCE

The need for social services to retarded children and/or their parents may present itself at a specific period of the child's development or may continue, as with other handicapped or emotionally disturbed children, throughout the child's life. As the child matures, however, and embarks upon experiences outside of the family unit, the casework focus may shift from the parent to the patient or at least include both in the treatment process.

The adjustment problems experienced by many normal children as they leave the security of their own homes and enter into the group learning situation of the school setting are probably even more severe for the retarded child. Recognizing that the latter has frequently been overprotected or rejected and has had little or no socializing experiences through normal play activities with peers, we can readily see how the retarded child's fear and insecurity may interfere with his adjustment. Whereas the normal child may compensate for feelings of anxiety through academic achievement and the recognition and status it provides, the retardate is lacking in these essential intellectual resources. Too often, because of inadequate diagnosis or the parents' unwillingness to accept the child's retardation, he is enrolled in a regular public school system and exposed to a competitive situation with which he is ill-equipped to cope. Teachers, social workers, and parents are all familiar with the problems that are soon manifested. The child reacts to his frustration with anger, aggression, or withdrawal; attempts at discipline or control are interpreted by him as rejection and further aggravate his emotional state. Segregation of the retarded child in special schools or even in special classes of the public school system may present a further enigma. There is the realistic danger that the child will identify himself as being "different," and that his peers may intensify his feelings of inferiority by directing his attention to his special class status. The possibility also exists that this manner of separation tends to emphasize the differences rather than similarities between retarded and normal children. There appears to be no ready solution to this dilemma, however, and considering the necessary intellectual focus of the school setting, the special class system would seem to pose the fewest problems. Frequently the problems encountered in the school setting carry over into the home and contribute to parental confusion or vice versa. The nature of the problem, as specifically related to brain-damaged children, has been well stated by Dr. Eisenberg: "His behavior, impulsive, demanding, often anti-social, is particularly apt to provoke rejection. . . . An impatient attitude and unjustified blame by the teacher increases the child's anxiety and results both in more disturbed behavior and in less ability to learn. Unless therapeutic intervention occurs, this self-perpetuating cycle is likely to end only with exclusion from school or persistent truancy."

The contributions of special education teachers have lessened to some degree the problems of the mentally retarded, but education alone cannot meet the total need. The important role of social factors in the behavior of retarded children would indicate that the integration of social services with educational training is of vital importance. The child's ability to profit from a school experience can be greatly influenced by the emotional atmosphere in the home; when overprotection characterizes the parent-child relationship, the latter will not learn self-sufficiency and the former will find it difficult to exert consistent discipline. The pre-existence of organically induced difficulty may make the child prone to forms of socially unacceptable behavior but psychogenic factors may be the primary disturbing force in his total adjustment.

It is fairly well established that the relation of the teacher to the retarded child will have considerable influence on his behavior and success in training. Yet, the substantial number of children who continue to show disturbed behavior in the classroom would suggest that in some cases a positive relationship cannot be established and in others that this in itself is not enough. It seems quite obvious that since children spend the major portion of their time in the home, habits learned in the classroom will not become part of the child's living pattern unless consistently re-enforced in the home. The capacity of parents to follow through on specific recommendations for discipline, control, or habit training is often dependent upon their own emotional maturity and/or feelings which may be quite unrelated to the child himself.

Teachers of the retarded are not always familiar with the child's environmental background and even where such information is available to them, usually have neither the time nor the professional skills to modify the home situation. For this reason, the teacher's activity with the child must be supplemented by casework services to the parents of a therapeutic nature where needed. The latter have to give up their unrealistic expectations for the child and must resolve the feelings aroused in them by the child's deficiency. To accomplish this objective, a great deal of effort must be directed toward the parents whose need for emotional support, understanding, and acceptance by their human environment is no less than that of their child.

In some of the more progressive areas, the needs of emotionally disturbed children have prompted the integration of social services into the total school program. The liaison thus made possible between the home and classroom serves many useful purposes. The social worker can interpret to the teacher the socio-economic conditions in the home, the intellectual and emotional resources of the parents, and the nature of the parent-child relationship. With such information available, teachers can develop better insight and understanding into the problems involved and individualize their approach to the child within the limitations of a group setting. Conversely, the child's classroom behavior, interpersonal relationships with peers, and responsiveness to certain forms of discipline as well as learning can be helpful to the parents in understanding the child's abilities and guiding his energies into constructive channels of activity.

The techniques of group discussions could also be utilized to good advantage. Parents, with or without professional leadership, can profit from ventilation of their anxieties, mutual support, a sharing of common experiences, and an ever expanding knowledge of mental retardation.

The needs described thus far may be continuous, and any division according to the child's age is admittedly arbitrary; however, the period of puberty and adolescence requires special consideration. In the adolescent retardate, unlike his normal counterpart, the struggle for emancipation from parental controls is not always manifested with the onset of puberty and its accompanying physical maturation, but frequently appears at a later date or perhaps not at all, depending on a variety of physical and mental factors. Whereas the adolescent's physical and social maturity may correspond to his chronological age, his level of emotional maturity may more closely approximate his mental development. The rebelliousness and negativism which are sometimes demonstrated are often the result of imitative behavior and identification with peer values rather than an innate desire for independence and the responsibilities of adulthood. In many cases this stems from overly rigid controls imposed by extremely anxious parents.

The courts and society tend to re-flect the attitude that the social misdeeds of the mental defective are due *wholly* or *primarily* to his limited intellect. This is an obvious conclusion which is certainly not altogether validated by the facts. We must remember that retarded adolescents have little social status and that normal social and recreational opportunities are not readily available to them. They seldom utilize community resources such as organized clubs and recreation centers because of the unequal competition and feelings of anxiety it provokes. They are also rejected by their peers and because of poor mental endowment find few compensatory outlets by which their needs for acceptance can be satisfied.

With this frame of reference, the importance of other factors as contributors to socially unacceptable behavior can be better understood. It is not uncommon that the misdeeds of a specific retardate are confined to only one form of delinquency. For example, a sexually promiscuous girl may be respectful and obedient, responsible around the home, and enjoy satisfactory inter-personal relationships. She may, in all other areas of functioning, reflect an ability to abide by the acceptable social codes and mores of society. In such cases, we cannot properly attribute her delinquent behavior to limited mentality or impaired moral judgment, but must look for underlying causes of an emotional nature.

We frequently forget that retarded persons are subject to the same range and variety of emotional reactions as are those of normal intelligence. This principle is often unconsciously disregarded by parents, too, who rationalize or justify all forms of social misconduct on the basis of the child's retardation or the negative influence of undesirable companions. In actuality, the incidence of delinquent behavior—as in the normal population—is greatest in homes characterized by marital discord, emotional instability, and socio-economic deprivation. Thus, we may conclude that limited comprehension or inadequate super ego development are only a few of the many factors contributing to maladjustive behavior. Retardates, because of their rejection by family and peers, are extremely vulnerable to the negative influences of others; anti-social conduct may seem the only means available to them for acting out their resentments toward society or gaining recognition and status.

The heightened sexual interest of puberty and adolescence is a frightening and perplexing experience to parents and of natural concern to society. Parents find it difficult to understand the relatively mature physical strivings of their children when compared with the very childlike, dependent behavior demonstrated in other areas. They recognize the dangers of exploitation and are often panicked into attitudes of rigid control or placement of the child in a more protective environment.

Though it would be a serious error to minimize the adjustment problems of the retarded adolescent, it is nevertheless very important to recognize that the dynamics involved are essentially the same as with normal children. In making differential diagnoses, we cannot confine ourselves solely to considerations of mental age and I.Q. but must also investigate social and environmental factors. Acceptance of these casework principles has many implications for treatment; it emphasizes the need for therapeutic services and the capacity of retarded persons to profit thereby.

Existing community resources for the treatment of disturbed children have thus far largely excluded the retarded from their case rolls. Diagnostic services are often provided, but the child and parents are deprived of other services because their potentialities for rehabilitation in the community are underestimated. It has been repeatedly demonstrated that institutionalized defectives can be returned to the community and restored to social competence. The stability of a protective milieu plus educational and vocational training programs are undoubtedly important factors in the rehabilitation process, yet one wonders whether these goals could not be accomplished for many retardates without resort to segregation from society. Guidance centers and social agencies can probably help many retarded persons in the community to achieve greater independence, develop more initiative, and incorporate more acceptable social codes. Efforts in this direction can preclude unnecessary institutional care and permit the use of state facilities for those for whom no other alternative is possible.

ADULTHOOD

The unmet needs of retarded children and their parents described in the foregoing sections are equally applicable to the retarded adult population and shall not be enlarged upon here. There are, however, problems specific to adulthood which require separate consideration. Inasmuch as the severely retarded and many of the moderately retarded are from a functional standpoint "children" throughout their lifetimes, our comments shall be directed primarily toward the high grade and borderline defective.

It is quite obvious that the prolonged dependency of mentally handicapped persons represents a severe drain on family financial resources in addition to some of the problems referred to earlier. Parents of retarded adults are in need of and entitled to the same considerations afforded parents of physically handicapped children. This has been expressly recognized by the Federal Government by its inclusion of the mentally handicapped as persons eligible for training and rehabilitation services. The Vocational Rehabilitation Amendments of 1954 states in part, "The term 'vocational rehabilitation services' means diagnostic and related services (including transportation) incidental to the determination of eligibility for and the nature and scope of services to be provided: training, guidance and placement services for physically handicapped individuals; ... (b) The term 'physically handicapped individual' means any individual who is under a physical or *mental* disability which constitutes a substantial handicap to employment, but which is of such a nature that vocational rehabilitation services may reasonably be expected to render him fit to engage in a remunerative occupation."

Employment of retarded persons offers many advantages to parents other than the obvious financial relief. As noted earlier, these individuals have little access to the social and recreational resources available to other adults. The lack of suitable outlets for physical and mental energies during leisure hours becomes a major problem when all one's time is spent in this fashion. A common complaint and source of frustration to parents is their inability to guide their son or daughter into constructive forms of activity. Enforced idleness in the home greatly magnifies supervisory needs; the mother is unable to explore outside interests and frequently must sacrifice her own social needs for those of the child. In situations of this kind, it is not unusual that feelings of martyrdom and resentment will develop, creating attitudes of rejection. The retardate, under such emotionally vulnerable conditions, is apt to seek stimulation, recognition, and acceptance outside of the home and thereby frequently falls prey to the exploitation of undesirable companions.

The success of work placement programs in institutions for the mentally retarded has effectively demonstrated the employability of this group. Our high degree of urbanization today has undoubtedly created complex problems of social adjustment for the retarded, but the accompanying industrialization has brought many jobs within their capacities. Technological change has reduced many work procedures to simple, repetitive tasks; these are particularly suited to the abilities and personality of retarded adults. Inasmuch as public institutions accommodate a very small percentage of high grade adult defectives (an estimated 5 per cent of all retardates, regardless of age or mental level, are institutionalized), it is reasonable to assume that a large majority of these persons are wholly or partially self-supporting.

Repeated job analyses in private industry have proven quite conclusively that personality factors rather than skill in work performance are of primary consideration in successful placement. Experience in institutions indicates this is true for the retarded as well. Relatively few individuals returned to the community on work placement have received vocational training as part of their rehabilitation program, and even those who have are seldom placed in jobs for which they have been trained. This would strongly suggest that the major benefit of any training program is the development of proper work habits, attitudes of responsibility, and satisfactory interpersonal relationships with co-workers.

It would seem that existing community programs except in a few areas are woefully inadequate in preparing the retarded for employment. Trade schools are frequently not geared to the learning capacities of the retarded, and in many instances, age limitations result in an individual's dismissal before he has had the opportunity to explore fully his potentials. The lack of follow-up training services after a child has reached his maximum academic achievement level has made institutional care necessary for many who might otherwise have remained in the community as productive, self-sufficient citizens.

The Federal Government has rec-ognized the mentally handicapped as persons eligible for services from the Office of Vocational Rehabilitation and has provided financial assistance to the states in their administration of this program. Some demonstration projects and studies have been undertaken in a few states, but these efforts have been widely scattered and in general this potentially excellent resource has been largely inaccessible to retarded adults and their parents.

The leadership provided by some institutional social services in the placement area should stimulate other social agencies to a reevaluation of their attitudes regarding retarded adults. Better use of the U.S. Employment Service facilities and the Office of Vocational Rehabilitation, establishment of sheltered workshops, and, above all, education of the public to the work abilities of this group, are some of the means by which the retarded can be helped to achieve a more constructive living experience.

There will, of course, always be a significant segment of the retarded population for whom institutional care must be considered. The above remarks are not intended to imply that all retarded children or adults can be habilitated or rehabilitated, as the case may be, through community planning. Severe retardation, physical disability, delinquent behavior, or inadequate home conditions are all factors which may necessitate institutional placement, but thorough evaluation and careful planning on the local level can effectively screen those in greatest need of this type of care. Only by a shared responsibility of local and state resources can we appreciably fulfill the many needs of our retarded population.

Of the many aspects of mental deficiency requiring the attention of society, the problems presented by the adult defective offender are unduly emphasized. States vary widely in their solution to this problem, depending on their concept of mental deficiency and what they regard to be the rehabilitation potentials of this group. Within different jurisdictions, such factors as the seriousness of the offense, the offender's previous criminal record, and his level of intelligence may be given unequal consideration in the disposition of the case. Furthermore, under the laws of some states, mental defectives are regarded in the same category as the mentally ill or psychopathic offender and are subject to confinement in hospitals for the criminally insane.

Our expanding knowledge and experience with retarded persons have demonstrated rather conclusively that intelligence is but one factor in social competency. In the experience of this writer with institutionalized defectives, the highest incidence of delinquency falls in the borderline range and declines markedly in the moderate and severely retarded group. This would suggest that personality maldevelopment and social or emotional factors are probably of primary importance.

The factors referred to in regard to intellectually normal offenders should be given equal consideration in planning for retarded offenders. Particularly in the upper moron and borderline ranges of intelligence, there is a need to thoroughly evaluate cultural and environmental factors and their impact on the individual's personality and behavior. On the basis of such investigation, the primary problem may emerge and the court can then properly determine whether a correctional institution, training school for defectives or probation in the community is the most suitable plan. Social workers connected with the courts or in the probation field can contribute greatly to a dynamic evaluation of social and personality factors and may through understanding supervision restore the retarded to social competency. . . .

REFERENCE

Eisenberg, Leon. 1956. *GP* no. 10.
[Four references not reprinted.]

7 Parents' Feelings About Retarded Children

Leo Kanner

There was a time when, confronted with the task of dealing with retarded children, the educator's, psychologist's, or physician's main effort consisted of an examination of the child and advice to the family. No matter how expertly and conscientiously this was done, it somehow did not take in the whole magnitude of the problem. Parents were told of the child's low I.Q. in mournful numbers and were urged to think in terms of ungraded classes or residential school placement. The I.Q. figures may have been correct and the suggestions may have been adequate, and yet very often a major, highly important and, in fact, indispensable part of the job was somehow neglected.

It is recognized more and more that professional and at the same time humane attention should be given to the attitudes and feelings of people who are understandably puzzled by the *lag* in their child's development and progress. Whenever parents are given an opportunity to express themselves, they invariably air their emotional involvements in the form of questions, utterances of guilt, open and sometimes impatient rebellion against destiny, stories of frantic search for causes, pathetic accounts of matrimonial dissensions about the child's condition, regret about the course that has been taken so far, anxious appraisals of the child's future, and tearful pleas for reassurance. It takes a considerable amount of cold, hard-boiled, pseudo-professorial detachment to turn a deaf ear on the anxieties, self-incriminations, and concerns about past, present, and future contained in such remarks. We have learned to take them into serious consideration and to treat them as the genuine, deep-seated, intrinsic perplexities that they are. We have learned to distinguish between abrupt, brutal frankness and a sympathetic statement of fact, between a dictatorial, take-it-or-leave-it kind of recommendation and the sort of presentation which would appeal to parents as the most constructive and helpful procedure, best suited under the existing circumstances.

I know that it is difficult to speak in generalities about a subject which entails individual sentiments. I know from experience that every couple who comes with a retarded child carries along a set of specific curiosities which must be understood and satisfied. For this reason, it may perhaps serve the purpose of this address if I were to introduce a few definite instances and, in so doing, to discuss the principal implications as they come along in the life of the retarded child and in the minds of his family.

Johnny Jones was brought to our clinic at the age of eight years. He was referred to us by his pediatrician with the request for a psychometric evaluation. Johnny was in his third year in school, had been demoted once, and after that had been given courtesy promotions, even though he did not master the required curriculum of his grade. The psychologist's examination showed that Johnny had a test age of six years and an I.Q. of 75. It was obvious that, with his endowment, he could not possibly be expected to do better than low first grade work. It would have seemed easy to say to the parents that Johnny should be in an ungraded class because of his low intelligence. It would have been very easy to give them the numerical result of the test and, if they balked, to offer them an authoritative explanation of the Binet-Simon or any other scale that had been employed. However, there was one big fly in the ointment. Mr. and Mrs. Jones were both college graduate people and moved in highly intellectual and sophisticated circles. Mr. Jones was a competent representative of a pharmaceutical firm and his wife had been a librarian prior to her marriage. They could see logically that their son had not been able to accomplish the scholastic functions expected of a child his age. But for years they had struggled against the very thought that something might be amiss with their Johnny's academic possibilities. As a result, they had kept looking for interpretations of his failures other than the one interpretation which they dreaded because they could not accept it emotionally. They had found fault with the "school system." There couldn't be anything wrong with the child; the problem must lie somewhere in the *method of instruction*: Johnny's teachers were either too young and inexperienced or too old and unfamiliar with modern education. They were alternately critical of what they chose to call either old-fashioned drilling or new-fangled frills. When, in the course of time, they had been convinced that the other children in Johnny's group got along all right under the same educational regime, they tried to seek the culprit in *Johnny's body*. After considerable search, they found one doctor who persuaded them that Johnny would do better if his tonsils and adenoids were taken out. They cherished this bit of wisdom because it fitted into their emotional pattern. They could say to themselves that, after all, their Johnny was all right and would learn better after the repair of a physical imperfection. This did not work. In order to satisfy their need for prestige, they began to pounce on *Johnny himself.* They decided that the child must be lazy. They scolded him, deprived him of privileges and sat with him for hours trying to hammer his homework into him. They pointed out to him how well his numerous cousins did without all the help such as he received from them. The child, smarting from the constant rebuff and rebuke, sat there, unable to grasp the parental instructions and, not knowing why he could not conform, came to think of himself as a wretched, miserable, ungrateful creature who let his parents down. He gave up completely. He lost all confidence in himself and, in order to find some compensation for his anguish, he took to daydreaming. Eventually, the parents thought that Johnny's salvation stared them in the face when they came upon an article in *The Reader's Digest* which told them that a certain drug, named glutamic acid, could brighten up children and make them learn better. They obtained the drug and got him to swallow tablet after tablet. For a time, they called off the dogs of daily tutoring and pushing, with the idea that glutamic acid would do the trick. Johnny, relieved of the pressures, perked up for a while and seemed brighter. He felt that being offered the tablets, however ill-tasting they were, was better than being hovered over impatiently at the desk. The parents came to feel that the money they paid to the druggist was about the best investment they had ever made. But in the long run they felt disillusioned and finally decided to take the child to the clinic.

Betty Brown was a placid, likable little girl whose physical characteristics and marked developmental retardation had led the child's pediatrician to make the correct diagnosis of mongolism. He was able to help the parents to understand and accept Betty's limitations. The Browns were warm-hearted people and genuinely fond of their three children, of whom Betty was the youngest. Michael and Anne were healthy and bright and held out every promise of good academic achievement. They sensed their sister's handicaps, were helped by their parents to make the necessary allowances and, being secure in the warmth of a comfortable emotional climate, adjusted nicely to Betty's need for her mother's special attention. Anne in fact welcomed and invited opportunities to be mother's little helper in her ministrations to Betty.

This constellation of attitudes might have made for an ideal mode of family living. But a "bull in the china shop" charged into this peaceful home in the shape of Betty's paternal grandmother who lived a few doors away from the Browns. The elder Mrs. Brown stubbornly refused to acknowledge the doctor's diagnosis. She had always been a bit critical of her daughter-in-law but had found it difficult to hold on to a specific hatrack on which to hang her expressions of disapproval. Betty's failure to develop properly came to her as a godsend. She made up her mind that there was nothing wrong with Betty herself and that the whole trouble stemmed from the child's mother's inadequate methods of training. She offered no concrete suggestions. She did not substantiate her recriminations. But every morning, with clock-like regularity, she appeared at the home, looked at the child with a mien of profound commiseration, and uttered the same reproachful phrase: "When are you going to start making something of the child?"

Mrs. Brown took this as long as she could. She discarded as utterly futile her initial attempts to convey to her tormentor the reality of Betty's condition. She decided to remain silent. But eventually she could stand it no longer. It is not easy to be confronted daily with insult added to painful injury. She turned for help to her husband, imploring him to do something about his mother's stereotyped antics. All that he had to offer was the advice that she "pay no attention." After a few months, she brought Betty to our clinic. In reality, she brought herself and her misery rather than the child. She was obviously depressed and was seeking help for herself, which by that time she needed desperately.

Alan Smith was his parents' only child. He was severely retarded in his development. The Smiths, feeling that Alan would need all of their attention, had decided to deprive themselves of further offspring. There was also the dread of a possible repetition of the tragedy. But most pathetic of all was the boy's mother's constant self-searching for some shortcomings of her own which might be responsible for her son's intellectual defect. When she brought him to the clinic, she asked: "Doctor, did I have something to do with it? Did I do something wrong?" She eagerly gulped down the acquittal but went on: "Well—maybe before he was born—did I do something then?" When told that her child's retardation was not determined by anything that she had done, she was still puzzled. She wondered: "If it isn't what I have *done,* maybe it's what I *am* that brought it about." Again she seemed grateful for authoritative absolution. But still she went on. If she had not contributed to the fact of Alan's retardation, then she was surely guilty of not recognizing it in time, of pushing him beyond his capacity, of losing patience with him, of doing things for him which he might have learned to do for himself. Furthermore, she had been ashamed of his backwardness and tried to hide it from her friends and neighbors, and then she was ashamed of having felt shame. Of course, she could not gain peace through mere verbal reassurance, however thirstily she lapped it up. She needed many opportunities to talk herself out, more chances for this confessional type of expiation, and help in the suggested efforts to return to her previous social and communal life from which she had removed herself in sacrificial isolation because of her feelings of shame and guilt and remorse.

Larry White was brought to our clinic at the age of 7½ years. His parents were distressed by his poor progress in school and by the suggestion that he be placed in an ungraded class. Larry was their only child who had come to them after eight years of married life. His birth, preceded by a miscarriage and much gynecological maneuvering, was greeted with jubilation. His mother, previously an efficient office manager, took Larry over as the biggest assignment of her career. Her feeding methods made and kept him nice and chubby. Speech development was somewhat delayed but this, she reasoned, is true of many children who later become regular chatterboxes. His faulty articulation was handled by sending him to a "teacher of expression and dramatics." He did well in nursery school and kindergarten. He was a happy, sociable, and well-mannered child.

Then the parents experienced their great shock. Larry could not do his first grade work, failed of promotion and finally was recommended for a special class. At first, the mother blamed his eyesight but three successive examinations convinced her that his vision was not at fault. The mother tried to do his homework with him, and each attempt made her more impatient. She then employed a tutor for him. When his scholastic performance showed no improvement, the parents began to transfer the blame to Larry himself. The father found comfort in the formula that Larry was "mentally lazy." The mother began to nag and punish him and deprive him of privileges. Larry became rebellious under the many-sided pressures, was increasingly restless, at times even destructive, and developed behavior ostensibly intended to get even with his critics and oppressors.

His I.Q. was 77.

The mother reported that her nephews and nieces all had superior intelligence and remarked significantly: "I can't understand. Why does this happen to me?" The father, more genuinely fond of the child, said: "I think he is perfect apart from school," and added that his wife was disturbed because Larry obviously was not a genius. Thereupon she said categorically: "I want him to go to college. We can afford it."

It is clear that one could not use a sledge hammer in dealing with Larry's parents. Merely telling them that their son was not ready for first grade work did not solve the essential problem. They had known this for some time. But they needed help in learning to accept the child as he was without a sense of personal shame and failure. Larry's mother felt ashamed and socially disgraced by having a child whom her society considers inferior. She felt guilty because the unpleasant thought must have kept obtruding itself that, after all her gynecological difficulties, she should perhaps have remained childless. She felt frustrated because her one great asset, her efficiency, had suffered defeat.

Examples such as these can be produced almost indefinitely. But even the small number of cited instances suffices to bring out a few highly important considerations. It is, of course, necessary for the expert to make the best possible use of the available test methods in order to obtain a scientifically valid assessment of a child's developmental potentialities. The application of these tests requires skill, experience, patience, and a setting in which the tested child would be at his ease and cooperate to his best ability. Many pitfalls must be avoided, such as testing a child during his regular naptime, failure to take into account an existing impairment of hearing or vision, psychometric examination immediately preceding or following a convulsion, or difficulty in allaying a child's acute anxiety which may manifest itself in speechless timidity or noisy defiance.

When a test has been completed satisfactorily and the child's intellectual endowment has been ascertained with reasonable accuracy, it is the expert's duty to report and explain his findings to the child's parents. It should hardly seem necessary to point out that such a report, if it involves the disclosure of a child's retardation, should be made tactfully, lucidly, and truthfully. But I have known parents who, without any concern for their emotional readiness, were thrown into a panic by the words feebleminded, imbecile, or moron hurled at them as if from an ambush. I have also known good-natured doctors who did not have the heart to confront the parents with the true state of affairs and mumbled something to the effect that Johnny or Janie may "outgrow" the developmental lag or "catch up" with other children of his or her age.

I once had a long-distance telephone call from a physician in a small town, who asked me to see a 6-year-old boy who was markedly retarded. For several years, he had "played along" with Billy's parents, who were his personal friends. He minimized, if not ridiculed, their apprehensions. When Billy did not begin to talk long past the expected time, he reminded the parents of a cousin of his who had not talked until the age of four years but then made up for lost time and eventually graduated from high school and college. He advised: "If Billy won't talk, just don't give him the things he wants unless he asks for them verbally." When this method did not work and the parents wondered whether they should have Billy tested, he said some unkind words about "all that psychology stuff." But when Billy was to be enrolled in the first grade, the school authorities refused to accept him. The heartbroken parents were enraged at the physician who, they felt, had either been inexcusably ignorant or had knowingly betrayed their trust in him. When I saw them, they asked again and again: "*Why* didn't he tell us?"

Adequate examination and the issuance of correct information are indeed indispensable. But they by no means constitute the whole of the expert's responsibility. The cited examples show that the mere procedure of Binetizing and Simonizing a child, the mere determination of an intelligence quotient, the mere pronouncement of the test result do not in themselves take care of the significant matter of family sentiments. It is true that each situation is unique and that different parents come with different problems.

Yet it is possible to pick out from the large welter of cases several recurrent puzzlements which are voiced almost invariably. Allow me to enumerate some of the questions which are asked regularly with a great deal of feeling and to which the inquirers hope to get straightforward answers, without evasion and without hedging:

What is the cause of our child's retardation?

Have we personally contributed to his condition?

Why did this have to happen to us?

What about heredity?

Is it safe to have another child?

Is there any danger that our normal children's offspring might be similarly affected?

How is his (or her) presence in the home likely to affect our normal children?

How shall we explain him (or her) to our normal children?

How shall we explain him (or her) to our friends and neighbors?

Is there anything that we can do to brighten him (or her) up?

Is there an operation which might help?

Is there any drug which might help?

What about glutamic acid?

Will our child *ever* talk?

What will our child be like when he (or she) grows up?

Can we expect graduation from high school? From grammar school?

Would you advise a private tutor?

Should we keep our child at home or place him (or her) in a residential school?

What specific school do you recommend?

If a residential school, how long will our child have to remain there?

Will our child become alienated from us if placed in a residential school?

Will our child ever be mature enough to marry?

Do you think that our child should be sterilized and, if so, at what age?

These are some of the questions asked commonly by the parents of retarded children. These questions vary, of course, depending on the degree of the child's retardation, on the presence or absence of other children in the family, on the parents' financial resources, on their ideas about social prestige, on their degree of acceptance or rejection of the child.

It is not possible to answer every one of these questions unequivocally. Science has not advanced sufficiently—and probably never will—to make omniscient persons of the consulted physician or psychologist. Aside from the fact that causes of retardation are not always the same in all instances and that there may be multiple contributing factors in the same instance, the search for an ultimate cause often runs against the barrier of our incomplete knowledge. I have never encountered a parent who respected me less because, in answer to the question about the cause of his or her child's retardation, I made no secret of my inability to supply a definite answer. Intelligent parents usually realize fully that would-be erudite terms, such as innate, congenital, or constitutional, though literally correct, often beg rather than answer their question. What most of them hope to hear is

indeed not so much a piece of etiological wisdom in words of Greek or Latin origin as an authoritative and sympathetic endorsement of themselves, of their human and parental competence, of their right not to blame themselves for what has happened.

Parents whose first child happens to be seriously retarded are almost invariably plagued by the question whether or not they should have another child. There is a conflict between the strong desire to enjoy the pleasure of having a healthy child and the simultaneous fear that things may go wrong again. The parents always wait for an opportunity to present this question to the person whom they consult about their handicapped offspring. They are disappointed if this opportunity is not forthcoming. It is not an easy thing to help in the solution of this conflict. For one thing, the question is not merely a desire for information. Behind it is sometimes a scheme, of which the parents themselves are not necessarily aware, to throw the whole burden of responsibility on the adviser. If the second child should also be afflicted, the parents are clear of any blame. They can point an accusing finger at the adviser who had told them what they wanted to hear. It has been my policy to remind parents that every childbirth entails a risk, that no one could possibly have predicted that their first child would be born handicapped. Though experience teaches that lightning does not usually strike twice in the same place, the risk, however small, must rest with the parents. But if they do decide in favor of having another child, they should do so only if they are capable of freeing themselves of any anticipation of disaster. Such constant dread before and after the arrival of the new baby would create an attitude not conducive to a wholesome relationship even with the healthiest and sturdiest child.

There is no time to go into a discussion of all the questions which have been enumerated above. But the introductory examples show how profoundly the feelings of parents are involved in their types of curiosity, in the handling of their retarded children, and in their need for understanding and guidance. Like all human beings, the parents of retarded children react to their feelings. Their own life experiences, which have helped to shape their personalities, have contributed to the manner in which they adjust to pleasant and unpleasant realities in general, and to the presence of a handicapped child in particular.

In essence, one may distinguish three principal types of reaction:

1. Mature acknowledgement of actuality makes it possible to assign to the child a place in the family in keeping with his specific peculiarities. The child is accepted as he is. The mother neither makes herself a slave to him, nor does she take her inevitable frustrations out on him. She goes on functioning in her accustomed way. She continues her associations with her friends and acquaintances. The father shares her fondness for the child. Both parents manage to appraise the needs of their normal children as well and to distribute their parental contributions accordingly.

2. Disguises of reality create artificialities of living and planning which tend to disarrange the family relationships. The fact of the handicap is seen clearly but is ascribed to some circumstances, the correction of which would restore the child to normalcy. Some culprit is assumed in the child's character or body or in the educational inadequacy of the trainers. The child's poor scholastic progress in the regular grades is interpreted as a manifestation of laziness or stubbornness which must be exorcised with painfully punitive methods; the full burden is placed on the child himself. His low marks, his failure of promotion, the school's recommendation that he be placed in an ungraded class, are taken as a result of the blameworthy effrontery of a willfully unaccommodating child. Parental pressures to speed up his lagging speech development, to correct his indistinct articulation, and to improve his homework heap misery on the child, who finds it impossible to gain parental approval.

Instead of, or in addition to, the child himself, his body comes in for frantic attempts at correction. Tongues are clipped, prepuces are amputated, tonsils are evicted with the notion that somehow such measures will undo the reality of his handicap. Thyroid extract, caused to be swallowed by some physicians with hazy etiologic notions, and chiropractic adjustments of an allegedly misplaced vertebra are still much too frequently employed as a means of disguising reality.

3. Complete inability to face reality in any form leads to its uncompromising denial. The formula goes something like this: "There is absolutely nothing the matter with the child. Those who are anxious about his development are merely pessimistic spreaders of gloom.

Some children walk or talk sooner than others, and some take their time." This is often the reaction especially of fathers who have no knowledge of children and do not wish to be bothered about them. They are away at work most of the day, have a glimpse of the child when he is asleep, hear the child's laughter on the rare occasion when they pick him up, and conclude with a shrug of the shoulder: "I can't see anything unusual."

A busy surgeon, the father of three children, could not see anything unusual about his youngest child, a severely withdrawn, autistic boy whom his mother brought to our clinic against her husband's wishes. The surgeon finally came, after several invitations. He had no idea of the child's developmental data; he left all this to his wife, he declared complacently. I tried to get an emotional rise at least by making him angry. I asked whether he would recognize any one of his three children if he met him unexpectedly in the street. He thought for a while, scratched his head, and then said calmly: "Well, I don't really know if I would." He felt that his wife's concern about the child was all nonsense but if she wanted to bring him to the clinic, that was all right, too; after all, this was her own business.

Any slightest acquaintance with the elementary principles of psychology is enough to indicate that all these different types of attitudes and resulting practices are deeply anchored in the emotional backgrounds of the individual parents and other relatives. Smothering overprotection, cold rejection, nagging coercion, or open neglect defended as proper tactics necessary to cope with the child's handicap, are in the main fundamental, dynamically evolved reactions which seize on the handicap with a readily accessible, superficial explanation.

All of this leads to the inescapable conclusion that the study and treatment of exceptional children would be sorely incomplete if the emotional factors of family relationships were left out of the consideration. In every instance, the place of the exceptional child in the family structure calls for a thorough overhauling, often with the urgent need for interviews with the parents. Frequently enough, the parents themselves beg for such an overhauling; they do so by asking seemingly specific or insignificant questions, and are most appreciative if such hints are understood and they are given an opportunity to talk themselves out before an experienced and sympathetic listener.

8 Modeling and Shaping by Parents to Develop Chewing Behavior in Their Retarded Child

William H. Butterfield

CASE HISTORY

A moderately retarded 8-year-old mongoloid child was referred by his parents who reported that their son ate only liquids, pureed baby foods, and semi-solid foods such as ice cream and cottage cheese.

A 1-week mealtime observation period established that the child did not bite down on, or chew any solid foods offered to him, and that the food the child most often asked for was creamed cottage cheese. The observations also revealed that the parents spent a great deal of time attempting to get the child to chew solid foods. A similar pattern of eating behavior was observed at school.

Attention has been shown to be a powerful reinforcer. Even attention that would be aversive to most children can be reinforcing for some children. The parents and the child's siblings were asked to quit urging the child to chew or to swallow and to quit shouting at the child when he did not chew.... [Instead] the family members employed the following procedure.

The mother gave the father a graham cracker and told him to make a "crunch." The father then took the cracker between his teeth and, with his lips spread apart so that his teeth were visible, bit down on the cracker producing an audible "crunch." Upon hearing the crunch, the mother immediately praised the father and reinforced him with a spoonful of creamed cottage cheese. This procedure was repeated until all the family members had modeled the behavior and had been reinforced.

Next, the mother offered the boy a graham cracker and asked him to produce a crunch. If he crunched within 15 sec, he was immediately reinforced with a spoonful of creamed cottage cheese and by copious praise from all the family members. When he responded he was given another cracker and the procedure was repeated. This procedure was continued until he had consumed a small jar of cottage cheese at which time the session was terminated. If a 15-sec interval passed without the boy "crunching" the family members "matter of factly" repeated the modeling procedure. If he failed to respond after five such rounds of modeling, the modeling session was terminated.

At first the mother was instructed to reinforce any approximation of a "crunch." She was then to successively increase the response requirement until the child bit completely through the cracker. The child was to be first reinforced for every bite. Later when he was biting regularly the requirement was increased to two bites per teaspoonful of creamed cottage cheese. From this point the response requirement was gradually increased until the cottage cheese reinforcement was eliminated and the behavior was maintained by social reinforcement alone. Following the same procedure, the level of social reinforcement was then reduced to a point where the child only occasionally received social reinforcement for proper eating behavior.

RESULTS

Prior to treatment the mother and other family members scolded the child on an average of eight times during a 20-min period. Upon the implementations of the program, the family successfully terminated their scolding behavior. The parents reported the following data: Sessions 1 and 2: "child cried." Sessions 3 and 4: "child attended to models and did not cry." Session 5: "child cried." Sessions 6 and 7 (first successful chewing session): "child happy." Session 8: "child sleepy and groggy." Session 9 through 13: "child happy." Session 14: "child sleepy and groggy." Session 15 on: "child happy." It did not appear to make any difference whether there were several models or only one during the treatment sessions. . . .

After the 24th day the parents found that their child had developed a "buzz saw"-like rate of crunching. At this point they discontinued counting "crunches" and discontinued the mod-

eling. After the 24th day they started reinforcing the boy for completing whole crackers. At the same time they began to introduce new solid foods and to reinforce him for eating them. During the week prior to termination of the formal treatment program, the boy was eating the following solid foods: Saltine crackers, Oreo cookies, graham crackers, cake, eggs, and meat.

DISCUSSION

The evidence strongly suggests that the treatment procedures were responsible for the boy's new behavior. This assumption is even more strongly supported when we examine the child's eating behavior at school. By the third week his eating behavior at home had progressed to the point where he was chewing at a high rate. However, at school there had been no change. At this point, a similar procedure was implemented at school with the teacher acting as the model. In about 3 weeks from the time the boy's teacher started the program, the child was also eating crackers, cookies, and cake at school without further modeling by the teacher.

Forty-two weeks after the termination of treatment the parents report that their son eats larger quantities of solid foods and that his eating behavior is being maintained without further reinforcement by them. They do report, however, that the variety of solid foods he eats has not further increased and they plan to reimplement the procedure to get him to eat a wider variety of foods. They also report that they have been unable to get the boy to eat with his mouth closed and want to consult with our staff in developing a treatment program to accomplish this goal. It would appear that this behavior is directly related to the modeling procedure, although it is not unusual for children of this age to chew in this fashion.

REFERENCES

[Seven references not reprinted.]

9 Health Insurance: A Dilemma for Parents of the Mentally Retarded

Frank Warner,
Thomas Golden,
and Maureen Henteleff

Although the cost of such medical care and treatment seems to be soaring in most areas of the country, little attention has been given to the nature of the restrictions imposed by health insurance companies on families with mentally retarded dependents. Therefore, this study was undertaken to obtain evidence concerning the extent of these limitations imposed by the health insurance industry.

METHOD

Twenty health insurance companies were randomly selected from an original list of 104 health insurance companies operating in the San Francisco Bay area during the summer of 1971. Two graduate students volunteered to personally interview executive personnel in each of the 20 health insurance companies. Primarily, the interview concerned itself with the following questions:
1. Does the health plan include dependents who are mentally retarded?
2. If not, why not?
3. If so, are the premium rates for families with mentally retarded dependents the same as for families without a mentally retarded dependent?
4. If a family is already enrolled in a health plan before the delivery of a mentally retarded child, is the child still excluded from all coverage?

RESULTS AND DISCUSSION

Fifteen (75 percent) of the 20 health insurance companies interviewed did not provide coverage for mentally retarded dependents in their health plans. Of the 5 health insurance companies that did cover mentally retarded dependents only 2, Kaiser Foundation and Blue Cross/Blue Shield, charge the same premium rates as they would to families without retarded dependents. However, this coverage does not include dental care or psychiatric treatment. The other 3 companies that cover mentally retarded dependents charge up to double the regular rates for families with mentally retarded dependents. The most frequently mentioned reasons why the health insurance companies either exclude mentally retarded dependents or charge higher premium rates were as

Reprinted from *Exceptional Children*, Vol. 39, September 1972, pp. 57–58 by permission of the Council for Exceptional Children. Copyright 1972 by The Council for Exceptional Children.

follows in frequency order: mentally retarded children require expensive diagnostic procedures; they are more in need of medical specialists; they are more accident prone; they are more apt to be emotionally disturbed; and they have a higher incidence of self-inflicted injuries.

The five health insurance companies that do insure mentally retarded dependents all require a medical examination to determine the extent of mental retardation. The degree of mental retardation determines the premium rates. A child who is considered to be mildly retarded would usually be classified under a lower rate than would a severely retarded child who is thought to be a greater risk. It appears then that a child's I.Q. rather than his present health status deter-mines the cost of the health insurance coverage.

It is understandable that health insurance companies would expect mentally retarded children to be more in need of medical care and treatment than nonretarded children. However, although many mentally retarded children have severe physical disabilities, a good number of the retarded, particularly the educable mentally retarded, do not have any gross or chronic physical disabilities. With an estimated 30 million Americans without any form of health insurance coverage, one wonders how many of these people are mentally retarded.

REFERENCES

[Two references not reprinted.]

10 Foster Family Care for the Retarded: Management Concerns of the Caretaker

Robert S. Justice,
Janice Bradley, and
Gail O'Connor

Care of the retarded has increasingly moved away from institutionalization and isolation within state hospitals. This national trend of expanding community services as alternatives to residential placement has intensified the need to examine the effectiveness of various hospital and community programs. As community placements continue to increase, and as innovative programs within the institution change its traditional custodial role, crucial questions arise concerning how best to interrelate specialized services to achieve maximum benefits for the retarded.

Recent California legislation designed to encourage alternatives to state institutionalization make it imperative to assess these placement programs. Foster family care was selected as the focus of this investigation as this program has the largest number of previously institutionalized patients placed in the community. In a nationwide survey, Morrisey (1966) presented statistics on the use of family care homes as an alternative placement. Approximately one-half of the 96 institutions reported they utilized such programs. Although in 1964, 8 of the 26 states employing foster family care accounted for 80% of the placements, wide variation occurs and not all institutions within the same state utilize this method of care.

Previous studies have been concerned primarily with attempts to define successful outcomes and to ascertain what variables are related to placement results. Those studies which focused on the characteristics of patients which led to successful placement have found that sex, age, I.Q., diagnosis, age at placement, race, length of hospitalization, and selected abilities did not differentiate between success and failure on foster family care placement (Carhill 1967; Tarjan 1959). However, within certain subgroups, age, sex, length of hospitalization, and toilet training interacted to discriminate placement outcome (Brown 1959; Carhill 1967). In a study of caretaker characteristics and placement success, Windle (1961) found that caretakers with high socioeconomic status, an estimated greater interest in the patient, and imputed altruistic motives, were given a higher rating by social workers. However, there were almost no significant correlations between the characteristics studied and a criterion based on measures of caretaker failure per patient month.

According to Windle (1962), studies that have attempted to assess the reasons of failure of patients when released into the community must be considered merely suggestive because of small sample size and other methodological difficulties. Windle did indicate, however, that the major reasons for retardates' failure in family care appear to be intolerable behavior and lack of environmental support.

The purpose of this study was to ascertain (1) the problems of caring for retarded foster children in the community as reported by the caretakers, and (2) the extent to which community resources were utilized to supplement the care and treatment provided by the foster family.

METHOD OF PROCEDURES

The sample consisted of caretakers who had at least one mentally retarded patient under 18 years of age on leave from Pacific State Hospital, and who resided in a geographically defined homogeneous service area. A structured interview was administered to 59 foster mothers caring for a total of 195 retardates. Respondents were asked what problems they have had in caring for retarded children in a family setting in the community and what community resources were used to aid in their care and training of the child.

Caretakers were asked if they had used specified public or private services for any patients in the home during the past six months. Public services were defined as being tax supported and administered by an official governmental agency. Private services were defined as those provided by nongovernmental agencies or private prac-

titioners, regardless of whether funding was from voluntary sources, from public funds for purchase of services, or both. A distinction was also made between professional and nonprofessional help; the latter included family members, relatives, friends, and the patient's family. A further question concerned what additional services or programs the caretakers believed would be helpful in meeting the children's needs.

For all patients in the study group, information was also recorded about school status and participation in community health, recreation, religious, and activity programs. With the exception of actual enrollment in summer programs the previous year, participation was defined as attendance within the past six months.

Patient characteristics were obtained from the updated census at Pacific State Hospital.

FINDINGS

The characteristics of the patients in the study group are presented in Tables 1 and 2. Although they ranged in age from 4 to 17 years, most of them were between 12 and 17. About one-half were profoundly or severely retarded. The medical diagnosis for slightly over one-half of the children was Down's syndrome. Although in general few were physically handicapped, over 60% had some difficulties with speech, and 50% had difficulty in dressing themselves without assistance. Although over one-third were hyperactive and/or aggressive, few other behavior problems were noted.

Table 1.   I.Q. and Age of Patients Placed in Foster Care Homes

| | | Chronological Age | | | | | | | |
| | | 0-5 | | 6-11 | | 12-17 | | Total | |
	I.Q.	(N)	(%)	(N)	(%)	(N)	(%)	(N)	(%)
Profound	(0-19)	0	0	4	2.1	12	6.1	16	8.2
Severe	(20-35)	1	.5	30	15.4	53	27.2	84	43.1
Moderate	(36-51)	5	2.6	33	16.9	26	13.3	64	32.8
Mild	(52-67)	2	1.0	6	3.1	16	8.2	24	12.3
Borderline	(68+)	0	0	2	1.0	5	2.5	7	3.5
Total		8	4.1	75	38.5	112	57.3	195	99.9

NOTE: Study included only patients ≤ 18 years (N = 195). Percents are based on N/195.

The caretakers interviewed had an impressive record of prior experience in the child care field. Seventy-one percent of them had institutional or foster care experience or both prior to participation in Pacific State Hospital's program. Of these, half had worked with retarded. Most caretakers were certified by the State Department of Social Welfare between 1966 and 1968, and 85% had cared for a total of ten patients or less. Although 93% of them had raised children of their own, almost half had no children living at home at the time of the study and only two households contained extended family members.

These caretakers could be charac-

Table 2.   Level of Patient Functioning Reported by Caretakers

Variables	N	%
Ambulation (no difficulty)	165	84.6
Toilet trained	178	91.3
Partially toilet trained	15	7.7
Full arm-hand use	177	90.8
Vision (no difficulty)[1]	154	79.0
Hearing (no difficulty)[1]	188	96.4
Speech understandable to a stranger	67	34.4
Speech difficult to understand	97	49.7
No intelligible speech	31	15.9
Can feed self	195	100.0
Can dress without help	98	50.3
Not hyperactive	127	65.1
Not aggressive	127	65.1

Note: Percents are based on N/195.
[1] Reported level of functioning with use of corrective devices when necessary.

Table 3. Number of Problems Reported by Caretakers

	N	%
No problems	18	30.5
One problem	23	39.0
Two problems	12	20.3
Three problems	5	8.5
Four or more problems	1	1.7
Total	59	100.0

terized as having been raised in large families, but very few were from families who had cared for foster children. However, 32% of the caretakers and 19% of the husbands did report personal experience with the problems of mental retardation in their own families.

Seventy percent of the caretakers specified one or more problems related to the care of the children. These are shown in Tables 3 and 4. It was possible for each caretaker to report more than one problem; therefore results are presented in terms of the number reporting each type of problem.

Public misconceptions about the mentally retarded and lack of community acceptance were the most frequently named problems. Examples reported to illustrate unfavorable public attitudes included open curiosity displayed toward patients, antagonism of neighbors and friends, discrimination against the caretaker's own children, exclusion of patients from community activities, and imposition of restrictive zoning regulations or other special requirements. Problems related to school and lack of other kinds of supportive services were also prevalent. Behavior problems with the patients and difficulties with the supervising agencies and natural parents accounted for most of the other problems reported.

Of the caretakers who identified problems, almost half had used professional counseling and referral services

Table 4. Number of Caretakers Reporting Each Type of Problem

	N	%
Public misconceptions about M.R. and lack of acceptance in the community	14	34.1
School problems[1]	11	26.8
Lack of other supportive programs[2]	11	26.8
Behavior problem of patient	9	21.9
Lack of medical and/or dental care in the community	7	17.0
Problems with supervising agencies	7	17.0
Problems with natural parents	7	17.0

Note: 41 caretakers reported a total of 66 problems. Percents are based on the number of caretakers reporting each type of problem divided by the total number reporting at least one problem (i.e., 14/41 = 34.1%). Therefore the columns do not total 100%.
[1] Program inadequacies, personnel conflicts.
[2] Recreation, day care, workshops, etc.

in relation to these problems and some of them also had received help from nonprofessionals. Nineteen percent had received help from non-professionals only; 37% reported no assistance.

Existing medical, educational, recreational and religious programs were heavily utilized by the caretakers. The reported use of these community resources is shown in Table 5. Private programs were heavily utilized, except for education. This is chiefly attributable to the large number of church-sponsored activities available in the area, and to the eligibility of patients for private medical care under Medi-Cal.

To ascertain the combination of resources used, no distinction was made between public or private resources. As is evident, most caretakers used school, medical services, and planned activity programs for patients. Only one caretaker reported no utilization of any community resources.

A look at the use of informal resources revealed that most of the caretakers in the study know other caretakers in the program, and a large percentage of these assist each other with the children's care. In addition to

Table 5.   Use of Resources by Caretakers

	N	%
Educational services		
None	9	15.3
Public education only	49	83.1
Private education only	0	0.0
Both public and private	1	1.6
Medical services		
None	1	1.7
Public only[1]	12	20.3
Private only[2]	21	35.6
Both public and private	25	42.4
Planned activity programs		
None	11	18.6
Public only[3]	8	13.6
Private only[4]	20	33.9
Both public and private	20	33.9
Combinations used		
None	1	1.7
Medical services only	4	6.8
Educational and medical services only	6	10.2
Medical services and activity programs only	4	6.8
All three resources	44	74.5

Note: Table refers to number of caretakers utilizing each type of resource for one or more of the patients in the home.
[1] Includes hospital outpatient care and County Health Department.
[2] Can be paid for under Medi-Cal.
[3] School, summer camp, park programs, etc.
[4] Church, Boy Scouts, etc.

the exchange of experiences and ideas, babysitting was the kind of mutual help most frequently reported. In areas where a number of foster care homes are located close together, some of the caretakers share joint recreation activities and transportation. In one instance they had developed a cooperative nursery school.

Recreation or activity programs was the type of service most caretakers stated would help them meet the children's needs. Recreation, day care and workshop programs were mentioned first if only one to three services were mentioned. Nineteen percent stated that it would also be helpful to have a vacation relief service available which would provide adequate care for the patients. Only five caretakers indicated that no additional services are needed

and seven said that they did not know of any that would help.

Since each foster family may have from one to six patients, it was considered necessary to ascertain the number of patients served by one or more community programs. The categories selected for the pattern analyses were the school, planned recreation activities, religious programs, and medical services. As shown in Table 6, the majority of patients utilized two or three of the defined programs. Only four children were total nonparticipants. The most frequent pattern of use was attendance at school, receipt of medical services, and participation in religious activities. Two-thirds of the study group were in school, the great majority attending classes for the trainable mentally retarded. Private

Table 6. Number and Combinations of Community Resources Used by Patients

	N	%
Total number used	195	100
None	4	2
One	33	17
Two	63	32
Three	68	35
Four	27	14
Combinations used	195	100
School, medical and religious	32	16
School, medical and planned recreation	29	15
Medical only	29	15
School and medical only	27	14
Medical and religious only	20	10
Medical and planned recreation only	9	5
All four resources	27	14
All other combinations	22	11

Note: Community resources were grouped into (1) educational, (2) medical, (3) planned recreation programs and (4) religious activities.

physicians' services under Medi-Cal and the hospital's aftercare services were the most frequently used medical resources.

When other types of services were reviewed, notable lacks were revealed such as the absence of day care programs for those not eligible for school, and sheltered workshops or vocational training programs. Seven of the 65 children not attending school were in the cooperative nursery school. There were no patients in sheltered workshops or receiving services from the State Vocational Rehabilitation Department, although some programs for the trainable mentally retarded included shop and craft activities. These individuals do not have severe physical disabilities or serious limitations in self-care, and they are in the age range when prevocational counseling and vocational training are important to future functioning. Therefore, the lack of availability of these programs is a serious service gap.

CONCLUSIONS

Experienced caretakers, expanded community programs, and supportive services provided by the Community Services Division and Pacific State Hospital have enabled profoundly and severely retarded young people to live in a home environment. The length of placement in the study homes varied from one month to nine years, but one-half of the children had been living in the community from two to four years.

Existing medical, educational, recreational, and religious programs were heavily utilized by the caretakers. However, notable service gaps were revealed by the study, such as the lack of available day care programs, prevocational counseling, vocational training programs, and sheltered workshops.

Retarded patients have been placed in foster care homes located in the study area for the past twenty years in rapidly increasing numbers. Forty percent of all the patients under eighteen who are in the Foster Family Care Program at Pacific State Hospital live in this area. However, this study provides evidence that acceptance of the mentally retarded has not kept pace with expanding community care. Achievement of fuller participation in local programs for these children will require increased involvement and communication among those persons active in the Family Care Program, related agencies, and the public.

REFERENCES

Brown, S. J.; Windle, C.; and Stewart, E. 1959. *American Journal of Mental Deficiency* 64:535-42.

Carhill, K. G.; Rader, L. C.; and Schonfeld, H. 1967. *Psychiatric Social Work Review* 1(9).

Morrisey, J. R. 1966. *Mental Retardation* 4(5):8-11.

Tarjan, G.; Dingman, H. F.; Eyman, R.; and Brown, S. J. 1959. *American Journal of Mental Deficiency* 64:609-17.

Windle, C. 1962. Monograph Supplement to the *American Journal of Mental Deficiency* 66(5).

Windle, C.; Stewart, E.; and Brown, S. J. 1961. *American Journal of Mental Deficiency* 66:213-17.

11 Home Care of Severely Retarded Children

K. S. Holt

The mental abilities of some children are so impaired that they require care and supervision throughout their lives. The recommendations for the management of these children are often influenced by the deep emotions that may be aroused by a consideration of this subject, so that it is very difficult to obtain a perspective of the various problems. The study described below was carried out to determine the nature and incidence of the problems in the care of retarded children.

PATIENT MATERIAL

It was necessary that the children and their families in the study should be selected only because of the child's retardation, and not, for example, because they were known to hospitals as unusual cases, or to social workers because their problems had caused them to seek assistance.

It is a legal responsibility of parents in England to ensure that their children receive suitable education from the age of 5 years, and equally, it is the duty of each Local Education Authority to see that this is possible. If a child is considered by the Education Authority to be unsuitable for education in either the ordinary school, or in a school for educationally subnormal children, then he is referred to the Local Mental Deficiency Authority as "ineducable," and they are then responsible for his ascertainment as a defective child.

Local Authorities are not case-finding organizations, but they are responsible for the ascertainment of those defectives who are "subject to be dealt with," as defined in the Mental Deficiency Act of 1927, and clarified in the Education Act of 1944.... The register of the Local Authority will not include some of the younger defectives, and those children whose parents make private arrangements for their care, but it will be increased by some whose abilities may not be severely impaired but whose behavior makes school attendance undesirable. The register of the Local Mental Deficiency Authority has its limitations as a source of case material but it is probably the most comprehensive list of severely retarded children in a community that can be obtained.

The material of the present study consisted of the families of those mentally retarded children in Sheffield who were born after July 1, 1939, and who had been ascertained to be mentally deficient by the Local Mental Deficiency Authority before July 1, 1955. There were 272 families with retarded children who had been ascertained in the specified period. Twenty-five children had died during these years, and 21 families had left the city. The information about 25 families was incomplete. Three refused to allow me to visit them; in nine instances the retarded children were orphans under the care of the Local Authority, and 13 families were not available, either because the parents had died, were in institutions, or had left the area.

There remained 201 families for the study. In three of these there were two ascertained children in the specified age range, but the data are related to the older of the two defective children in each family.

In 31 families the retarded child had been admitted to an institution, but in the remaining 170 families the child was still at home at the time of the study. The proportion of children admitted to an institution is no measure of the extent of the problems because of the extreme shortage of accommodation. In these families, admission to an institution was the last measure, and was often far too late to help the families.

Of the 201 defective children, 101 were boys and 100 girls. None were less than 3 years of age. Seven were from 3 to 5½ years of age, 86 from 5½ to 10½ years of age, and 108 from 10½ to 15 years of age. When ascertained, 84 had been classed as feebleminded, 100 as imbeciles, and 17 as idiots.

The size of the families is shown in Table 1. The retarded child was the only child in 32 families (16%). There were 19 families with five or more children in addition to the retarded child; two of these families had as many as 12 other children each.

The social class of the families was determined from the father's occupation (Census, 1951). Table 2 shows the distribution of the families by social class, with the distribution of the adult population of Sheffield for comparison (Census, 1951). This table shows that, despite the qualifications described above, the case material is reasonably representative of the general population as regards social classes.

PROCEDURE

Visits to the homes of the families with retarded children formed the main part of this study. A letter was sent to each family explaining the purpose of the visit, and making an appointment for several days ahead. The families were visited when most of the members would be at home. The best times were found to be in the later afternoon when the children had returned from school, or early evening after the parents' meal.

The interviews with the parents were conducted informally. Free discussion was encouraged, and notes were never produced. The discussion was directed along the lines of a schedule that had been memorized, and whenever unusual opinions were expressed the conversation was returned to that topic later to confirm the views. In this way all pertinent points

Table 1.   Size of Families

Number of other children in addition to the defective child	0	1	2	3	4	5 or more
Number of families	32	64	43	28	15	19

Table 2. Social Class of the Families

Social Class	Families Visited Number	%	Adult Population of Sheffield, %
I and II	23	11.5	14.2
III	125	62.5	56.0
IV and V	51	25.0	29.0
Insufficient data	2	1.0	0.8

were covered in the interviews. Careful notes were made at the end of each interview.

I conducted all the interviews personally. This meant uniformity of observation, but there was always a possibility that the observations might be biased by my own views. I tried constantly to guard against any personal bias.

The interviews lasted from half an hour to over an hour. The mother was always seen, but sometimes the father was not at home at the time of the visit. Arrangements were made to see the fathers later if I felt that this would add to, or clarify, the information obtained. Although each family was interviewed only once, many were seen at other times—at hospital clinics, collecting their children from occupation centers, and at meetings of the Association of Parents of Backward Children.

The information obtained from the home visits was supplemented by reference to the notes of the Mental Health Department and the Children's Hospital, and by discussions with Mental Health Visitors and Hospital Almoners. The home visits were carried out before these additional data were collected so that I would not be influenced by other opinions. I found that my observations coincided closely with the views of others working with these children.

Much of the information related to the other children in the family. Whenever possible the parents' information about their children was checked by watching and talking to the children. Also, in the case of those children attending schools in Sheffield, the Principal School Medical Officer told me about any who had frequent absences from school, or showed unusual behavior, or exhibited any unusual features, that might be due to the presence in the home of a defective child.

THE PRACTICAL PROBLEMS

The problems presented by retarded children may be considered in two parts: the practical problems, and the emotional disturbances. Obviously, the two are interrelated, but this division forms a useful basis for discussion . . .

The retarded children required more care and attention than normal children. Some, however, were exceptionally troublesome, and these can be considered in three groups: those requiring nursing care; those needing constant supervision because of their aggressiveness or restlessness; and those needing attention at night. These problems exhausted the parents, resulted in the neglect of the fathers and siblings by the mothers, curtailed relaxation and holidays, caused difficulties with shopping and travelling, and gave rise to extra expense (Table 3).

Care of the Child

Fourteen of the two hundred one children required nursing care. They could not walk; they had to be fed, bathed and dressed, and they were incontinent. The mothers showed intense devotion to these children, and the children, although of such low intelligence, seemed to foster this attention by showing resentment if unfamiliar persons dealt with them.

In 63 families the children's behavior was so difficult that constant surveillance was essential. Destructiveness was the main problem in 39 children; 9 were exceptionally aggressive; 8 were restless; and 7 often wandered away from home. Several parents had to resort to extreme measures. One mother fastened her son to a rope that was pegged down in the garden. Another kept a toilet bucket for her own use downstairs, carrying it from room to room, so that she never need leave the child unattended. Many parents had erected high fencing around their gardens, or divided up the courtyard at the back of the house.

Thirty-one of the two hundred one

Table 3. The Incidence of Some Practical Problems Observed in 201 Families with Retarded Children

Problems and Needs	Families	(%)
Of retarded children		
Nursing care	14	7
Constant supervision	63	31
Attention at night	31	15
Of families		
Exhaustion of mother	38	19
Exhaustion of father	11	5
Father's work affected	6	3
Siblings attacked	24	12
Siblings suffering through helping	11	5
Mother never leaving child	6	3
Parents never out together	82	11
Parents never taking a holiday	34	17
Additional expense	59	29

children often needed attention at night. In all but one of these cases the mothers attended to the child, with help from the father in only five cases. In one family, however, the father always attended to his son at night as he felt that his wife needed her rest to be able to look after the child in the daytime.

The parents arranged for restless children to sleep conveniently near to them. Thus, 6 of the 31 children slept with their parents. Although these arrangements made it easier for the parents to attend to their children at night, they also tended to perpetuate the restlessness. Each of the six children sleeping in the parents' bed could have slept elsewhere, and better arrangements could have been made for 14 of the 17 sleeping in the same room as the parents. It follows that while the strain caused by these restless children can be appreciated, the possibility that parents' overanxiety perpetuated or aggravated the situation must be recognized.

The Parents' Health

In most of the families the mother bore the heaviest burden of work. Many of them appeared to be in poor health. They were pale and worn out by the strain of caring for their retarded children. Thirty-eight severe examples were noted. Some of these 38 mothers had large families and were from the poorer classes. They might have been exhausted anyway, but their condition appeared to be aggravated by the extra care needed for the retarded child.

Stories of weight loss were common. One mother had lost 31 kg in weight in the first 4 years of the child's life. Several broke down completely and had to be treated in hospital. Two mothers with serious chronic illnesses refused to have treatment rather than leave their children.

Two mothers attempted suicide. One was abnormally devoted to her child. She had no time either for her husband or other children, and refused to allow anyone into the house lest the retarded son catch an infection. She attempted suicide at a time when she appeared to be experiencing an intense conflict between devotion to the child and guilt caused by realization of the extent she had neglected her husband and normal children. The other mother was not very intelligent and she was unable to manage her microcephalic idiot son and her other children. She attempted suicide at a moment of complete despair.

The father's health was adversely affected by the presence of the retarded child less often than was that of the mother. This was seen in 11 families. In 7 of the 11 the strain of caring for the retarded child had exhausted both parents. In six families the presence of the retarded child affected the father's work. He was unable to do his work and did not feel able to take opportunities for advancement.

The Siblings

Of the 201 families studied, there were 169 with other children in addition to the retarded child, and these families provided a total of 434 siblings. Twenty-four children suffered from physical attacks that were often unexpected, unreasonable and persistent. In addition to the physical harm, the victims of these attacks were often reduced to a state of constant fear. Siblings younger than the defective child usually suffered in this way. Nineteen of the twenty-four children were younger siblings. One defective child was found with his hand thrust down his small brother's throat. Another pushed his brother through an upper window. Several children had to be admitted to hospital with injuries.

In some families, especially in the working classes, the children were expected to help a great deal. It might be anticipated that an older sister would become a "second mother," as was observed in 11 families; but almost as often, in 8 families, a boy had to do a large share of the work. Eleven children suffered seriously through this burden. The school teachers remarked that their work was very poor because they were always so tired, and one older boy lost a good post in a laboratory through his frequent absences looking after a defective sister.

Relaxation and Holidays

Some mothers never left the defective child. This was especially noticeable in the group with children needing nursing care. Six of the fourteen mothers in this group had stayed with the child constantly for several years.

In many families, the mother was able to have a break only by her husband taking over the work. Thus there were 82 families in which the parents were never able to go out together. There were many other families in which relaxation and other activities were very considerably restricted.

Apart from the group of children needing nursing care, the severity of the retarded child's condition did not always appear to be the most important factor affecting the ability of the parents to obtain relaxation. Whether the parents went out together in the evenings or not depended more upon their own wishes to do so, and their ability to have someone to look after the children. Only seven families employed paid child minders, and only five were helped by neighbors. In all the other families where the parents had occasional relaxation, they relied upon relatives to look after the children. In two-thirds of the cases other children in the families did the task, and in many of the others the help came from a grandmother.

It was difficult for many of the parents to obtain the benefits of an annual holiday. For most of them a holiday meant the added strain of caring for the defective child in different and often strange surroundings. The parents in 34 families felt that the retarded child prevented them from taking holidays. Problems of travelling and the antisocial behavior of the children did in fact make holidays impossible for many of these families, but there were 11 families where holidays should have been possible if the parents had been able to bring themselves to make the effort. It appeared that in these cases the holidays were prevented more by the parents' reactions than by the retarded child. The majority of the parents who did take holidays preferred to go to cottages or caravans, or to stay with relatives, rather than face the embarrassment of mixing with other people.

Shopping, Traveling, and Expense

Those mothers who were tied to the house with the child had to rely upon the husband, other children, or neighbors to do the shopping. This was a satisfactory arrangement in only a few cases. Other mothers had to take the defective child with them to the shops. For some this was a nightmare. They had to go to shops where they were well known so that they could be served quickly before the child became restless or did some damage. Many said that they returned home with only half the things they wanted.

Traveling with the defective children was often time-consuming and difficult. Those children who were attending a training center had to be taken on the bus, thus taking up much of the mothers' time for domestic work. Many of the children became restless if they had to wait for a bus, and some were noisy and excitable when traveling.

Fifty-nine parents complained about the expense incurred in caring for their children and these claims did not appear to be exaggerated. The causes of the extra expense could be grouped as follows:

No. of Families

Seeking advice or training for
the child in the hope that it would
be beneficial 23
Damage 20
Worn out clothing, because of
roughness or frequent soiling 9
Traveling expenses 5
Alterations to house 2

THE EMOTIONAL DISTURBANCES

The observations relating to the emotional disturbances are summarized in Table 4. It was not possible to talk to the parents of these children without realizing the deep disturbances created by their child's condition. In not one

Table 4. Emotional Disturbances and Their Consequences in 201 Families with Retarded Children

Problems	Number of Families	Proportion (%)
Parental relations		
Quarrelling	12	6
Separation	10	5
Sibling reactions		
Resentment	20	10
Shame	10	5
Imitation	1	<1
Social reactions		
Isolation	126	63
Neighbors objectionable or reserved	148	74

of the families I visited did I consider that the parents had made a full emotional adjustment to the problems, and were able to lead a normal life within the community. Some had come near to doing so by very gallant efforts.

The parents were usually bitterly disappointed that their cherished hopes had ended in this way. One mother showed this very clearly when she explained that she and her friends had all had their babies about the same time. Now her friends were worrying about their children passing the eleven plus examination, when her daughter could never hope to pass any test.

The emotions of guilt and shame were very noticeable in most parents, with the exception of a small number whose children had been normal, and had then become retarded after an illness such as meningitis or encephalitis. These parents were much better adjusted to their problems than the others.

Two mothers showed very open guilt reactions, regarding the child's condition as a punishment for previous transgressions. In others the basic reactions were changed to marked overanxiety and a desire to devote themselves entirely to their retarded children. The impression one got from these mothers was a sense of inadequacy and failure in having produced a retarded child.

The diagnosis of retardation would not be accepted by some parents. Two families rejected the possibility outright, while others avoid it by emphasizing other physical defects. Thus one said, "it's his speech," another, "He's not mentally defective but spastic."

Many parents showed resentment. This was sometimes against a doctor who had failed to tell them about the child's condition, or who had told them brusquely. Others directed their resentment against neighbors, or an impersonal "they" who failed to help the family.

Parental Relations

The parents were forever seeking reasons why their child was mentally defective. It was surprising to find that in not one family did a parent openly lay the blame for the handicap upon the other, although it is possible that such feelings were present but were not expressed. In several cases, however, other relatives would pursue this question of apportioning the blame upon the parents either directly, or indirectly by insinuations about the handling of the child. The mother was blamed in these cases, and the paternal grandmother was the principal offender. Three mothers had been completely rejected by their relatives in this way, the presence of the retarded child giving them an excuse to oppress and dominate the mother.

In 12 families the parents quarrelled with each other severely, frequently, and persistently, and this marked unrest appeared to be directly attributable to the presence of the handicapped child. Quarreling occurred from time to time in varying degrees in other families, but this was particularly serious in the 12 families. There were three main reasons for the unrest: (1) the mother's, and less often the father's, extreme exhaustion; (2) the mother's extreme devotion to the child with the rejection of her husband; (3) the fear of further pregnancies.

In 10 families the parents had separated. This group of parents was rather different from the group who quarrelled. One mother would not divulge the reason for the separation, but she was emphatic that it was in no way connected with the retarded child. In two families the separation occurred as a direct result of the mother's complete devotion to the handicapped child. But in the other seven families it was uncertain whether the presence of the child brought about the separation, for these were low-grade families whose houses were dirty and who neglected responsibilities and the children, and who would probably have broken up in any case.

It seemed then that the mother's devotion to the child, with consequent neglect of the family, was the most potent factor in causing unrest in the home, and separation of the parents in a few cases. In most families of reasonable integrity the burdens were shouldered, even though this led to quarrelling, and only in the less secure families was separation observed.

Sibling Reactions

The reactions of the other children in the families might be considered in three aspects: resentment at the lack of attention they received; shame and embarrassment; and imitation of the defective child.

Twenty children were extremely resentful of the attention given to the retarded child. This was most noticeable in older children, and was seen in only one child in the pre-school age period. Some children developed attention-seeking devices, but others appeared to retire into themselves. One girl was interested only in schoolwork. She had no friends, and the parents had found her on several occasions sobbing in her room because, she said, they did not love her. The rejection of the normal children by their mothers for the sake of the defective ones could be very marked. Two mothers, for example, had completely rejected their normal children, who were being brought up by relatives, and had been legally adopted by them. The difficulties these reactions of the siblings create for parents are illustrated by the following case history.

Mrs. A. is an intelligent woman who appreciated that problems would arise if she neglected her normal child. However, she found that if she did not give her attention to the retarded child his behavior became very obstreperous. So finding that the attention-seeking behavior of the normal child was less disturbing than the behavior of the retarded child when he did not get attention, she came to give more and more of her time to the handicapped one.

The shame and embarrassment shown by the siblings was, to some extent, a measure of the parent's own adjustments. These reactions were severe, and affected the child's life in 10 cases.

Imitation of the defective child by his normal sibling is recorded because of its infrequency. Only in one family was this a serious problem. It seemed that in other cases where imitation had occurred it was usually a transient reaction.

Social Reactions

There is a strong social stigma against mentally retarded individuals. This is evident in the stares and comments that follow a defective child down the street. This stigma tended to isolate the families from the community. The parents mixed only with a small group of friends, were not eager to make new friendships, and had little wish to join communal activities. Social isolation was a very noticeable feature, being found in 126 of the 201 families. This prevalent reaction tended to unite the parents together into a unit struggling against society. It was impossible to say to what extent this reaction was due to rejection of the family by the community and how much it was due to the parents' own desire to isolate themselves. That the latter factor played some part is suggested by the observations that the reaction was observed in families from all social classes, in families with friendly and helpful neighbors, and that it tended to persist in families after the children had been admitted to an institution.

The reactions of the neighbors to the families with retarded children could be divided into three groups: those who were helpful; those who were objectionable in that they avoided and would not let their children play with the child, or complained about the family, or quarrelled with them; and those who hid behind a barrier of "respectability," showing little interest in the child, and avoiding the family.

Fifty-three families found their neighbors to be helpful. This was evident more in the higher than in the lower social classes. Even these neighbors sometimes limited their helpfulness, and preferred to have little to do with the retarded child himself. This is well illustrated by one neighbor who would take out the normal children to help the mother, but who would never take out the retarded child.

The remaining 148 families found the neighbors to be either objectionable or reserved. The most hurtful act that many of them did was not to allow their own children to play with the retarded ones. Not only did this upset the parents but it meant that their retarded children usually had to play alone when they might have benefited from play with others.

INCIDENCE OF PROBLEMS

It is very easy to obtain distorted views of the problems when considering a subject like mental deficiency. This survey was carried out in order to determine the nature and incidence of problems arising in the home care of retarded children, and for this purpose the families were selected because they had a retarded child, and not because they had problems. It is always possible that when one embarks upon a study of problems in families one finds more of those particular things for which one is searching. It is also possible that any problems that arise will be attributed to the child as a suitable scapegoat. Every care was taken, however, to ensure that the problems found were definitely due to the presence of the retarded child. Consequently, many minor problems have not been included although they may well have been created or aggravated by the presence of the child. It is my belief that in this study I have been able to obtain a reasonably representative picture of the nature and extent of the principal problems created by retarded children.

It would have been interesting to pair the 201 families with similar ones without retarded children, and to contrast the difficulties in the two groups. Such pairing is extremely complex and was outside the scope of this study. It would be fallacious to compare the reports of problems in other family groups without retarded children, for these have been carried out at different times and places than the present study. . . .

REQUIREMENTS OF HOME CARE

This study indicates some of the requirements of home care. The parents should have a reasonable appreciation of the child's condition, and feelings of guilt and shame should be resolved. It is difficult, if not impossible, to overcome the feeling of disappointment, but this may be reduced by attention to the positive assets of the child. Many of the parents, especially the mothers, have a feeling of inadequacy, and this is increased as they experience successive difficulties in rearing their children, such as problems of feeding and training.

The parents' emotional difficulties can be helped by careful counselling. This begins with the first interview, the correct timing of which is probably one of the most difficult problems in this sphere of medicine. Some suggest that the parents should be allowed to suspect the condition before anything is said to them, but . . . many parents do not appear to realize the child's backwardness until much later than one would expect . . . . There is no doubt that in most cases there is much to be gained by telling the parents quite early.

A single interview is not sufficient . . . . Some advantages may be derived from group counselling, and there is no doubt that many parents benefit by joining Parents' Associations where they can meet and talk to others with similar burdens.

Very few of the mothers had received advice from their doctors. Only 30 families (15%) found their doctor helpful. Others often commented adversely, "the doctor had to call often during my husband's illness but he never once looked at him, or asked about him (the retarded child)," "the doctor never told us about his condition, and even now we have found out, he will not talk to us about it"; "the doctor said she would never be any use and did not bother anymore." A greater appreciation of the difficulties of these parents by the doctors would make them more attentive to advising about the care and management of retarded children. . . .

I once felt that it was important for the parents to appreciate fully their child's condition and disabilities. Unreasonable hopefulness can lead to considerable difficulties and is clearly undesirable, but I have come to feel that it is only some spark of hope, or possibly faith, that enables these parents to bear their heavy burdens year after year. It is important to remember the part that religion can play in these families. . . .

Another requirement of home care is reasonable accommodation. It is a great help if there is somewhere safe for the children to play. Eleven families in this study had neither garden, yard, nor court. Poor living conditions, poverty, and parents of low caliber often go together, and there were 30 families living in appalling conditions that were not fit for rearing any children. Another finding in the lower class families was a tendency to have large families. The lack of advice on family limitation was combined here with an inability to assimilate and follow instructions. The presence of a retarded child in these families was just one facet of the many social problems they presented.

The enlightenment of the general public about mental retardation in recent years has been quite remarkable, but there is still a great deal of stigma attached to defective individuals. If only this attitude could be further changed, more would be willing to help these families. That these families do need help is only too evident, and it is to be hoped that the activities of the various organizations interested in the problem will reduce the antipathy and antagonism of the community to the problem.

These families with retarded children often looked for help from their normal children, or from relatives living either with them or near at hand. The advantages of a family and their relatives living closely together have been recognized by others and were well illustrated by several cases in this study. . . .

It is difficult to formulate a scheme for help that would be applicable to all families. An increased availability of home helps . . . would be expensive, and they would not always be present at the most suitable times. These families need help with many of the small tasks: helping to feed the child; looking after the child while the mother does her shopping, or has a break in the evenings; carrying the child to bed; taking the child to clinics, and so forth. There is surely a place here for the Voluntary Organizations.

Although some of the parents complained about the extra costs, an all-round money grant for these families would be undesirable. It would be too impersonal: these people need an understanding and helping hand. It would lead to the feeling that once money has been given them other efforts can be lessened.

Throughout this discussion the impression may have been given that the problems and requirements of home care are constant and stationary. This is not so. The demands placed upon the family by the handicapped child, and the ability of the family to meet these demands, are in a constant state of flux. A dynamic equilibrium may be reached, but at any time the balance may be upset with consequent temporary or permanent failure of the family to manage the difficulties.

It must have been a recognition of these changing situations that inspired the Ministry of Health to recommend that temporary institutional care should be available so that parents might have periods of rest and be relieved at times of illness and pregnancy. Very few of the families in this study took advantage of this provision, however, partly because they disliked the thought of their child going to an institution, however short the period, and partly because of a shortage of institutional accommodation. It is also possible that the authorities feared that this arrangement might lead to the "dumping" of the children.

HOME CARE AND INSTITUTIONAL CARE

Institutional care for defective individuals was introduced originally largely as a means of segregation from the community.... admission to an institution is seldom for the benefit of the child, but mostly for social reasons. It is little wonder then that many now feel that home care of retarded children is the better form of care whenever possible. Home care will always be necessary for most retarded children, and will be the first form of care for most of those who are later admitted to an institution. It has been shown that home care is often associated with difficulties, and this underlines recent recommendations that every assistance should be given to these families to enable home care to be successful.

Institutional care should not be considered as an all or none proposition. There should not be the thought that the retarded children have to be grouped into those for home care and those for institutional care. Institutional care is not an alternative to home care, but is complementary. Institutional care is one of the many means available to help these families and should be invoked whenever there is extreme family failure, either temporary or permanent. The attitude that these families should be allowed to manage as best they can for as long as they can until they finally break up, and institutional care becomes inevitable, is to be deprecated most strongly.

SUCCESSFUL FAMILIES

This study was designed to show the problems experienced by these families, and the report dwells upon this aspect. Nevertheless, mention must be made that there were families who managed very well and who showed emotional and spiritual reserves that suggested that outside help would be superfluous. The families who managed best were not those in the upper social classes. These parents were usually ambitious for their children and never overcame their frustration and disappointment. The ideal parents were those who, while sufficiently intelligent to appreciate the needs of the child and to have some insight into his difficulties, did not have great ambitions, and so they did not constantly display their disappointment. They were perhaps rather fatalistic in their outlook. They looked upon a child as a gift for which to be thankful whatever his condition. Those families were better adjusted who had not concentrated all their hopes and desires upon one child, and who had other things to think about, often other problems, so that the defective child was not forever in their minds.

It is possible that the home care of retarded children can have beneficial results for both parents and siblings. This is difficult to assess, and the present study does not give information on this point. One got the impression, however, that in some families the parents and other children had come to a deeper understanding of life through their worries and burdens. . . .

REFERENCES

[Thirty references not reprinted.]

12 Parents of the Mentally Retarded Child: Emotionally Overwhelmed or Informationally Deprived?

Adam P. Matheny, Jr.
and Joel Vernick

There is an abundance of articles related to the crisis and concomitant emotional impact of a mentally retarded child upon his parents and to the need for adequate professional counseling of these parents. In general, adequate counseling is depicted as focusing on (1) the parents' acceptance of the reality of having a retarded child; (2) their needs in planning for their child's schooling or residential care, home life, and occupation; and (3) their need for support in the face of possible limitations of life plans for themselves and for their child.

The professional person purportedly faces a formidable task when he counsels these parents, encountering a host of reactions: chronic sorrow, loss of self-esteem, anxiety, guilt, denial, mourning, hostility, rejection, frustration, helplessness, shame, and disorganization of personality. It is suggested that these reactions require some degree of resolution so that the parents can accept help in mobilizing themselves to cope with their child's retardation.

One gains the impression from some of the articles reviewed that when the child is brought to a diagnostic clinic, it is the role of the staff to help provide amelioration of these reactions through short-term, psychotherapeutic approaches. It is not enough for the staff to show, through sympathetic regard, that they are aware of the parents' feelings; they are enjoined to explore actively those feelings. On theoretical grounds alone, emotional morbidity is not only assumed to exist in these parents, but it is often explored and sometimes treated.

To take another point of view, the crisis of having an exceptional child is one which parents can and do work through without professional help. It is our contention that a learning process involving an emotional reorganization has already been embarked upon by the parents from the instant they become aware or are told that their child is different. What the parents require most from diagnostic or informative counseling is specific, clearly transmitted, honest information about the child, implications for his future, and knowledge of what concrete steps they can take to deal with the problems. Although this approach does not exclude the counselor's concern or sympathy, it avoids the pervasive exploration of suspected emotional dis-

Reproduced with permission from the *Journal of Pediatrics* 74: 953–959, 1968. Copyrighted by the C. V. Mosby Company, St. Louis, Missouri.

orders and places the greatest emphasis on helping essentially mature and rational people to learn more about their child.

Unfortunately, few studies of the effects of counseling are available, and most are related to measures of changes in parental attitudes toward their child, clinics, institutionalization, etc. The relation between clinical strategies for giving information and consequent changes in parental knowledge and expectations is virtually unexplored.

We have examined the effects of an informational-educational approach for providing help to parents of the retarded child. Based on previous pilot data and our experience, this study was undertaken to determine whether: (1) when parents initially seek help from a clinic, their presumed emotional reactions do not generally distort or obfuscate an accurate appraisal of their child's present behavior; and (2) when parents have over- or underoptimistic anticipations of their child's future, a brief clinical experience based on an information-learning approach helps them change toward more realistic expectations.

RESEARCH APPROACH

The clinical setting in which this study was carried out is one in which military dependents below the age of seven years are evaluated for suspected mental retardation. Routine diagnostic practices include a home visit by a social worker and a nurse, and medical and behavioral procedures carried out at the clinic. After the evaluation, which requires about two days per family, the child's case is discussed by the staff. Both parents are then given the clinical information and recommendations by a pediatrician during a session lasting from one to two hours.

For the purposes of this study, additional procedures were added; these will be described in some detail since the findings underscore the conclusions presented in this paper.

Prior to the initial visit to the clinic, the social worker interviewed *both* parents at their home for one to two hours. During this period he first administered, independently to each parent, a questionnaire which could be completed in five minutes. On this pre-clinic questionnaire the parents were asked to subscribe to items in content areas about: (1) the expected grade level of the child's future educational achievement, (2) the expected degree of future independence as an adult, (3) the expected degree of success in maintaining a family, and (4) the expected level or type of occupation for which the child could be proficient as an adult.

The social worker then obtained medical and social information pertinent to the clinical evaluation. Although the first impression of the stability of the family unit was gained during this session, little or no time was spent trying to discuss feelings and emotions centered about the child.

Since it was the feeling of the authors that the "major item we had to sell to both parents was information," the social worker made it quite clear that we would discuss with the parents everything that we would find out about their child. Further, the parents were told that they would be present during all aspects of the evaluation and that they should feel free to ask questions of each staff member encountered. The social worker suggested that the parents should not hesitate to put pressure on the staff members to communicate with them about their child. In discussing the communication process with the parents, the social worker indicated that, as with any group of people, some staff members would be better "communicators" than others and that some would be more willing to communicate than others. The parents were encouraged to let the social worker know about any communication problems and told that he would "manage" the communication process until the parents were satisfied. (The establishment of the social worker as an "Evaluation Manager" *for this study* was an attempt to assure ourselves and the parents that a frequent experience with physicians at clinics— the parents being given unclear, little, or no information—would not occur.) Finally, the social worker made it clear that, despite any difficulties of communication encountered by the parents during the evaluation, they would be given a final integration of the information during the counseling session.

About one month after the parents had been counseled by the pediatrician, the social worker again visited the parents for the purpose of evaluating changes following the clinical experience. By means of an interview the parents were asked: (1) what they had learned about their child; (2) what actions they had taken or were going to take regarding school placement, institutional placement, etc.; (3) what areas of information the parents still had questions or doubts about; and

(4) what degree of satisfaction the parents had gained from the experience. They were also given a postclinic questionnaire which duplicated the content areas of the preclinic questionnaire.

METHOD

The parents of 40 children were selected for study. Each family was included as it was referred unless both parents were not available throughout the evaluation—a qualification which excluded less than 6 per cent of all families seen at the clinic. Table 1 contains a description of the families studied.

During the social worker's initial interview with the family, the parents were asked to describe any previously gained diagnostic information. They were also asked to assess their child's developmental level (mental or ability age) in years and months. Several studies have shown that such estimates of ability may provide some indication of the parents' realistic appraisal and acceptance of their child's disability. In the main, these studies indicate that parental judgment agrees well with professional judgment of ability; however, one study suggests that mothers are prone to "distort" (i.e., overestimate) children's abilities.

The questionnaire items were keyed to reflect an Expectation Score (ES) ranging from 0 to 50. The highest ES would indicate that the child was expected to have future accomplishments at a superior adult level, such as becoming a teacher or lawyer, going to college, etc. The lowest ES would indicate that the child was expected to be a completely dependent adult with no

Table 1. Descriptive Statistics of Families

Data	Statistics
Number of parent pairs studied	40
Percentage of retarded children by sex	Boys, 65% Girls, 35%
Mean age of retarded children	47 mo.
Mean age of parents	Fathers, 35 yr. Mothers, 33 yr.
Mean educational level of parents	Fathers, 14 yr. Mothers, 12 yr.
Range of educational level of parents	Fathers, 8 to 18 yr. Mothers, 6 to 14 yr.
Mean number of children in the family	3

prospects of training, family, or job. The questionnaire items were also scored by the staff so as to reflect their expectations of the child's future as based on clinical evaluation. Response reliability of the parents and scoring reliability of the staff yielded correlation coefficients of 0.83 and 0.92, respectively.

The staff's estimate of the child's present ability level and the staff's expectations of the child's future accomplishments were used respectively as the standards of comparison for: (1) the parents' estimate of the child's present ability level, and (2) the parents' preclinic and postclinic expectations of their child's future accomplishments.

RESULTS

The mean of the maternal estimates of the children's present developmental ages (converted to an I.Q.) was 67.4,

and the mean of the paternal estimates was 65.8; the correlation coefficient between the I.Q. estimates of both parents was 0.89 ($p < 0.01$). The difference between the means was not significant. The mean of the clinical estimates of the children's developmental ages (converted to an I.Q.) was 65.1, which was not significantly different from the means of the parental estimates. These findings indicate that our parents' assessments of their children's developmental ages were reasonably accurate when compared with the clinical assessments.

In Table 2 are listed the means of the preclinical and postclinical ES's for mothers, fathers, and parents-composite (an average of the paternal and the maternal ES's). The table also gives the mean of the clinical ES's which were used as the standard of comparison.

No significant difference was found between the means of the paternal and maternal preclinic ES's. Also,

Table 2. Mean Expectation Scores Derived from the Families and Clinic before and after the Clinical Experience

Questionnaire	Clinic	Paternal	Maternal	Parents-composite
Preclinic	30.5	37.2	37.3	37.2
Postclinic	30.5	30.4	30.7	30.6

no significant difference was found between the means of the paternal and maternal postclinic ES's. Additional analyses were made on the basis of the parents-composite scores.

A comparison between the mean of the clinic's ES's and the mean of the parents-composite preclinic ES's indicates that, prior to the clinical experience, the parents tended to have higher expectations for their children's futures than the staff had. The difference between these means was significant ($t = 2.04$, $p < 0.05$). After the experience in the clinic, however, the parents' expectations tended to be congruent with the expectations of the staff; the difference between these mean ES's was not significant at the 10 per cent level. . . .

It seemed clear from these data that parents of the retarded child: (1) are generally in agreement with the staff in appraising their child's present abilities, (2) have unrealistic overestimates of their child's future usage of these abilities, and (3) can be brought to realistic expectations of their child's future capabilities after counseling. These data do not, of course, indicate that the staff's assessment is valid, since only a long-range study could show that the diagnoses and recommendations were appropriate.

What remained to be shown was that the parents translated their new information into actions recommended by the clinic as being appropriate for the child. The parents could, after all, pay lip service to the information they had received but continue to act on the basis of the expectations held prior to coming to the clinic.

Recommendations advanced by the staff to the 40 families included: (1) institutionalization (7 children), (2) special schooling in a nursery or kindergarten for the retarded (21 children), (3) special schooling for the brain-injured (3 children), (4) further medical or paramedical evaluations (4 children), and (5) no specific program other than a follow-up evaluation because the child was not retarded or too young (5 children). Thus, in our study population, 33 families could demonstrate that the diagnostic information was of some consequence to them by actions other than answering appropriately in an interview. Of these families, all but two had initiated or carried out the clinic's recommended actions by the time of completion of this study. These two families received recommendations for special education for the retarded. One family continued to maintain their child in a nursery school for normal children; the other family sought a special educational program centered around psychotherapy for emotional disorders. Clearly, after counseling, most parents' expectations for and knowledge about their children were mirrored in their immediate actions.

DISCUSSION

Our findings qualify some of the generalizations frequently made about the extent and effect of emotional morbidity presumed to exist in families with retarded children. If emotional factors existed in our parent population, these factors were not so disruptive that the parents invariably distorted perceptions of their child's behavior. Furthermore, emotional factors generally did not prevent these parents from receiving new information and acting appropriately on it. These findings, which need further verification in less educated, nonmilitary populations, suggest to us that many parents' lack of acceptance of limitations on their child's life might result from nonemotional constraints— e.g., the parents' level of education, lack of knowledge about retarded children, existing expectations based on normal children, inability to translate the child's present abilities into future capabilities—which can be attenuated by a well-structured delivery of pertinent information about the child.

Clinical contact with parents of the retarded has been laden with an emphasis on emotional factors which are said to cause further retardation, prevent effective management, disrupt family relations, and disallow planning of a realistic future for the child. The counseling of parents is often an extension of this preoccupation, and counselors approach the situation with a theoretical point of view that parents must be helped by slow steps, involving various degrees of "insight." Within this framework, counseling practices vary: Some counselors equate "insight" with the parents finally making the diagnosis—"you are trying to tell me my child is retarded . . ." Some counselors expect tears; some do not. Parents who "shop around," parents who ask too many or too few questions or argue about some point, parents who seem to be ignorant of what other professionals have told them—all are suspect. Implicitly, it is always the parents' and usually the mothers' emotionality which is to blame. The manner by which counselors give information to parents is seldom investigated as being a contributing factor.

We recognize that there are parents who, in fact, *do* fail to receive or act upon properly given information for emotional, intellectual, or other reasons. But, more often than we would want to believe, counseling also fails because of the counselor. The counselor's difficulties—inexperience in communication techniques, hesitancy to give "bad news," protection or "sheltering" of the family, pursuit of the parents' having a positive image of him, and lack of expertise with or confidence in diagnostic information— interfere with his role as an effective communicator (or teacher). Moreover, the consequences of the counselor's difficulties are likely to be attributed to difficulties in the parents when they return to the clinic or go elsewhere. By this process, the parents' continued ignorance can easily be described as psychopathology, and indeed it may become so.

Having a retarded child is a unique learning experience for almost all parents. The guidelines for parental behaviors and expectations are altered; the knowledge gained from having other children in the home or acquired from neighbors is of limited usefulness. Consequently, parents become confused. In the face of this confusion the parents, whether overwrought or calm, will be seeking information for new guidelines and expectations. We are convinced, on the basis of this preliminary study, that many parents can be helped to learn appropriate guidelines for action and expectations when we place the primary emphasis on effective communication rather than on effective short-term psychotherapy.

Undoubtedly more studies are needed to show how and what kind of clinical contacts influence parents of the retarded to alter their behavior and expectations. We also needed to know more about the "styles" of counselors, the dynamics of counseling, and the familial factors which limit the counselor and the counseling. The authors are presently engaged in studies related to these topics. It is hoped that these and similar studies will provide us with new approaches for improving clinical services to parents of the retarded. . . .

REFERENCES

[Twenty-eight references not reprinted.]

13 Shopping Parents: Patient Problem or Professional Problem?

Those of us working with the mentally retarded child and his family are constantly being called upon to reassess our knowledge and skills in meeting human needs. Indeed, in our profession a person frequently re-examines basic concepts and attitudes. In the process of one such examination, I found myself becoming increasingly puzzled as to what was meant by the term *shopping parent.* Various clinicians with whom I spoke had different definitions of what constituted a *shopping parent.*

DEFINITION OF THE TERM

In order to better delineate what is meant by the term and what some causal factors might be, a study was made of all parents of mentally retarded children who contacted the U.C.L.A. Neuropsychiatric Institute, Child Outpatient Clinic, Mental Retardation Unit during the six months between July, 1970 and December, 1970. The problem of defining such a parent became immediately evident when the question arose as to how many times did parents see a professional before becoming *shopping parents.* For instance, after their child had been seen initially at one facility, parents would often go to additional professional people or clinics seeking yet other opinions regarding their child.

Often, friends or relatives would advise the parents to seek another opinion.

This desire for a reassuring second opinion seemed a realistic course of action for a parent, because of the tremendous emotional impact of, and responsibilities implied in, a diagnosis of mental retardation. Thus, after careful consideration of these factors, the following definition, for the purpose of this study, was made: a parent who pursues a third professional evaluation after receiving at least two others on previous occasions is a *shopping parent.*

There were 218 children who received initial screening diagnoses of mental retardation during the study period. Of this total number, only six of the families fell within the range of the definition of *shopping parents.* It therefore appears that the *shopping parent* constitutes less than 3% of this population of parents.

In a publication on mental retardation it was suggested that parents who shop are doing so out of a strong wish for a magical cure (American Medical Association 1965). This did not appear to be the case with the six sets of *shopping parents* we studied, because all six of their children were brought to the clinic for treatment of severe aggressive behavior problems encountered in the home. The patient histories were ones in which the behavior, over a period of years, had become increasingly difficult for both parents and therapists to manage. In fact, at this point in time, the parents' request for evaluation was based upon a realistic desire for help in coping with this behavior.

SUMMARY AND CONCLUSIONS

It is recognized that the above number of *shopping parents* is very small, and that any conclusions made are done so with the reservation of this small number. However, the total population surveyed provided enough data to explore several areas. Because of this, there seemed to be several possibilities for consideration:

1. The term *shopping parent* may be a stereotype that is stultifying and pejorative in that it seems to be used only in reference to parents of mentally retarded children. It appears to reflect a negative professional bias and it obfuscates the larger problem—the parents' request for help.

2. It has been postulated that these parents do not misuse the services, but come out of a sincere desire to obtain help (MacKinnon and Frederick 1970). The parents in this study would seem to support that postulate.

3. Such requests from parents may indicate a severe behavior management problem, where effective intervention in the home through parent education programs or placement of the child in institutions may be required.

4. Parents who have been through several previous evaluations can be effectively helped by a consolidation of the previous evaluations, discussion of the present and previous evaluations, and strong encouragement that they contact the clinic at any future time.

In conclusion, it would appear to me that the term *shopping parent* is really a misnomer in that the parent does not simply flit from one professional to another, rejecting recommendations and information. Rather, it has been suggested that such misnamed parents come to professionals requesting different services than those they have had previously. They can best be helped by meeting that request.

REFERENCES

[Two references not reprinted.]

Part III

ROLE OF THE PROFESSIONS

14 Introduction to Part III

When the literature search for this work began, I did not intend to examine the roles of individual professions relative to families with retarded children. However, the identified literature contained many and varied works on the roles of various professions. Since the literature had been selected for its focus on parents of retarded children, these studies constitute a unique literature on how various professions see themselves relative to parents of retarded children.

Of the articles listed in the "Guide to Further Reading," thirty-nine can be considered as falling under the head "Role of the Professions." Although ranging from 1945 to 1973, they tend to concentrate in the early and mid-1960's. Prior to World War II, the principal service was institutionalization, which removed professionals from intensive interaction with families. After World War II, emphasis on community based services, reinforced by community demonstration grants from Federal agencies such as the Children's Bureau, placed large numbers of professionals in the unfamiliar role of serving families in the community, and the roles of the professions needed clarification. The rash of articles in the 1960's seems to have satisfied the professions about the basic elements of their roles since frequency has declined since 1968.

The thirty-nine articles cite roles for the psychologist, physician, marriage counselor, teacher, home economist, social worker, genetic counselor, nurse, clergyman, and occupational therapist. The physician and the social worker dominate the literature, however; 17 of the articles are on the physician's role, 9 on the social worker's role, and next in frequency are the nurse and psychologist. This is not surprising. Every case of retardation is seen by at least one physician, and several subspecialties in medicine contribute to the overall diagnosis and management of a case. The social worker is exclusively family oriented, so that nearly everything written about the retarded by social workers would qualify for this book.

Most of the roles are defined parochially; that is, the role of a given profession is defined without reference to the role of other professions which may be sharing case management. Many authors allude to the need for coordinating services but this is secondary to the definition of the role for a given profession. A 1973 article by Howell (not reprinted) may be introducing a new dimension to the literature on roles. She discusses the role of the psychiatrist, but she does so in the context of an interdisciplinary team.

The articles reprinted here deal with those professionals who are in most frequent contact with families with retarded members: physicians, psychologists, nurses, social workers, educators, and clergymen. Jensen (1950) describes the role of the physician. This is one of the earliest works on a profession's role and has been frequently cited by later authors. Deisher (1957) also describes the role of the physician, but his article was selected because it describes in more detail than any other the need for continuous service over time and the need for dovetailing any professional's activities with those offered by other professions.

In contrast to Deisher, Rheingold (1945) focuses solely on the informing interview, and does so from the point of view of a psychologist. She provides much detail on the actual conduct of an informing interview and stresses the need to extend service beyond the interview. Schild (1964) describes the role of the social worker. As with Rheingold, casework is seen as a process over time, focusing on periodic crises to an extent but also emphasizing various benefits from continuing support.

The Noble (1970) article covers the role of the nurse. Like the Begab article in Part II, the family's problems over the life cycle are described, and the role of the nurse is fitted to the long-term needs of the family.

As the retarded child grows older, he may be in less frequent contact with professions such as medicine, social work and nursing, and in more frequent contact with teachers and clergymen. Mullen (1960) examines the role of the teacher relative to parents of children with any type of handicap. This author stresses "teamwork" with the parents and expresses an interesting attitude toward the occasionally belligerent parent. Stubblefield (1964) considers the extent and nature of the clergyman's contact with families. Although his findings may not describe the current scene, they provide the only data available.

In any consumer-provider relationship, there is always an element of dominance. The following represent the extremes and the middle ground: (1) consumer-dominant relationship: The consumer decides what he needs and it is the role of the provider to satisfy those needs. (2) egalitarian relationship: The consumer and provider collaborate in decisions on what the problems are and what must be done. (3) provider-dominant relationship: The provider decides what the problems are and what must be done, and it is the role of the consumer to comply with the expectations of the provider.

It is difficult to imagine a situation in which the consumer is completely dominant. For instance, a mother may or may not elect to send her retarded child to a summer day camp for which the child is eligible. But in such circumstances the provider does control the eligibility criteria. The other extreme, provider dominance, would generally require court participation. For instance, a parent who is taken to court for the neglect or abuse of a retarded child may be required to consume various social, psychiatric, or probationary services. Most of the encounters between consumer and provider, however, fall between the extremes, on one side or the other of the egalitarian relationship.

None of the literature embraces the ideal of consumer dominance on the clinical level. Consumer dominance at the program level is found in programs sponsored by parent groups, but in this circumstance the consumer collectively has become the provider. Hersey and Lapidus in Part I describe the egalitarian relationship which, in their words, is a contract explicitly and equally arrived at by consumer and provider. However, works that advocate a completely egalitarian relationship are quite rare. Nearly all fall between an egalitarian and a provider-dominant relationship.

Kysar in Part I reports a parent's disenchantment with excessive and damaging dominance. Many articles, by virtue of their concern about the gaps in service, imply that the service system dominates simply by having the power to offer or to withhold service. Most articles, however, suggest only a general tone of dominance. The ability of parents to participate in rational decision making determines the degree to which an egalitarian relationship is possible. But many authors who write from clinical experiences—probably from highly select populations—are impressed by morbidity in the clientele. (Matheny and Vernick (Part II) doubted this, but they too were dealing with a special sample.) For instance, the following words are applied to parents in an article not selected for reprinting.

problems	inner conflict	irritable
cannot cope	intense	blame
stress	hurt	worried
breaking point	pain	overworked
chronic problem	distorted	fears
pressure	guilt	anxieties
overwhelmed	sin	ashamed
strain	alcoholic	taunted
shocked	angry	guilt
bitter	upset	confusion
hate	monsters	distraught
suffer	cruel	fatigued
turmoil	wrong	doubts

Authors of this and similar works clearly do not view the parent as capable of partnership in rational decision making; the role of benevolent dictator is deemed necessary out of a sense of humanitarianism.

The articles selected for this Part do not go to such an extreme. The authors believe that the capacity to act rationally and constructively varies enormously from family to family and, for a given family, may vary enormously from time to time. Consequently, the egalitarian relationship may be the goal, but the professional must realize when it is necessary to assume leadership because a family is at least partially incapacitated by its problems. (Articles on professional roles tend to favor an egalitarian relationship more than the literature as a whole. As the literature moves away from a consideration of professional roles, it may more easily accept a provider-dominant relationship.)

15 Clinical Management of the Mentally Retarded Child and the Parents

Reynold A. Jensen

The magnitude of the general problem of mental retardation is brought home by the fact that we have an estimated total of 950,000 to 4,500,000 such retarded individuals in our country. But this is only the most obvious consideration. Even more sobering is the realization that there are nearly as many *families* involved. It is difficult to estimate the tragic suffering in a family that has a mentally retarded member. Such suffering is too often aggravated by generous advice from sympathetic relatives, friends, and even professional workers. In all probability our errors are due to (1) lack of understanding of the basic issues inherent in each case, and (2) inadequate techniques in assisting parents to plan more objectively.

It seems obvious that in any program designed to help deficient individuals the emphasis must be placed on the family, for upon the family's attitudes and thinking, particularly that of the parents, depends the ultimate success of the program.

The task of helping parents who have a retarded child is complicated. It is not enough to sidestep the issue or to "tell" them that their child is "feeble-minded" and should be institutionalized. In our experience at the University of Minnesota Hospitals the three most frequently encountered errors are: (1) delay in defining the problem early in the patient's life;

(2) encouragement of parents by holding out false hopes, which naturally results in disillusionment later when the patient is not cordially received in school or becomes a social problem requiring immediate planning for his management; and (3) too much direct advice and/or urging adoption of a specific plan—too often institutionalization. We physicians sometimes assume that this alone will adequately solve the problem. However, our assumptions usually result in failure for we have not fully appreciated the strong emotional ties that bind most parents to the mentally handicapped person. Our own hastily formulated plan often complicates the situation because it increases parental resistance.

Since we have become cognizant of the real and widespread need to offer help to the parents of retarded children we have given serious thought to the development of a *workable* method of doing so. We believe the keynote is the approach to the parents. Several important factors require consideration. Unfortunately most parents still regard mental deficiency as a stigma. In addition they have much real anxiety usually closely related to feelings of guilt. In the majority of instances they try to resolve these emotional problems by assuming an attitude of overconcern and overprotectiveness toward the defective child. This, in a measure, may be protection of themselves. For these reasons we believe, with few exceptions, management of the strong emotional ties that bind the average parent to the defective child is the core of the problem.

Average parents are aware that their child is retarded. We avoid, insofar as possible, directly telling them what they already know. Parents come to us primarily for confirmation of their suspicions and doubts. Our task is to help parents define their own problems and possible solutions to them. In the process we are able to help reorient parental emotional ties with the defective child and give support and justification to the parents' knowledge.

Our approach to the *study* of any individual suspected of being mentally retarded requires acceptance of several basic principles. We try not to deviate from them.

1. Ample time is provided. If justice is to be done not only to the child involved but also to the parents, it is impossible to hurry. A frequent complaint made by many parents who have been disappointed is, "How does he know our problem? He was with him only a few moments. How does he know our problem?"

2. The study is thorough. *All* factors bearing on the case are carefully considered.

3. Care is exercised in the choice of words used during the interviews with the parents. Each word in our language has associated with it its own peculiar emotional colorings. Some are more emotionally charged than others. Such expressions as "feeble-minded," "moron," "imbecile," and "idiot" are avoided. In their places are substituted "backward," "slow," and "retarded in development."

4. Parents have not only the *right* but the *responsibility* for deciding what is to be done for or with their child. This right is respected by the physician.

5. Parents are encouraged to reveal their own questions and doubts. The success of the study depends in a large measure upon how completely and satisfactorily their questions are answered.

6. The physician's attitude in dealing with this problem is no different from that in dealing with any other medical problem. He approaches the problem analytically allowing no personal feelings to interfere with a sound, critical evaluation.

7. The orientation of the social worker and psychologist associated with the physician is also of paramount importance. Each must have a thorough knowledge of his field, and an appreciation of his own responsibilities is essential. At no point should anyone become overaggressive.

A complete study of each case involves the following procedures:

1. Initial interview with parents to obtain a complete medical history.

2. Evaluation of the physical status of the child.

3. Psychological testing.

4. Clinical observation of the child.

5. Summary interview with parents.

The initial step in the study is securing a detailed medical history from the parents. More than one full hour is often required. Parents seldom mention the possibility of retardation in presenting a complaint. They usually offer some other trouble to explain their seeking help. Recognition of this fact by the physician often encourages parents to reveal unconsciously more than was intended. This is anticipated and encouraged.

A complete case history includes detailed consideration of the following items:

1. Pregnancy history. In the light of recent researches into the influences of various common infectious diseases and dietary deficiencies on the fetus during gestation, this is becoming increasingly significant.

2. Labor, birth, and postdelivery history.

3. Health and accident history.

4. Developmental history, which includes such items as neuromuscular maturation and activity, feeding experiences, speech development, play habits, curiosity, and the unfolding capacity of the child to relate himself meaningfully to parents and others.

5. Family history.

6. Definition of the child's present capacities and abilities: "In terms of everyday activities what can your child do?"

By this time it has become clear to both parents and physician that the child is not functioning at anticipated performance levels.

At this point the parents are asked *"How is your child different from others of comparable age?"* This simple question yields surprising results because it enables parents to delineate more objectively their own thinking and at the same time to evaluate the child himself. As differences are elaborated, the final question, "On the basis of our discussion, how old would you estimate your child to be?" is asked. *The accuracy with which average parents estimate their child's developmental age is remarkable.* Their answer helps them by more sharply bringing to focus their own evaluation of the problem. It also provides a logical focus for beginning the final interview.

In the second step of the survey, thorough physical and neurological studies are made together with all essential laboratory procedures. Necessary psychological testing is next undertaken. Such tests are very useful. However, they must be used with caution and interpretation, and always in relation to the rest of the study. It is always essential to know at least three things about any psychological testing that is done: (1) What tests were used? (2) What were the conditions of the tests? (3) Who was the examiner? Unless these essentials are known, the test results are of no particular value.

Clinical observation of the child himself is important. In our experience this is best accomplished if the child is admitted to the hospital for a day or two. The child's reaction to separation from parents, his capacity to adapt to new surroundings, his acceptance by other children in the hospital, and the manner in which he handles his own inter-personal relationships are helpful guideposts. In addition, it provides for continuous 24-hour study. Following this complete survey, the parents are seen in a final interview.

The general plan of the interview is as follows:

1. The parents' suspicions are confirmed.

2. The most likely explanation is given for the child's retardation.

3. Prognosis for the future is considered.

4. Possible solutions to the problem are discussed.

5. Opportunity for parents to ask questions is provided.

In recognition of the increased parental emotional tensions during this final conference, it is the usual rule to review carefully some of the data obtained during the first visit. Parents often are able to supply additional information which in itself is not only helpful but serves to ease their own tensions of the moment.

As stated earlier, parents are helped to estimate the actual attained developmental age of their child during the initial interview. This serves as a starting point for the physician in making his final report. If the study has substantiated the suspicion of retardation, it becomes easy and natural to state, "We agree with you that your child is delayed in his development." Many times one can go a stop further by complimenting the parents for their accurate estimate of the child's developmental age.

The fact of confirmation often yields surprising results in itself, for it relieves the parents of anxiety and enables them to consider plans that otherwise would not have been possible. This is well illustrated by the immediate response of one mother who spontaneously burst out with, "I've known from the time my child was but a few weeks old that she was not developing normally but I couldn't get anyone to confirm it." The child was nearly five years old when the study was undertaken. Once the mother's suspicions were confirmed, she was actually freed to "do something about it." This youngster is now satisfactorily placed in a school for backward children.

Next in order is the discussion of probable etiology. Parents want an explanation for the child's retardation. Either consciously or unconsciously they individually feel much personal guilt. As you know, the cause of mental retardation can be placed in one or more of the following large groups: (1) hereditary, (2) congenital, (3) accidents associated with labor or delivery, (4) accidents or illnesses that follow birth, and (5) a miscellaneous group that is related to little understood central nervous system deterioration. It is admitted that such a classification may have some deficiencies. However, it is one that parents can easily understand and accept.

The next step in the final interview is a full consideration of "What can we do about it?" As was suggested, no one has any right to tell a parent what he must do with or for a defective child. However, the physician has the responsibility to help the parents think through their problems. He does this by considering all possible plans of action and the effect these plans may have on all members of the family. Immeasurable suffering has been initiated by a too hasty suggestion that you "ought to put your child in an institution." Such procedure disregards completely the parents' emotional problems.

No one likes to feel alone with his

troubles. At this point we make two direct suggestions, stated in the following manner: "The many people who face this same problem have found it helpful in planning for a retarded child to make two major decisions. One is to accept the child and his deficiencies; the other is to accept the fact that medical science has nothing to offer that will *substantially* alter the developmental pattern of the child."

The four possible solutions to their problem are then outlined to them as follows:

1. The child may be kept at home. Offering this plan first tends to reduce resistance later.

2. An appropriate boarding home may be found—usually in the case of infants.

3. The child may be placed in a church or private school for care.

4. The parents "can take advantage of the facilities which the state offers" by considering "placement" at the state school. Stressing the "advantages" and suggesting "placement" rather than "sending the child away" help parents over rough spots in this portion of the interview.

Before the family finally decides on a plan that is "right" for them, further suggestions are elaborated in the following order:

1. The child will continue to grow physically. The unevenness of the total growth due to the persistent lag in social and intellectual maturation is carefully considered. In addition, parents are reminded that the differences already noted will become more marked as the child grows older.

2. No parents should undertake the responsibility of planning for one member of the family until the *total needs* of every member of the family, including themselves, are fully considered. Care is taken to speak directly at this point. Trouble usually ensues when parents have disregarded the needs of the other members of the family.

3. In consideration of the above questions, emphasis is placed on the point that all good parents consider fully the needs of each child in the family and try to the best of their ability and circumstances to meet them as adequately as possible. This point is made as it serves the dual purpose of (a) compelling the parents to consider freely the child's own particular needs for deriving as much satisfaction from living as possible and (b) protecting themselves should they decide on a placement plan.

The conference is ended by providing an opportunity for the parents to ask questions and bring out related problems. This is most essential as it makes possible full discussion of issues peculiar to the case and family. In addition, it is possible to deal with the parent's own emotional problems. It is during this phase of the interview that many parents deal directly with the real sources of their guilt and anxiety.

In general, this is our approach to the study and management of every problem of mental retardation. The approach is often varied to meet the emotional needs of the parents. Frequently the child's progress is checked at periodic intervals. In the interim, parents, benefiting from sympathetic understanding of the total problem, gradually develop for themselves greater understanding and more complete acceptance of the reality of the situation. Careful and considerate management on our part enables the parents to deal more effectively with the child and his problems as well as their own.

The question is often raised, "Doesn't this procedure seem to involve a great deal of time?" The answer is "yes," but by spending time on any one patient situation, in doing a thorough, careful analysis, time is actually saved. As parent's doubts and suspicions are confirmed, as their many questions are answered, they are gently freed of their own binding emotional problems. This lessens the need "to shop around," which means in itself a saving of time. But more than that, as parents develop insight and understanding, the child himself benefits by the change in their attitude toward him. Excessive pressures on him are lessened, and, being freed of these, in many instances he responds more favorably than would have been possible otherwise. Finally, if placement is eventually decided upon, parents have the pleasant feeling that their own rights and privileges have been respected.

Three important results have emerged following the use of this approach over the past five years: (1) Parents, when given a chance, do make good decisions. (2) Should parents decide on a specific plan such as placement, they can use more constructively the services of the social worker and others who assist the parents in carrying out the plan they have decided upon. (3) This, in turn, has made it possible for the social worker to make a greater contribution to the total welfare of the family. Of equal importance is the feeling of comfortableness the physician has in dealing with a problem that, at best, is most trying and difficult. The confidence he has in understanding the basic problem and his responsibility is of material help in assisting parents with an unpleasant task.

As we all work toward this common end, society is benefited, for its fundamental unit, the family, will have been protected and, in many instances, strengthened.

16 Role of the Physician in Maintaining Continuity of Care and Guidance

Robert W. Deisher

A physician who has the opportunity to work with retarded children and their parents sees many children after they have already visited a great many doctors. The help these parents and children require is something quite different from that needed by the average patient. The physician who stops with making the diagnosis of retardation in a child has missed an opportunity to accomplish something of value to the patient and of satisfaction to himself. It is not difficult to make a diagnosis on a retarded child with the aid, if necessary, of laboratory work, x-rays, and perhaps a consultation or two. Then, even though the findings are communicated to the parents in such a way that they accept the diagnosis and are not angry with the doctor, there is still much more that the physician has to contribute.

No physician would, for a moment, examine a child suspected of having rheumatic fever and, when the examination was complete and the diagnosis established, simply tell the parent that the child had rheumatic fever and let them go on their way. He would follow the rheumatic fever child for the duration of his disease and keep him under close surveillance for some years afterward. He would have no question about doing this, and yet, with the retarded child, an altogether different approach is used. The re-

tarded child and his parents have just as much need for the physician's continuing interest and follow-up as the child with rheumatic fever.

Let us consider some of the things that the physician might do that would be helpful to the parents and to the child. If the diagnosis of retardation is made at birth or shortly thereafter, as is sometimes the case in mongolism, the physician has a very important role to play. He would not recommend that these children be institutionalized immediately except perhaps in extreme cases where the mother, for physical or psychologic reasons, might be unable to care for the infant. Even then, there often are better places for infants than institutions. This situation is rare and the physician should continue to help the mother raise the child in the way best for the child. A mongoloid child who is seriously retarded has some potential; if his needs are met during the first few years of life he will be able to better utilize the limited potential he has.

What do these children need during their first few years? For one thing they need the same sort of relationship with the mother as that needed by any normal child. So often, because the child is different, the mother feels different about him and treats him differently. Mothers often say they just do not know how to handle such a child. These mothers need to be seen periodically just like the mothers of normal children. They need to have their questions answered, to be told about feeding, development, and all the points with which any unsure mother needs help.

The physician can call on other persons for help. He may find the public health nurse useful in demonstrating physical care of the infant, discussing feeding problems, giving suggestions about appropriate toys, or any of the things that a trained person can do who has the time to talk in a relaxed manner with the mother in her own home and to make on-the-spot suggestions. Often a good public health nurse can do a tremendous amount of good just by letting the mother talk and offering understanding and sympathy.

Again, a mother may have a hard time accepting her child's retardation and may be emotionally upset. Sometimes the father and mother are at odds over what to do about the child and are not of any mutual support. The physician, by talking to the father and helping him to accept the situation and be more supportive to the mother, can contribute much to lessening of family tension. If the doctor feels that the situation needs more time than he can give, the family can be referred to a social agency, such as Family Society. If there is no family agency in the community, then perhaps the social worker in the children's division of the welfare department might help. The children's worker in the welfare department can be a most interested and helpful person in many ways.

The important thing is that the physician keep aware of the needs of the retarded child and his parents and know what resource persons his community has, in order to make effective use of them. He must not, however, turn the family over to them and step out of the case, but should continue to play an active part, integrating and coordinating the work of different people and agencies. He must know what the other persons are doing and when an agency has fulfilled a need and another type of help is indicated.

In addition one should follow closely the child's physical condition, because of his susceptibility to illness. Many retarded children have dental, nutritional, orthopedic, or speech problems, and the like. It is important that defects be corrected and the child be in as good physical condition as possible. A child who is already limited mentally can have his functional ability much further reduced by physical problems. Conversely, by correcting physical defects one can often increase the child's total functional capacity.

The retarded infant needs to be loved and cared for, just as any other baby does. If the mother has difficulty accepting the child or feels that he is different and therefore does not need affection, the physician can help her with this adjustment. A few weeks ago I saw a mongoloid girl fifteen months of age. This child had remained in the hospital since birth. It was a good hospital and the child had had good physical care and probably a little more attention and affection than are usual in most hospitals. The mother had visited her two or three times a week. The child was in good physical condition and had had a minimum of infections during her life. However, the parents were concerned because they felt this child was more seriously retarded than most mongoloids. They told me that the child never smiled nor seemed happy and did not appear to know the mother or the nurses.

It became obvious as we studied the child that she was not really more retarded than the usual mongoloid child—in fact the child tested somewhat higher than average for this group—but, having been raised in such an unstimulating atmosphere as even the best hospital can offer, the child was simply showing the apparent retardation due to lack of stimulation. This is a situation a physician should try to prevent. There was, in this case, some reason for the mother's not taking the child home with her. She had a number of other children and had had, in the past, a mental breakdown. She did not want to take the child home and was able to afford private care. A much better solution would have been to place this child in a foster home where she could have had the love and warmth from one person that are so important for any baby's emotional growth.

If the physician's first contact comes when the child is of preschool age, or as the child he has followed reaches this age, he must be aware of the changing needs of child and parent. With the retarded child, just as with the normal one in preschool years, experiences outside the home and with other children become important. It is also important for the mother of the retarded child to get some time away from her child. If the child is retarded to such a degree that he is unacceptable in a normal nursery school, it may be possible for the mother to get together with other mothers of retarded children and organize a special nursery school.

An important resource in such an effort would be the local association of parents of retarded children. Such a nursery school might already be in operation or perhaps mothers in that group could establish one. This, or course, is not the only use of the parents' organization but I shall not at this time go into detail concerning the many ways this organization can be of help to parents. Let me say, however, that getting the parents of patients in contact with the association does not mean that the physician's continued interest and coordinating efforts are less needed.

The physician will sometimes find that his chief task is to convince the parents that a child is not defective. Many children have been referred to our clinic by physicians, teachers, and social agencies where there was no doubt in the minds of the parents or referring person that the children were mentally retarded. A thorough study, including psychologic and psychiatric examination, has revealed that the children were not defective at all, but emotionally disturbed. In many cases the condition could be reversed but, in order to accomplish this, it was necessary that an active psychotherapy program be started immediately. Again, the physician is in the best position to cause such an evaluation or re-evaluation to be made.

Recently a seven-year-old boy who illustrates this type of problem was referred to our clinic. The boy was attending the School for Retarded Children in his local area and, inasmuch as he had never been thoroughly studied, was sent for evaluation. There was no question in the minds of the personnel of the school or in that of the mother that he was retarded. The mother planned to place him in the state training school for retarded children as soon as he could be accepted. Our diagnostic procedures revealed nothing medically to indicate a basis for retardation. The boy's I.Q. score was only in the sixties but it was obvious that his fearfulness and tremendous anxiety on being separated from his mother were large factors in his poor performance. The child had had a traumatic life. At two years of age a sibling had been born. Shortly after that, his father died. The mother moved, while being emotionally upset herself, into her grandparents' home, where the child was cared for by a doting great-grandmother. The mother felt that her grandmother spoiled him too much; so after a few months she moved out. The emotional trauma, in addition to being raised by a rather unhappy, rigid mother, contributed to the boy's condition. He needed psychiatric help and not placement in the state institution for retarded children.

Unfortunately, there is a sizable number of children who are thought to be retarded but who really have emotional problems. In this case we were able to get the school guidance department, the school principal, and the teacher, as well as the social worker from the local child guidance clinic, together and plan a program to help this boy. The coordination was done by our clinic. Many children, however, are not going to be seen in a special clinic for retarded children. The physician can meet with school and guidance people and help plan an effective program.

Schoolteachers and administrators are generally interested and cooperative concerning the problems of the retarded child and can do a lot to help. Usually they need and appreciate the interest and guidance of a physician. Most feel uncertain about the physical aspects of the case and work more effectively as a member of a team focused on helping the child rather than alone, having the entire responsibility left to them.

There are also some children who are merely slow in maturing and need only time, together with the parents' patience and understanding, to function in a more adequate manner. Here again the physician is in the best position to help the parents carry out such a program of waiting. The resources one utilizes depend not only on the needs of the child, but also on those available in the community. Some areas are much more fortunate than others. There are always public health nurses, at least a child welfare worker connected with the local welfare department, and, of course, people within the school system who can and will work effectively with the physician. Of course, personalities must always be considered. Some people naturally work well with children who have mental problems and others do not. It is up to the physician whenever possible to determine what individual will best meet the needs of his patient. . . .

17 Interpreting Mental Retardation to Parents

Harriet L. Rheingold

A frequent and important task of the psychologist in the child guidance clinic is to give to the parents of a child an interpretation of his retardation. The interpretation is considered as much a part of the service rendered as is the determination of the child's retardation by examination. Often a guidance clinic's services are requested by parents solely to obtain an interpretation of the retardation, the examinations having been administered elsewhere. This suggests that school, court, and medical workers have limited their interviews with parents to reporting the diagnosis or to giving advice concerning commitment or special school placement. This practice too often injures the parents' feelings or arouses their antagonism. Neither attitude is a salutary one for the child or for his parents, for the antagonism causes them to dispute the findings, while disturbed emotions render them less able to consider the welfare of the child.

At the Institute for Juvenile Research it has been customary for the psychologist to interview the parents subsequent to the child's physical and psychological examinations. We are learning, however, that in many instances where other evidence of retardation is sufficient, we can render parents the assistance they need without complete psychometric examination of the child prior to the interview. What the parent wants is not only help in handling the child's problems, but also the psychologist's understanding of his own emotional needs; he does not always require an accurate measure of his child's mental status in years and months. Psychometric and other examinations should be administered, not as a routine procedure, but to meet the requirements of each situation, to aid the psychologist, or to satisfy the parents' needs. This should not be understood to minimize the importance of actual observation of the child's behavior.

The purpose of the initial interview should be to guide the parents toward an emotional acceptance of the child together with his mental defect, since wise planning for such a child is impossible if the parents do not accept his retardation. There is little likelihood that they will act upon the advice given them until this goal is attained. Emotional acceptance in this sense may be defined as: sufficient agreement between the subjective facts (the parents' feelings) and the objective facts (the reality situation) to make wise handling and planning possible. Emotional acceptance of the child with his defect enables the parents not only to accept the psychologist's statements today, but also to feel a month from now that the conclusions are as wise as they appeared at the close of the interview. That is to say, they are able to change and adapt plans as the child or the situation changes. A realistic orientation of effort is a result of emotional acceptance. While this acceptance is the main purpose of the interview, the assistance rendered the parent in planning for the child is the chief by-product. The extent to which parents can utilize this assistance depends upon the success with which the primary purpose is achieved. Stating the diagnosis, answering questions about etiology and treatment, discussing habit training and educational plans are only the materials out of which the interviews are woven.

The interview, to be successful, should resemble closely any other therapeutic interview in which the gaining of insight is the objective. This means that the psychologist should not be, and should not allow himself to be, forced into the role of an authoritative person whose sole function is to give advice. As in all therapeutic interviews, both persons—here psychologist and patient—must play active roles. The parent should feel not that he is being forced to accept what he has been told, but that he has worked in equal measure with the psychologist toward a solution of his problem. At least he should feel that having obtained a basis for action he can carry on independently.

This interview differs in some respects from the typical therapeutic interview. The psychologist possesses information which the parent needs. This means that the parent's questions cannot be turned back upon himself at every point, although at many points they need to be. The psychologist's role is therefore the more active one. Throughout the interview he should help the parent to clarify his own feelings about his problem, but if asked a question concerning test findings, private schools, and so forth, he should give a direct answer. The attitude of the psychologist should be that of any psychotherapeutic worker—interested, sympathetic, understanding.

From experimentation and experience we have found that a successful interpretive interview follows a sequence almost as orderly and regular as that of the psychometric examination itself. It possesses a logic of its own. Its development can be predicted. The content of the interview will vary, of course, according to the age and sex of the child, the degree of retardation, the physical symptoms, and the emotional needs of the parents, but this does not alter the sequence. Furthermore, each parent has been conditioned to some extent by the number of examinations his child has already had and by his own experiences with examiners. This, however, does not affect the orderly progression of the interview although it may increase the relative prominence of one step or reduce that of another, even to negligible proportions.

The writer finds that the therapeutic nature of the interviews can be facilitated by the character of the psychologist's opening remarks. As the first step, there should be a simple restatement of the problem: "You are worried about John's development, aren't you?" or, "I can see that Mary's care has been difficult for you." Such a beginning possesses several advantages. It assures the parent of the psychologist's understanding and sympathy from the first moment of the interview. It gives proper importance to the feelings of the parent, designates an active role for him, and makes him a protagonist.

Almost invariably the parent agrees that he has been worried about John for some time, or that Mary's care has been exhausting. Thus, at the very beginning of the interview the simple restatement has secured an exposure of the parent's recognition of the child's problem and avoided antagonism which would hinder the therapeutic nature of the interview. This admission is necessary for the steps to follow; without it the parent's full cooperation cannot be secured. In contrast, if the interview is opened by giving a diagnosis, the parent's verbal admission that the child is retarded may never be attained, even up to the conclusion of the interview.

The admission itself stimulates the parent to take the next step, a description of the child's behavior. In this the parent can be assisted by the psychologist's asking, "What concerns you about Mary's development?" or, "Tell me more about John." In their descriptions parents find it easier to begin with the less serious and less stigmatizing symptoms; this is usual and should be accepted. One parent will begin with, "What bothers me most is that Anita is so clumsy. She's always falling down." Another will say, "I can't get Tom to chew his food." Other symptoms frequently given prominence at the beginning of the interview are: inability to play with other children, enuresis, day-dreaming, nervousness, lack of concentration, stubbornness, temper tantrums, and speech defects. As the psychologist

verbally, and more importantly by attitude, shows his acceptance of these complaints as worthy of concern, the parent works through the less serious symptoms and finally arrives at the most serious, the child's inability to learn at a normal rate.

If the psychologist seems to reject the first symptoms as of minor importance, and if he presses the parents to describe the more serious ones, the parent may limit his recital to the less stigmatizing and never approach the more serious. The desirable progress of the discussion is insured by the psychologist's attitude of interest and sympathy at every point. No more is required of the psychologist by way of a verbal response than, "Yes," or "I can understand that." Only occasionally a more specific comment may be needed, such as, "That embarrasses you, doesn't it?" or "That worries a mother."

Throughout this sequence runs an evaluation of the child's development in terms of the achievements of other children of comparable age or of the parent's own older children as he recalls their behavior at the patient's age. While this comparison is usually spontaneous, in the few cases in which it is not, such questions as, "Do any of your friend's have a child about John's age?" or, "What was your older daughter like at his age?" serve to produce the evaluation for the steps to follow.

A few questions such as, "How was it from the time he was a baby?" or, "When did you first notice his slowness?" stimulate the parents to relate a history of the child's development. The gathering of a detailed history prior to the interview possesses no especial advantage for this type of interview; history taking has then become an integral part of the interview.

At this point the psychologist becomes more active and asks, "What age child do you think Margaret resembles now?" In our experience, parents then estimate an age very close to the mental age indicated by the tests. Surprisingly, underestimation is somewhat more common than overestimation. This occasionally may be an expression of parental rejection of the child.

At this point we may review the processes of this step. The parent himself has given sufficient material for a diagnosis. Since this has been given in terms of the development of other children, he has supplied a measuring rod which has meaning for him. He has been led a long way towards an understanding of the child's retardation; he will not now reject the psychologist's diagnosis. He has been forced to accept nothing; he has been allowed to evalute the problem himself.

The parent will usually ask the psychologist at this point, "What do you think?" This leads to the third step in the sequence of the interview. The psychologist answers the question, but refrains from discussing the child's retardation in terms of future development or present planning. One should keep pace with the parent's progress in grasping the implications of the problem and avoid giving him more information than he can assimilate at the time. The results of tests should be presented to the parents in terms of mental age. In our interviews it has always been sufficient to give the mental age, not in years and months, but as "about four years, " or, "between

seven and eight years." The terms "idiot," "imbecile," or even "high grade mental defective" are never used. The psychologist from now on usually talks about the child as one who is "slow to learn"; occasionally, as a "mentally retarded child."

How far it is wise to spare the parent's feelings must be considered, for sometimes parents ask, "But he isn't feeble-minded, is he?" One mother, seen at our clinic recently, decided to arrange for her son's commitment to a state school. The county clerk to whom she had to apply asked her if the boy were feeble-minded. Although his I.Q. was 50, we had not reported this to the mother or used the term "feeble-minded" in our interview. She answered, "No, he isn't feeble-minded," whereupon the county clerk replied, "Well, then he doesn't belong there." Since then we have modified our procedure. We now tell parents who are thinking of commitment that "feeble-mindedness" is a legal term used by officials.

Parents will ask next about the child's future: "Will he be able to go to school?" "Will he ever learn to talk?" "How far can he go in school?" "Will he be able to get a job?" This we have recognized as the fourth step of the interview. The parent is asking now about the implications of the mental retardation; he is attempting to translate them into terms of future development. In general, the psychologist waits until the parent asks the question, answers only the questions asked of him. He refrains from predicting the child's entire life history. For example, if the parent is worried only about the speech development of a young retarded child, the psychologist does not add that the child will never be able to support himself. In the manner suggested, the worker keeps pace with the parent's needs and feelings.

The parent next asks questions about etiology and treatment—the fifth step in the sequence. Parents are forever seeking a specific statement of cause. There are two reasons for this desire: first, that a definition of cause will relieve them of the responsibility for the defect; second, that a discovery of cause will indicate an effective method of treatment to correct the defect. In the discussion of etiology, the psychologist should encourage the parents to review verbally their own attempts to account for the retardation. Often they have sought to relate it to heredity, to accidents of birth, to prenatal or neo-natal experiences. If the explanation offered seems reasonable or constructive, the psychologist encourages the parent's belief. If it seems warranted the psychologist may offer a tentative diagnosis of mongolism, cretinism, or birth injury, to be checked by medical examination. More often, however, the psychologist can only point out the lack of definite etiologic knowledge, emphasizing points which tend to relieve feelings of responsibility, such as the many different causes advanced by medical science, the universality of the problem, the possibility of attributing it to fortuitous circumstances in the absence of more definite etiology. While the psychologist's statements in this area must be as accurate as possible, his attitudes and comments should be directed more toward allowing the parents an opportunity to bring out into the open their own thoughts on the subject rather than towards presenting them with a detailed review of medical knowledge.

The discussion of etiology leads directly into a consideration of treatment. Even if no specific statement of etiology is possible, parents hope desperately that somewhere a cure is available. They usually think of surgical measures first, then, in order, other medical, educational, and social measures. Here again the parent should be encouraged to express the hopes he has cherished; again the psychologist should answer directly and as accurately as his knowledge and experience permit; for painful as it may be, most parents are seeking the truth.

For the most part parents of retarded children feel in some way responsible for the retardation. If the psychologist allows the parent the more active role during the discussion of etiology and treatment, the parent himself will raise the question of his responsibility. If he does not, the psychologist may say, "I suppose you sometimes wonder if you are to blame."

A sense of responsibility may stem from feelings of inadequacy or guilt, or both. Some parents feel that they are being punished for sins, real or imagined. The intelligent father of a very retarded child felt that he was being punished for his love of gambling. A mother may be haunted by her attempt to abort the child; another, by having entertained the idea; and still another fears that her ambivalent feelings about her pregnancy may have been the causative factor. A parent may feel that his own personal inadequacy as a man or as a woman is the cause of his child's retardation. Some parents blame themselves for not playing more with the child, or for not reading to him more often. In the latter instance, however, the self-reproaches usually mask more serious feelings of inadequacy or guilt. Associated with these feelings may be the fear of loss of status and prestige which seriously threatens the parent's emotional security.

The importance of encouraging the parent to express his feelings of responsibility can scarcely be overestimated, for the success of the interview may depend upon it. A parent does not parade these feelings; in fact, he struggles to repress them and hesitates to admit them, even to himself. But until he can obtain relief for feelings of guilt, inadequacy, or humiliation, he cannot view reality with sufficient objectivity to develop emotional acceptance of his child.

At some time during the discussion of etiology, treatment, and feelings of responsibility, the parent usually succumbs to an overt expression of his grief. Tears may come to his eyes; more often he weeps openly. This show of emotion need not disconcert the psychologist. It has cathartic value for the parent, while for the psychologist it is another indication of the successful progress of the interview. It requires no direct handling. Sometimes the psychologist need only wait until the parent gains control of himself; at other times he may say, "I understand how you feel." Frequently, following an emotional outburst, the parent will bring up what troubles him most: feel-ings of responsibility, fear of personal inadequacy, loss of status in the community. If the psychologist takes alarm at the show of feeling, or if he becomes too solicitous, the parent may retreat. Thus the psychologist may cut off an expression of the chief sources of the parent's anxiety.

At this point the parent usually returns to a consideration of the present situation. This is the sixth step. He asks, "What shall I do now?" He is attempting to express his clarified feelings in action. As a rule this question can be returned to the parent. The psychologist will ask, "What do you want to do?" or, "What do you think?" In this way the psychologist encourages the parent to plan for the child in accordance with the reorientation in thinking effected so far by the interview.

Since the purpose of this paper is to define the interview as a therapeutic process and to delineate its orderly progression, it is considered unnecessary to include here a discussion of the psychologist's thinking about the advantages and disadvantages of care at home vs. public institutional care; regular vs. special room placement; local resources; the tendency of most parents to press the mentally retarded child for academic achievement, at the same time requiring too little in social and emotional maturity; the possibilities for good personality development in spite of the mental defect. These are some of the considerations which arise at this point in the interview. The psychologist must be familiar with them for he will be called upon to answer questions. He should offer information freely; the decisions, however, must rest with the parent.

As the interview draws to its close, most parents begin to feel guilty because their objective discussion of the child seems to suggest their rejection of him. This attitude they express by an enumeration of the child's assets and especially of bits of behavior which seem to them bright and hopeful. They will say of a young child: "But he points out all the parts of an automobile," or of an older child, "But he can travel all over the city by himself." One should not feel at this point that the interview is of dubious success because this is only an expression of the parent's attempt to relieve his feelings of guilt. The psychologist in response verbalizes the parent's ambivalence. He may say, "You are afraid that you haven't been fair to your child," or, "It is natural for you to see that in some ways he is not as slow as in others."

Fear of seeming to reject the child becomes an even more serious matter when the parent considers committing the child to a state school. Moral censure arises both from within—his feelings of responsibility—and from without—his fear of community disapproval. Fear of loss of prestige and status arises here, too, for it is difficult for the parent to admit that he must resort to a state agency for the care of his child. Often a parent is unwilling to accept public assistance, and feels obliged to spend his own money on the child's care. When the parent can ill afford private care, and especially when the expense may be detrimental to the welfare of other children in the family, the psychologist should explain the meaning of this sacrifice as a compensation for the parent's feelings of guilt or inadequacy.

This type of interview leads to emotional acceptance of the problem and helps the parent plan for the immediate situation. His own personality needs, the severity of the retardation, the age of the child, the awareness and insight brought to the interview—these determine the extent of his acceptance. The psychologist may be skillful but he constitutes only half of the interview situation. While most parents can be carried through the interview with profit for themselves and the child, there are some who obtain only limited benefits. Occasionally a parent may seem to have arrived at emotional acceptance and to be able to plan more or less wisely for the child, yet at the end bring up his conviction that a tonsillectomy may still effect a cure. Sometimes this may represent no more than a temporary lapse into an earlier pattern of thought. At other times it may indicate that the parent is not yet able to plan wisely for the child's future. Occasionally one parent will leave the interview with apparent insight, but at home will be influenced by the other parent to return to the original hope that the child needs only speech therapy. These parents "shop around" from doctor to doctor, from clinic to clinic, seeking corroboration of their hopes. Some parents can only be regarded as untreatable.

Then, too, there are parents who, in one interview, achieve only partial emotional acceptance and objective insight into the needs of the child. The problem has proved too great and too damaging to the parent's ego, too bound up with feelings of personal inadequacy and guilt. For this reason we close each interview with an assurance of our interest and availability whenever the parent wishes to discuss any aspects of the problem. If the mother was interviewed, and it appears from her conversation that the father finds it difficult to accept the child's limitation, we offer an interview to the father and vice versa. Parents of young children are invited to return at six-month intervals for re-examination and interviews; parents of older children are invited to return at yearly intervals. Occasionally the parent's anxiety will appear disturbing enough to warrant our offering several interviews in succession. The general invitation is always given; more definite appointments depend upon his need and his desire for further help.

18 Counseling with Parents of Retarded Children Living at Home

Sylvia Schild

In the light of the emergent philosophy and prevailing practice of encouraging home care of mentally retarded children, a re-examination of the casework counseling technique with parents is indicated. Until recent years, social workers in the field of mental retardation were primarily located in institutions and the focus of casework with families was usually geared around the problems of placement planning. With the advent of special clinics for early diagnosis and evaluation of retarded children, attention shifted to parental feelings and reactions and to ways of counseling parents more satisfactorily. The need for a sympathetic, supportive approach to the parents has been well established with the recognition that the impact of the retarded child is deeply disturbing to the ego-functioning of the parent. The importance of having as complete a knowledge and evaluation of the child's problem as possible has been accepted as a necessary counterpart to being able to provide a meaningful explanation to the parents of the child's difficulty and to give consideration to the parental questions and emotional involvements related to having a retarded child.

Social workers in specialized clinics and social agencies are now dealing not only with the areas of diagnosis and placement, but with the complex task of helping the family and child live together more comfortably in the home. The purpose of providing maximum benefit to the child needs to be interlocked with minimal stress to total parental needs and family functioning. Both the child and the family are faced with making adequate adjustments to and in the community in which they live. Unless these ends are achieved, maintenance of the child in the home serves little purpose.

Professional workers, in supporting a philosophy of home care for retarded children, must be keenly aware of the responsibility to know how to help families achieve this goal with maximum ease. This paper proposes to examine some aspects of counseling with parents of retarded children living at home that are characteristic of the problem and that may lead to a better understanding of how to work with these families. These observations are drawn from experience in counseling with families receiving services in the Child Development Clinic at the Children's Hospital of Los Angeles. The clinic is a diagnostic and counseling center primarily for retarded children less than age six. The observations thus are related to the early adjustment of the preschool child and his family, although they may be generic to the problems of the older retardate as well.

AMBIVALENCE OF PARENTS' FEELINGS

Enormous ambivalence of feeling is evoked in a parent when he learns that his child is retarded. Feelings of rejection, dejection, and disappointment collide with anxious hopefulness, doubt, anger, and self-pity. Strong emotions of guilt mix with protective parental reactions; resentment, confusion, and insecurity become pervasive. It is this ambivalence that characterizes initial work with families of retarded children. These conflicting emotions are never completely resolved, as the long-term aspect of the problem and the repeated crises that stem directly from the fact of the child's handicap stir up the ambivalence from time to time. To help the parent, it is necessary to ferret out the positive aspects of the ambivalence and help him to build on these so as to find some answers to the problem immediately at hand. Thus, ambivalence is dealt with in relation to the immediate crisis situation on a reality basis and by focusing on the areas that are conducive to meeting the needs of the family. The following case illustrates this point:

A young couple had just heard the diagnosis of retardation for the first time. In the hostile tirade the mother loosed on the social worker, she vehemently denied that this catastrophe could be true, attacked the doctors, blamed herself. Toward the end of the outburst, she cried out, "Nothing I ever do is perfect. How will I ever be able to raise this child?" In this plea for help the social worker recognized the mother's immediate fear and denial of the diagnosis as resulting from her shaken confidence in being able to successfully handle her mothering role with the defective child. The positive aspect of the ambivalence, underlying the fear of inadequacy, was her intense desire to be a good mother. This was an area that could be worked with realistically in counseling, since she was indeed performing successfully in her mothering role with her two older children. The husband's support to his wife was encouraged. With help and attitudinal change, this mother was enabled to depend again on her own inner strengths and resources in coping with the child; this in turn paved the way toward better understanding of the child's limitations and freed her to work on other aspects of the problem.

A factor accounting for sustained ambivalence toward a retarded child is that the parents are deprived of the opportunity to project any blame for the problem onto the child himself. It is too difficult in any rational way to blame the child for his own defect. This differs from situations in which, when social pathology exists and becomes reflected in disturbed parent-child relationships (for example, in emotional disturbance and delinquency), the parent realistically is able to hold the child partially responsible for a share of the problem. This serves to alleviate some parental guilt and lowers resistance to accepting help. In the area of mental retardation the self-accusatory parent, who feels that he alone is in some way accountable for his child's limitations, is very well known.

It is an accepted fact that part of the resistance of the person seeking help stems from his feeling of responsibility for the problem. When guilt is intensified, the resistance to help will be proportionately increased. Because of this, those endeavoring to help parents of retarded children must be aware that heightened resistance is usually due to the inwardly projected guilt of the parent. In counseling, this guilt needs to be alleviated and an emphatic understanding of the problem area imparted to lower the parent's resistance, freeing him to benefit from the offered help. Most parents hope to hear an authoritative and sympathetic endorsement of themselves, of their human and parental competence, and of their right not to blame themselves for what has happened.

One way of ameliorating the guilt of parents is to counsel them together in joint interviews. This helps to focus on the mutuality of feelings and responsibility shared by each parent and aids to shift away from individual parents the assumption of self-blame for the problem. The joint interview technique often may help to restore the marital balance around the mutual concern for the child so that the parents are better able to mobilize all their strengths to handle crisis situations. Although mothers are generally entrusted with the major care of the child, management is a joint responsibility of both parents. Too often the father's role and share of responsibility are overlooked, especially when it is the mother who assumes the task of taking the child for his medical care and transmitting the medical information and advice to her husband. Joint interviewing frequently serves as a device to engage the father actively and to give due consideration to his concerns and attitudes, as well as to those of his wife. Counseling parents together is supportive and enables them to concentrate their energies, not as much on the fruitless searching for why this has happened to them, but more productively on how they can better perform in their parental roles in order to benefit their child.

CHANGES REQUIRED OF PARENTS

The hard reality that needs to be faced is that with the presence of a retarded child the family is no longer the same and it cannot be reconstructed as it was before the arrival and impact of the defective child. Perhaps the area of greatest difficulty that needs to be resolved in the counseling process is the changes required on the part of the parents to meet the special needs of the retarded child. These often conflict with parental functioning that heretofore was considered satisfactory.

Often the management of the retarded child is perceived by the parents as being no different from their performance with their normal offspring. Counseling needs to be directed toward helping parents to see that their attitudes and feelings relative to mental retardation per se have indeed shifted their own parental behavior.

One mother complained constantly of her child's temper tantrums. The disturbance the child was creating was upsetting to the entire household, and the mother felt at her wit's end. The parents were beginning to feel that to keep the child in the home was almost impossible. The mother stated she was handling the problem behavior exactly as she had in the past coped with similar behavior in an older child.

Closer examination revealed that in reality the mother, caught up in her disappointment and her attitude that a mentally retarded child was totally worthless, considered the child not worth bothering to discipline. Also, the father was unsupportive, leaving all discipline to his wife. Hence, the mother responded to the tantrums with anger and helplessness, and was permitting herself to be manipulated by the child. The youngster, having no external controls put on his behavior, became increasingly infantile and difficult. This gave validation to the low value placed on him by his mother.

When the mother gained some insight and understanding that she was reacting differently to this child than to her normal offspring, she began to cope with the problem. Her self-esteem increased with her more effective management of the child. In addition, the father was helped to participate more meaningfully in the child's discipline, thereby giving his wife emotional support. As the child's behavior improved, the parents acquired a new appreciation of him. This in turn helped them to evaluate better the considerable potential latent in their mildly retarded son and to enjoy a more favorable relationship with him in the home situation.

The resistance and ambivalence of the parents in counseling are amplified also by the nature of the new stresses encountered merely by virtue of being the parent of a retarded child. The problem of keeping the retarded child at home is determined by a number of factors, such as sibling relationships, social status, family attitudes, the degree of deficiency in the child, and so on. These are all potential problem areas and the ability with which problems that might arise in these areas are handled and solved vary from family to family, situation to situation.

The new stresses arising from the presence in the family of a retarded child are not pathological as such, but should be viewed as a normal complement of problems for the situation that may affect the parent-child relationship and to which adjustments need to be made. When a pathological situation (i.e., divorce) is imposed on a family and is disruptive to family functioning, the focus in counseling must be directed toward the realistic problems that occur as a result of the pathology. It has been pointed out that the presence of a retarded child in the home is often a precipitating factor in individual or family maladjustment or breakdown. The family that is able to adjust satisfactorily to the impact on it of a retarded child has also to deal adequately with the many normal problems that occur in relation to the situation. Their attitudes, feelings, care and management of the child, and the like must all be taken into account.

These normal problems attending the presence of a retarded child in the home must be dealt with on a reality basis to permit the best possible solutions to be effected. Some of these problems are met often in other handicapping conditions of childhood; the increased dependence of the child on the parent, confusion and lack of finiteness in medical diagnosis, crumbling of parental aspirations for the child, rehabilitation and training problems, and the like. However, there are some conditions that occur uniquely in the case of the mentally retarded child and his parents.

One solution, which is culturally sanctioned, is often freely available to parents of the severely and moderately retarded. This is the opportunity to relinquish responsibility for care of the child to an institution if, considering the degree of his intellectual impairment, the child is eligible. Granted that placement holds the parents to a modicum of responsibility and is indeed an appropriate solution in many situations, there still is a need for recognition that this alternative presents conflict for the parents and may impair efforts to effect a successful adjustment in the home. From the time that parents are told that their child is eligible for institutionalization the ambivalence about the child and the problem increases. Again, this am-

bivalence needs to be handled in counseling, with the focus geared to the positive aspects inherent in the successful fulfillment of parental roles and responsibilities.

COUNSELING SHOULD BE SPACED

One difficulty occurring in counseling with parents is that the resistance of the parent is sometimes insidiously supported by the behavior of the child himself. The parents may move well initially in shifting to more positive attitudes and methods of handling the child only to be thwarted by the slow movement of the child in responding to improved parental functioning. Although intellectually the parents can relate the slow pace to the child's mental limitations, they often become frustrated emotionally and can react by feeling that the counseling is unproductive. This can cause reversion to easier, more familiar patterns of behavior. The counselor, too, can become uneasy and impatient because of the slow pace of the child's response and may fail to support the parents' efforts adequately or project blame on the parents for failure to utilize the counseling.

The most immediate help, consequently, occurs when the parents are having critical emotional distress and help can be directed toward easing their personal difficulty rather than being geared to change in the child himself. Casework for this later goal, which is focused around the management and behavior of the child, can perhaps be best provided when spread out over proper and widely spaced intervals to give the child an opportunity to react and develop at his own speed.

A review of the reactions of forty parents to diagnosis and counseling emphasized that the parents needed time to take in the extent of their problem and solutions needed to be worked out step by step. Also, parental questions did not arise in an organized, crystallized fashion but gradually, as the child grew. When the element of time is taken into consideration and work with the family is structured over appropriate intervals, the parents are able to bring into counseling some growth on the part of the child that might not otherwise have been apparent if counseling around the child had been sustained on an intensive basis. In other words, parents need intensive casework help at times of crisis situations but, in addition, they need a continued contact. The latter can be less intensive and made available to them over a longer period of time. Such counseling should be properly spaced and educationally focused, to help the parents with the practical problems of daily living with their retarded child. This help is often crucial in determining if the child can live in his own home and in strengthening and sustaining the mental health of the total family unit.

Counseling related to everyday living experiences with the retarded child helps to sustain the parents' motivation to continue in a program designed to improve the child's behavior and to develop his potential. Parents need to deal with concrete situations—the success they achieve in such common daily experiences tends to ameliorate the problems of living with a retarded child. For this kind of approach the caseworker must have a keen knowledge and awareness of normal growth and development. To help the parents understand their child's behavior, it is important to assist them in relating behavior to normal functioning and expectations of children as well as to comprehend the limitations in their own child and its implications. . . .

19 Nursing's Concern for the Mentally Retarded is Overdue

Mary Anne Noble

Approximately three percent of the population of the United States is considered to be psychometrically retarded and one percent is thought to require some form of service because of mental retardation. These data indicate that mental retardation is a significant problem in our society. Yet hitherto the needs of the mentally retarded have received attention from only a few—long-suffering parents, custodians in state institutions, and special education teachers. Avoidance of the problem by the majority has resulted in great inadequacies of care and treatment. Our society's lack of concern for the retarded and their families is certainly inconsistent with the humanitarian principles it professes to hold.

Mental retardation is a health, social, educational, vocational, and legal problem which calls for the services of physicians, nurses, social workers, psychologists, educators, lawyers, rehabilitation counselors, and other professionals. This array of manpower is needed to prevent retardation and to cope with it when it does occur. Nurses have an important role in both these types of efforts.

Traditionally, nurses have served the retarded in institutional settings, including general hospitals, since retarded persons are often afflicted with multiple physical handicaps. To some extent, nurses have provided services to the retarded and their families in the home. However, a survey of the needs of the retarded and the services they require throughout their lives indicates that the nurse's role in serving this group must take on new dimensions and be extended to other settings.

Even before a child is conceived steps may be taken to prevent mental retardation. Theoretically, this preconception period begins at birth of the prospective parents and extends to the end of their child-bearing age. The risk of their having a retarded child is related to their general health. Factors having a particular relationship to retardation are the expectant mother's nutrition, the drugs which she takes, the radiation to which she is exposed, and the contraction of rubella.

Many persons in this country are undernourished. Because of her role in community health teaching, the nurse is in a strategic position to correct poor nutritional practices. She can also assist in the prevention of drug and radiation abuses which lead to congenital abnormalities, including retardation. The rubella vaccine which has recently been perfected holds promise of eradicating a disease that is so dangerous for pregnant women, and the nurse can promote rubella vaccination of at least the grade school population, although its use among adolescent girls and pregnant women is controversial.

A significant percentage of mental retardation is believed to be the result of complications of pregnancy, labor, and delivery. For example, toxemia and Rh incompatibility frequently lead to retardation, and recent studies point to a positive correlation between prematurity and retardation. These complications are largely preventable. The nurse can help to prevent many of these complications in her role of teaching and supervising pregnant women in physicians' offices, obstetric clinics, community centers, and patients' homes. In her community work she can be instrumental in the detection of pregnancies which might otherwise proceed without medical supervision. Neglected antepartal care is common among the culturally deprived. Children of these mothers suffer greater than average risks of retardation.

After the child is born, and before mother and child leave the hospital, the nurse has an important part to play in helping the parents to recognize their responsibility to provide an environment which is conducive to the child's growth and development. She can also identify mental illness and economic deprivation of the parents—two factors which may contribute to cultural or functional retardation of the child—and intervene by working with mental health and social services to find ways of providing psychological and economic assistance to the parents. If the child is born prematurely, the nurse who provides intensive care for him can be instrumental in overcoming respiratory and nutritional difficulties.

When a baby is noticeably retarded at birth, the nurse who is in close contact with the mother during the immediate postpartum period has a unique opportunity to assist the family in this crisis situation. The parents, particularly the mother, need support and understanding. If a decision must be made concerning the baby's disposition, the parents need to explore all possibilities. It is especially important that they be made aware of the advantages of keeping their offspring in the family at least during his childhood. The decision is theirs to make, however, and they must be afforded the freedom to do so.

The child's first year of life is important because it is the organic base upon which environment builds to affect the future. Retardation is usually not detectable at this early age, except when the retardation is severe and coupled with physical handicaps, as serious retardation frequently is. Milder retardation is detected at a later period when the child's development falls behind that of his peers.

The nurse who works in the community should pay particular attention to babies who are subject to potential retardation. In addition to those who were born prematurely, this group includes those who are afflicted with phyenylketonuria or who suffer from other inborn errors of metabolism. The undernourished and the culturally or economically deprived child also runs a high risk of retardation. The community nurse has an opportunity to instruct mothers in principles of good nutrition and diet management of metabolic disorders. She may be involved in the supervision of premature babies during their first few crucial months at home. She can help parents to provide a stimulating environment for their children—one which fosters intellectual growth and mental development.

The nurse can also help the parents of retarded children to come to an acceptance and an understanding of retardation and assist them in the difficult task of caring for their babies. As for the retarded infant who is unfortunate enough to be institutionalized, in addition to physical nursing care, the nurse may be able to provide some of the mothering and stimulation which he so desperately needs in order to develop to a degree that approaches his capacity.

When the retarded child reaches preschool age his condition becomes more apparent. Typically, both his motor and his speech development are delayed and he does not show appropriate social and emotional responses for his age. Ongoing social and developmental stimulation is important to help him make the most of his potential. Conditioning and social training are necessary so that in later life he may be able to care for himself. A number of services are available for helping the retarded child during the preschool years. Preschool nursery programs can provide both social training and stimulation. Head Start programs prepare children suffering from cultural retardation for future school achievement by whetting their intellectual curiosity. Play and recreational services fulfill strong needs for socialization, stimulation, and relaxation. There is opportunity in a variety of settings for the nurse to serve the retarded child during his preschool years. In a residential center she can help to provide an environment which is developmentally constructive and stimulating, thereby reducing the untoward effects of institutionalization. In the child's home and in community agencies she can teach the family health and developmental principles. She can assist in identifying children who may be culturally deprived.

The largest group of retarded persons—those who are categorized as the mildly, or educable, retarded—usually are detected when they enter school and fall behind their peers. Some children of this age are falsely classified and treated as retarded; often the learning disability is due to a physical, perceptual, or emotional handicap. Irrespective of the causative factors, these slow-learning children require unique educational programs, services, and techniques ranging from traditional special classes in school to more individualized methods of instruction.

In addition, retarded children also need special health care throughout their years in school because they are often more prone to illness and physical handicaps than are normal children. The nurse working in the school must therefore maintain close health supervision over retarded and slow-learning children. She can assist in teaching the principles of health and safety which retarded children often find difficult to learn and practice. When the child has a physical handicap or suffers from mental illness, the nurse should work closely with educators in reaching a differential diagnosis of learning disability and assist them in planning the proper educational placement of the child. She also has a pivotal role in finding medical or psychiatric treatment for the child.

The transition to adulthood may be an especially trying time for retarded persons and their families. The severely retarded whose families are no longer able to care for them may now have to be institutionalized. The mildly retarded may need further educational and vocational preparation before they can live independently. When they are ready to move into the community, they may require financial support, family-life counseling, transitional living arrangements, provision for leisure-time activities, and supportive mental health services. When adjustments become difficult, the nurse may be called upon to give support both to the retarded person and to his family. She should make emergency home visits and be able to intervene in crises. She may have a role to play in referring the retarded person to prevocational services focused upon his psychological preparation for employment.

Retarded parents deserve special attention. The nurse can be instrumental in helping such persons to adjust to their new and difficult role. The pregnant retarded mother has particular need of the nurse's supervision and assistance during the antepartal period and, later, in caring for her newborn infant.

The needs of the elderly retarded person are similar to, but perhaps more accentuated than, those of the general geriatric population. He is likely to be more subject to illness and other health problems. If he has been supporting himself in the community, he may need special guidance and emotional support to maintain his independence. The nurse must put into practice the principles of health supervision and mental health practice in assisting retarded persons to accommodate to the aging process.

From this longitudinal approach to the needs of the mentally retarded, it is clear that no clinical specialty in nursing can be excluded when comprehensive care of the retarded is considered. Are nurses prepared for this task? How much do they know about the problem of mental retardation? How much has it been considered in their basic nursing curriculum? What are their attitudes toward the mentally retarded?

Two additional issues confront nurses preparing to care adequately for the retarded. First, they must be experts in working within the multidisciplinary team. Team functioning is not a new concept to nursing, but it is frequently more an ideal than a reality. When team functioning is for the benefit of retarded patients, the members of each profession must realize that the complexities of retardation necessitate a wide range of knowledge and skills and must be cognizant of the expertise and merits of the other professionals.

Finally, a new role for the nurse appears to be emerging—that of health and social planner. Community planning involves working with many persons, both professional and nonprofessional, to influence social policy. It requires an understanding of political mechanisms and the way in which decisions are made at every level of government, knowledge of how bureaucracy responds to political decisions in allocating resources.

Community planning and community organization are quite familiar to many of the other professions, but to nurses this area of activity is relatively new. In particular, nursing is as yet sparsely represented among the many professions that have become involved in preparing comprehensive plans for caring for retarded persons from birth to death. Since nurses are so intimately involved in providing services for the retarded, it is important that they take part in the planning process. Only then can their insights and expertise be brought to bear on the development of new and better programs for the long neglected retarded segment of the population.

REFERENCES

[Twenty-two references not reprinted.

20 The Teacher Works with the Parent of the Exceptional Child

Frances A. Mullen

Teamwork between the home and school is basic for effective service to any child. When the child is exceptional, such teamwork is doubly needed and, sometimes, doubly difficult.

When Johnny is very bright or very dull; when Judith's schoolwork lags because of a visual or hearing defect or a speech impediment; when any physical condition interrupts attendance or interferes with learning; when Jerry persistently misbehaves and Joe retreats into frightened silence—when any one of these problems arises, the teacher should not have to solve it alone. The child who differs significantly from the average in mental ability, in physical traits, or in emotional adjustment needs teachers and parents who understand each other, who believe in each other, and who can work together.

Exceptional Johnny's first teacher normally is not a specialist in work with the handicapped or gifted. It is in the regular grades that most exceptionalities are recognized, that diagnostic processes are started, and that much work with parents takes place. The blind child, the profoundly deaf, the severely retarded, disturbed, or physically handicapped may start school in a special class, but children with these extreme disabilities constitute a small percentage of the exceptional. Many more children with somewhat less serious defects in vision, hearing, speech, or motor ability, and children with deviations in mental ability or emotional stability enter the regular classes and stay there for considerable periods of time for a variety of reasons, even though they are eligible for special classes or services. Still more children (many times more) with less serious exceptionalities remain, as they should, in the regular stream of the American public school system. For all of them, school and home need intimate and continuing contacts more frequently than for the "average" child.

Teamwork implies interdependence. The school has as much to learn from the parent as it has to give. Each can help the other to understand the child more fully and to meet the problems each day brings forth.

Sometimes we in the school resent a barrier which the parent seems to erect in the face of inquiries. We forget that the parent feels equally frustrated when he or she tries to get some information from us. Frankness begets frankness. When the teacher is willing to discuss facts realistically in words the parent can understand, without glossing over the possible seriousness of symptoms noted, when she can admit difficulties and failures, and when she can face fears that the trouble may be deep seated, she can expect similar reactions from the parent.

TEACHER AND SPECIALIST

It is the responsibility of a teacher to note symptoms but not to diagnose and evaluate exceptionalities. While she is alert for symptoms, she is aware that there are many possible causes of each symptom and that diagnosis is the province of appropriate professional people.

Her group tests may suggest that the child is so bright that he needs much more than the usual school program provides or so slow that special classes or special techniques should be employed. Therefore, she calls in the psychologist to make a diagnosis that will differentiate between innate ability level and a variety of spurious factors, which might produce temporarily a very high or low written test score. The psychologist, in turn, depends on both teacher and parent for information about the child. He may find it necessary to refer the child to a neurologist, psychiatrist, or other specialist.

With another child, the teacher may suspect a visual or hearing defect or a physical basis for laziness and inattentiveness or restlessness. The parent is entitled to a frank explanation and preparation for referral to appropriate diagnostic facilities.

VALUE OF FORTHRIGHTNESS

Too often this frankness is lacking. The teacher surrounds her suggestions with weasel words that do not tell the story. Her mistaken kindness in "softening the blow" gives the parent an excuse for not facing up to the full possibilities and, therefore, for putting off further diagnosis. Frankness does not need to be brutal, if it is approached in the spirit of mutual concern. "We both have a problem. We both need more help and more information before we can know how best to help Johnny." Frankness indeed may well restore confidence and reduce tension.

The resistance parents sometimes show to suggestions for diagnostic referrals or to changes in educational plans to meet the needs of a child may stem from unspoken, unacknowledged fears that something still worse is wrong with the child, something for which the parents are to blame in some obscure but fundamental fashion. Real frankness conveys with it a desire to help and a lack of blame that can be a relief to the most disturbed parent.

Counseling parents is a long-term project. It is not a job accomplished in one interview, whether by classroom teacher, principal, counselor, or school psychologist. Ideas need time to sink in. The school person learns as well as the parent. The pieces of the puzzle fall into place gradually as both work toward more understanding of the child and both seek better ways of handling him in the school and the home.

It is unlikely that the teacher will have all the answers ready to hand over to the parent for obedient action. Even if she did, it would avail little to handle the interview in such fashion. It is much better to provide the information and lead the parent to work through the steps by which the school arrived at a given conclusion. By the time the school and parent have gone through this process together, the teacher as well as the parent will see the child in a somewhat different light.

The belligerent parent who blames all the child's problems on his present teacher, or last year's teacher, or the principal, who threatens to call the alderman, or writes to the governor, who screams that no one is going to call her child crazy when a child guidance clinic is mentioned is not the typical parent of the exceptional child, but she is a parent all teachers of the exceptional meet sooner or later. The more deeply a parent is inwardly disturbed about his child, the more insecure he feels, the more need he has to project his fears into resentment against any convenient outside person.

"YES, BUT . . ."

Some readers who started this paper, I am sure, have discarded it before this point, with a heartfelt, "I'd like to see the author talk frankly to my Mrs. Z." Let the author say only that she knows Mrs. Z very well, indeed many Mrs. Z's, and she still believes that rapport can be established with almost all. Mrs. Z eventually will come around to a reasonable discussion—if we have the time and the patience and the skill to let her talk herself out and to express her feelings to a person who listens with respect and with concern. After Mrs. Z has made clear her resentment of the school, or the doctor, or

the social worker, she will begin to tell the counselor that she never could do anything with Johnny. A basis for beginning to work together on a mutual problem is then established.

The catch in this optimistic view is the proviso of time and patience. Where do we find the patience when the emotional resources of the teacher are battered day in and day out with the pressures of an inhuman teaching load? Where do we find the time when school administrators or school boards or patrons still think there is something wasteful, if not sinful, about a few minutes of "free time" on a teacher's class schedule?

There are other reasons why counseling the parent of the exceptional child cannot be accomplished in a single interview, or a few interviews. Ambivalence in attitude toward one's child is common to all parents. Any honest mother or father would have to admit to the times when he or she has resented the burden of parenthood and felt like rejecting the child. The exceptional child puts a double burden on the parent, while, at the same time, he makes the parent feel doubly guilty if a normal resentment temporarily wells up in him. Because of the depth of the emotions that center in all parent-child relationships, and particularly surrounding the child that is different, there may well be a long gap between intellectual and emotional acceptance of the facts as presented by the school. When acceptance has not gone below the intellectual level, the parent appears to understand and agree; but action does not follow, because the parent is not yet ready to accept fully on the emotional and personal level.

OTHER SOURCES OF HELP

The school is only one of the sources of professional help that parents of handicapped or exceptional children need. The kind of counseling that we have been talking about frequently begins in the school, because many exceptionalities are not clearly recognized until the child comes into direct comparison with his peers in the classroom, or because the family physician has been too busy to focus on the problem, or because other community resources are lacking. However, the responsibility of the teacher and the principal, in many of these cases, is primarily to get the family to the professional who should take over much of the further diagnosis, counseling, and treatment. This may be the family or clinic physician; it may be a social agency to which the family is already known; it may be a community child-guidance clinic or family-life clinic; it may be the school psychologist or school nurse or school social worker if these are available.

When community resources needed by a number of families are lacking, it may well fall to the lot of school people, as interested citizens, to take an active role in working with community leaders to develop an appropriate source of help. Even when a facility is available, referral does not absolve the school of responsibility.

Diagnosis and counseling are a teamwork responsibility. All too often many professional persons and agencies (school, medical, or social) work independently with a family, with little interchange of experience and information. Because almost every agency engaged in service to people is overburdened and understaffed, communication breaks down. Ways to keep in touch should be planned from the beginning of almost all referrals.

GROUP TECHNIQUES

There are many techniques for working with parents. This discussion has so far referred chiefly to the individual conference between the parent and a school person, whether teacher, principal, counselor, psychologist, or social worker on the school staff. But this is by no means the sole means of accomplishing the ends we have been discussing.

Group techniques range all the way from work with community mass meetings or the meeting of the local P.T.A., to a small group of two or three parents with similar problems. The technique may range from a formal lecture by a visiting expert, to a down-to-earth presentation, autocratic perhaps, by a school person, to a continuing democratic work-group experience, in which real interchange of ideas and experiences and feelings takes place. There are some things that can be accomplished better in the group situation than in individual counseling.

The way the school reports to parents can increase or retard the parents' recognition of the success or failure of different ways of working with a child. Radio, TV, and other media of mass communication have their place in the total program of the school for working with parents of exceptional children.

The task is difficult, sometimes thorny and troublesome. Effectively discharged, it is among the most rewarding of the opportunities open to school people. As we come to know parents of exceptional children as co-workers, we find them (even some of the difficult ones) to be the most courageous, the most devoted, and the most responsive of all the parents with whom we deal. From them we in the schools have much to learn.

21 The Ministry and Mental Retardation

Harold W. Stubblefield

In the growing volume of literature on the church and mental retardation, the role of the minister in the religious care of the mentally retarded and their families has been recognized. Recent publications have also suggested that religious factors are sometimes involved in the parental acceptance of a retarded child. However, no research dealing with the actual work of pastors in mental retardation is available. The present exploratory study was undertaken in an effort to sample the thinking of pastors regarding mental retardation and to survey the actual ministries performed. No formal hypotheses were advanced.

METHOD

A questionnaire survey was made of all the pastors in Davidson County, Tennessee, a metropolitan area with a population of approximately 416,000 persons. A questionnaire, together with a letter explaining the nature of the study, was mailed to 645 ministers on the mailing list of the Nashville Association of Churches. A follow-up led to a total return of 229 questionnaires. The total number of Negro and Jewish respondents represented a relatively minute proportion of the total returns. Therefore, in order to allow for more adequate generalizations from present findings, responses from the Jewish and Negro clergymen were not included in the final analysis of

data. The present report is based on an analysis of the returns of 220 white Protestant ministers and Catholic priests, together representing 46 per cent of such clergymen in Davidson County.

In an effort to encourage the return of completed questionnaires, the ministers were not asked to identify themselves by name. However, they were requested to give the following general information concerning themselves: church affiliation, ministerial training, size of church membership, and location of church.

Table 1 gives the denominational affiliation of the respondents, indicating that over 10 denominations were represented in the sample. The distribution of denominations represented in the returns closely corresponded with the distribution of these denominations in Davidson County.

The ministerial training of the clergymen is outlined in Table 2. . . . Table 3 lists the size of church membership. Table 4 describes the location of the churches.

The questionnaire consisted of items pertaining to: (1) the extent of the minister's contact with mentally retarded persons and their families; (2) the ministry to parents of retarded persons; (3) the nature and scope of the church's responsibility; (4) the effect that the birth of a retarded child has on the religious faith and practice of parents; (5) theological issues in mental retardation; (6) the ministry to

Table 1. Number and Percentages of Respondents According to Denomination

Denomination	Number	%
Baptist	53	24
Methodist	43	19
Church of Christ	38	17
Presbyterian	20	9
Nazarene	16	7
Catholic	11	5
Lutheran	8	4
Episcopalian	6	4
Disciples of Christ	7	3
Others	18	8
Total	220	100

Table 2. Ministerial Training of Respondents

Level	Number	%
Seminary*	154	70
College graduate training	11	5
College	44	20
High school or less	6	3
No response	5	2
Total	220	100

*12 per cent had received some form of clinical pastoral education.

retarded persons; and (7) the religious responsibility of the retarded. The responses were scored quantitatively and qualitatively.

RESULTS

Some previous contact with mentally retarded persons and their families was indicated by 92 per cent of the ministers. However, only 62 per cent of the total currently have parents of retarded persons in either their present or previous pastorates; 47 percent learned about the retardation during a routine pastoral call in the home; 42 per cent were approached by the parents; 10 per cent became aware of the retardation when the child created problems in some church organization; and 5 per cent heard about it through community sources, including friends, neighbors, church workers, and professional persons. In other instances, the minister became aware that a child was

Table 3. Size of Church Membership

Size	Number	%
100 or less	27	12
100-250	58	26
250-500	55	25
500-750	26	12
750-1000	16	7
1000-2000	10	4
2000 or more	9	4
No response	19	4
Total	220	100

Table 4. Location of Church

Type	Number	%
Suburban	151	69
Downtown	31	14
Rural	15	7
Other	14	6
No response	9	4
Total	220	100

retarded by observing him in church activities.

The ministers reported having learned of the retarded child's condition at different stages in his development. Thirty per cent first learned that a child was retarded through the parents' concern over his slow development; 22 per cent reported that of the retarded children they knew, the condition was recognizable at birth; 18 per cent became involved when the family considered institutionalization of the child; and 4 per cent learned of the child's condition when he presented problems in the sexual area or became aggressive in behavior.

Ministry to Parents

Fifty per cent of the ministers had engaged in pastoral conversation with parents regarding their retarded child, and 42 per cent served parents by offering comfort and support. Intensive counseling, i.e., helping the family work through their feelings, was reported by 17 per cent, while 23 per cent had ministered by referring the parents to community agencies or other professional persons.

In the respondents' description of actual ministries performed, a variety of approaches in ministering to parents of retarded persons was reported. For some clergymen, the primary ministry was to recommend that the family seek professional help, and in some cases the pastors recommended that the child be institutionalized. Other ministers characterized their ministry as one of pastoral care. For example, one pastor said that he always sought to get the parents to accept this situation, to recognize that it existed, and to integrate the child into the home life as far as possible.

However, several pastors reported performing no ministries at all for parents. In some situations, the family had already adjusted to the problem and/or had received professional help when the minister first met the family. In other instances, the minister's perception of his role prevented his taking initiative in offering pastoral services to the family. For example, one pastor with considerable graduate training in psychology said: "Being non-directive and knowing the parents knew of my qualifications, I left any attempts at counseling up to their initiation, and they made none." Other clergymen were prevented from offering services because of the unwillingness of certain families "to face up to the problem."

What were the ministers' personal feelings in regard to their ministry to parents? Only 25 per cent of the clergymen indicated that they felt competent to help parents with this problem, while 10 per cent said they felt helpless while working with parents of retarded children; 50 per cent perceived that this would be a problem of long duration, but only 1 per cent said that this was not a problem of concern to a minister. Most clergymen reported that their feelings of inadequacy stemmed from a lack of preparation and training for ministering to this specific problem and from a lack of information regarding resources available to the parents. However, on the whole, the respondents reported that they felt competent to minister to parents as pastors, to offer meaningful pastoral relationships, and to advise the parents to seek professional services.

Nature and Scope of the Church's Responsibility

Of the respondents, 96 per cent believed that the minister and church do have a responsibility to the retarded and their families; 87 per cent replied that the ministry should include pastoral counseling to help families work through their feelings and make responsible decisions concerning the child. A supportive ministry to encourage and strengthen parents was advocated by 78 per cent, and 76 per cent said that the pastor should serve as a referral source to community agencies. Sixty per cent believed that the church should provide special religious education classes for the retarded, while 62 per cent felt that the church's ministry should include pastoral care and/or counseling of retarded persons.

Several clergymen suggested that the ministry of the church in mental retardation was only one part of the church's ministry to all persons and should not be considered as a special ministry. Other respondents noted that the effective fulfillment of this responsibility was limited by the lack of trained personnel in the church. A small minority of the ministers said that the church has no responsibility for a ministry to retarded persons and their families.

Effect on Religious Beliefs and Practices

Varying degrees of awareness regarding the effects of the birth of a retarded child on the religious faith and practice of the parents were evidenced by the clergymen. Forty-one per cent of the respondents had observed that a retarded child stimulated greater faith in the parents, and 15 per cent had observed no effect at all in other parents. On the other hand, 15 per cent of the ministers believed that having a retarded child had caused doubt about the goodness of God in the parents known to them, and 13 per cent had observed that the birth of a retarded child created guilt in the parents.

With reference to the effect of the retarded child on the church attendance of the parents, 12 per cent of the ministers indicated that families with retarded children known to them became irregular in church attendance, and 3 per cent knew families who ceased attending altogether. However, 33 per cent of the clergymen had noted no change in the degree of attendance at church, while 28 per cent had observed families who were brought closer to the church as a result of having a retarded child.

In the comments of several respondents, there was a variety of interpretations of the religious dynamics involved in the parental response to a retarded child. In the opinion of some ministers, the faith manifested by parents after the birth of a retarded child was simply an extension of a prior faith. Other pastors, however, reported having observed various "ups and downs" in the faith. In many parents a positive religious response was not automatically attained, but was achieved after a struggle. In still other cases, completely negative religious responses were observed by the respondents.

Theological Issues

In answer to the question: "Do you believe that there are any theological or religious issues in the problem of mental retardation?" 47 per cent replied "Yes," 36 per cent replied "No," and 17 per cent did not respond to the question. In an analysis of the data from the standpoint of the denominational affiliation of the respondents, suggestive differences were found. Theological issues in mental retardation were acknowledged by 67 per cent of the Methodist ministers, 57 per cent of the Disciples of Christ ministers, and 54 per cent of the Catholic priests. However, only 40 per cent of the Baptist ministers, 38 per cent of the Lutherans, 37 per cent of the Church of Christ respondents, and 19 per cent of the Nazarenes believed that there were theological issues in mental retardation. The responses of the Presbyterian and Episcopal clergymen were equally distributed among positive and negative replies.

In order to determine what the ministers perceived these theological issues to be, it was requested that they be listed. The theological issue most often cited related to the causation of mental retardation, and more Methodists listed this than did ministers of any other denomination. Mental retardation was attributed by some ministers to the sins of the parents, though this was usually qualified so as to exclude personal sin. Others disclaimed any belief that God punished parents through the birth of a retarded child. Mental retardation, however, did pose real questions for the respondents about the will and purpose of God and His control over the creative processes. As one minister put it: "To many church people mental retardation is basically a religious matter as to why."

The effect on the religious faith of parents as a result of giving birth to a retarded child seemed to be the second most crucial issue. Several ministers interpreted the birth of a retarded child as an occasion that could cause the parents to doubt the goodness of God and to become hostile toward religion and rebellious against God.

The religious responsibility of the retarded was seen as another theological issue; ministers of the Baptist, Church of Christ, and Nazarene denominations cited this more often than did ministers of other denominations. As each of these denominations practices "believer's baptism," these ministers were apparently concerned about the retarded person's degree of competency in religious matters and the nature of the retardates' responsibility before God. One Church of Christ minister expressed the issue as "determining the advisability of confronting the subject with obedience to the gospel." A Lutheran pastor asked what constituted sufficient knowledge on the part of the retarded for participation in the sacraments of the church.

Other religious issues included: (1) the theological motivation for the church's responsibility to minister to the retarded and their families; (2) the religious resources that could strengthen parents as they cared for a retarded child; and (3) the degree of the parents' responsibility for the care of a retarded child. Only one minister inquired about the ethics of sterilization for parents who have produced several mentally defective children.

Many clergymen stated that all of life involves theological and religious values, but they did not believe that there were any religious issues in mental retardation that were not present in good health as well. Other respondents commented that mental retardation presented no theological problems for them, but that it raised unspecified theological questions in the minds of parents and church members.

Ministry to the Retarded

What specific ministries did the churches actually offer to mentally retarded persons? Ninety-six per cent of the clergymen felt that the church was responsible for the religious care and training of the retarded. However, only 9 per cent reported that their church made any special provision for the retarded in its educational program, and only 4 per cent indicated that they planned to do so in the near future. In several churches, the retarded were integrated into the regular Sunday School classes or placed in the nursery. Reasons offered for failure to make special provision included an insufficient number of retarded children to warrant a special class, lack of trained teachers to staff the classes, and lack of space in the church facilities. Several ministers expressed the need for interchurch co-operation in order to make adequate provision for the retarded.

Ninety per cent of the respondents felt that a pastoral ministry to the retarded was impossible. Sixty-three per cent of the ministers reported having made pastoral conversation with retarded persons; 54 per cent made pastoral visits at time of sickness; 35 per cent counseled about personal problems; 25 per cent counseled about vocational problems; and 5 per cent had taught a special religious education class. In general, the clergymen indicated that a pastoral ministry to

the retarded was limited by the degree to which the person was retarded as well as by the minister's lack of training for work with these individuals.

Religious Responsibility of the Retarded

Ninety per cent of the ministers believed that mentally retarded persons are capable of understanding what it means to be a Christian and of becoming members of the church; 43 per cent of the ministers had already received retarded persons as members of their churches, and an additional 49 per cent indicated they would be willing to do so in the future.

The general consensus was that reception of a retarded person into the membership of the church was conditional on the degree of retardation, but that retardation, in and of itself, should not be a reason for exclusion. It was held that the retarded should be accepted or rejected according to their ability or inability to understand the meaning of being a Christian and a church member. The demand for a responsible religious decision on the part of retarded persons was most pronounced in, but not limited to, the Baptist and Church of Christ ministers. The ability of the retarded to make a responsible religious decision did not present as great a problem to ministers of the Presbyterian, Lutheran, and Catholic faiths.

CONCLUSIONS AND IMPLICATIONS

On the basis of the data compiled in this exploratory study, several pertinent conclusions concerning the work of ministers in mental retardation can be drawn. The most obvious finding was that almost every clergyman had had some contact with mental retardation and that the majority had performed some type of pastoral service either to retarded persons or to their parents. The respondents tended to define the minister's work with parents as that of offering meaningful pastoral relationships and of making referrals to other professional persons. The clergymen characterized their work as pastoral care, i.e., short-term, unstructured, supportive relationships, rather than long-term, intensive counseling. However, no clear consensus regarding what it means to be a pastor to parents of mentally retarded persons was evident. Some apprehension about the role of the pastor seemed apparent; only one-fourth of the clergymen indicated that they felt competent to help parents with this problem. Also, the respondents felt that a pastor should have special training before working with parents of retarded children. Apparently, the ministers had not identified the needs of parents with which a minister could be of help; consequently, they were apprehensive and confused about their role. The clergymen's work was also influenced by the stage in the family's adjustment to the problem at the time the pastor became involved as well as by the parents' willingness to receive help.

With respect to mental retardation and the religious faith of parents, the clergymen had reportedly observed that the birth of a retarded child more often stimulated greater faith than it created guilt or doubt about the goodness of God. In contrast to the experience of the ministers . . . psychologists and social workers indicate that guilt is quite prevalent among parents of retarded children and is a major factor impeding parental acceptance. One explanation for the difference in the perception of the dynamics operating in the parental response to retarded children may be that professional persons such as psychologists and social workers tend to see parents in crisis situations, when they are more expressive of their deeper feelings. Also, these workers are better trained to observe psychodynamics of behavior. Ministers, on the other hand, most often work with parents in an unstructured, pastoral-care situation that may not allow for the expression of deeper feelings. Moreover, many of the clergymen indicated that they came in contact with the parents only after some adjustment to the problem had already been made.

As might have been expected, many clergymen had grappled with the theological issues in mental retardation. The religious aspect of the causes of mental retardation was the crucial concern. The ministers seemed to be struggling with the relation of retardation to the sovereignty of God and man's responsibility. Retardation raised real questions about the nature of God and His control of the creative processes. Although retardation was not directly attributed to the sins of the parents, there seemed to be some feeling that "sin" was the ultimate cause. Essentially, the ministers were grappling with the "meaning" of mental retardation in relation to the Christian faith and with the religious basis for the acceptance of retarded persons.

In the current literature on the church and mental retardation, the emphasis has centered on the responsibility of the church to provide special religious education classes. However, the present survey indicated that the clergymen were more often involved in two other types of ministry: pastoral care of individual retardates and the ministry at the time of religious decision. Surprisingly, the pastoral ministry to the retarded was more prevalent among present respondents than was the ministry to parents. Although one of the crucial theological issues concerned the degree of the religious responsibility of the retarded, almost half of the clergymen said that they had already received mentally retarded persons as members of their churches. In contrast to the frequency of ministry through pastoral care and at the time of religious decision, only a minute proportion of the respondents had taught a special religious education class themselves and provided such classes in their churches.

The clergymen seemed quite clear as to what should be the nature and scope of the church's responsibility. They believed that the ministry to parents should include pastoral counseling, a supportive ministry, and referral to appropriate community agencies. It was generally agreed that the church should provide special religious education classes and pastoral care and counseling for the retarded. However, only in the area of pastoral care to the retarded and their families did the actual services performed approximate what the respondents perceived to be an adequate church ministry. The areas of greatest disparity between actual and idealized services were the pastoral counseling of parents and special religious education classes for the retarded.

The results of the present study suggest two significant implications relevant to the future ministry of the church. First, the church must conceive of its ministry in a broad and comprehensive fashion. Because only four significant disabling conditions (mental illness, cardiac disease, arthritis, and cancer) exceed mental retardation in prevalence, almost every minister and church can expect to be involved with this problem at some time. To meet this challenge responsibly, the church must first "make sense" of mental retardation in relation to Christian theology. Moreover, parents of retarded persons need sensitive pastoral care to help them accept the child, to secure competent professional services, and to reconcile the event with their religious faith. The church is responsible for ministering to retarded persons individually through pastoral care, for guiding them to participate in the life of the church, and for providing religious training. In essence, then, the ministry of the church to the retarded and their families is no different from its ministry to any other person or group.

The second implication is that additional research on almost every topic covered in this survey is needed. The areas that apparently need further research are: (1) the theological aspects of mental retardation; (2) the role of the pastor in the religious care of the parents; and (3) the effect that the birth of a retarded child has on the faith of parents. In the absence of basic research on these and other vital areas, the literature on the church and mental retardation is becoming repetitious, tending to rephrase old ideas without producing new knowledge.

Part IV

DETECTION
AND DIAGNOSIS

22 Introduction to Part IV

Detection refers to the recognition that something "may be wrong" with a child and *diagnosis* is the judgment based on a professional examination that the child is or is not retarded. In all cases detection obviously precedes diagnosis. The literature on detection is quite small. Indeed, not one article was found to deal exclusively with the topic of detection from the perspective of this book, so that is was necessary to combine it with the only other logical topic, diagnosis, for which there is an abundant literature.

Detection is sometimes followed closely by diagnosis: Down's syndrome (mongolism), for instance, is apparent at birth and the specialist who makes a definitive diagnosis may be called into action in the first hour of the infant's life. Sometimes the interval from detection to diagnosis is quite long; a pediatrician, for instance, may detect disturbing signs in a six-month-old infant, but a definitive diagnosis may not be possible for years. In all circumstances, however, detection precedes diagnosis.

The consumer and the provider usually have a logical division of labor in regard to detection. Parents who notice problems are expected to bring those problems to the attention of the appropriate specialists. In some cases, however, a parent may detect some disturbing signs which she does not communicate to professionals because she is afraid of being considered overconcerned or the anxieties aroused may be so intense that her observations are suppressed. When a provider finally detects the disturbing developmental signs, he is technically the one who made the detection although the parent was fully aware of what he detected long before he did so.

Professional detection results from systematic or nonsystematic efforts. One form of systematic detection effort is the standard routines employed by professions and service systems. Pediatricians, for instance, have routines that automatically detect many acute and chronic deviations from normalcy. Another agent for systematic detection is the screening test. It divides the screened population into two groups—those who probably do and those who probably do not have the condition screened for. Those who are indicated as probably having the condition are subjected to full diagnostic procedures. The Denver Developmental Screening Test is one device which feeds thousands of detected cases into diagnostic clinics each year.

Nonsystematic detection of mental retardation may occur in a multitude of situations. A caseworker in a child-abuse program may detect symptoms which

141

average parents would have detected but which many abusing parents would not. A teacher may observe in the course of her day-to-day work symptoms of subnormal intellectual functioning. A physician may detect developmental lag as he treats a child with measles or other conditions not associated with mental functioning. And so forth.

The articles of Rosen (1955), Schonell (1956), and Oppenheimer (1966) provide more detail on detection than any others in the literature. However, each article considers several other subjects as well, especially diagnosis and counseling. Rosen offers the only conceptualization of detection in the literature from the perspective of the parent. It is an exploratory study of thirty-six mothers of retarded children, with an interview schedule based on Dewey's "five steps in thinking." These five steps trace the mother's process of becoming aware of the problem to the final step of acceptance of the problem. Interestingly, the majority of the mothers detected developmental problems before the service system. Schonell's findings on fifty families support those of Rosen. (Only the sections concerned with detection are presented in excerpt form here.) Oppenheimer focuses on the full process from detection through treatment. Interestingly, the type of counseling a family needs is seen to be determined in part by whether the family detected the problem first. Except for these three articles, the literature on detection is quite meager and does not explain just how cases of retardation enter the service system or how the interdependence of consumer and provider determines the entry.

In *diagnosis* the parent is much less involved than in detection. Yet the parent does have two tasks beyond bringing the child to the diagnosticians. First, the parent may be an important source of information for the diagnostic process, and Schulman and Stern (1959) demonstrate this. Second, the parent has to understand and accept the diagnosis before any treatment plan may be formulated, and Keogh (1966) provides case examples of just how difficult this is for parents and how important professional support (nursing in this case) is beyond the act of communicating the diagnosis. Menolascino (1968) supplements Keogh by classifying the family crises surrounding diagnosis, each of which has different implications for case management. Finally, Wolfensberger (1965) offers a delightful respite from the usual literature and points out five widespread deficiencies in diagnosis.

23 Selected Aspects in the Development of the Mother's Understanding of Her Mentally Retarded Child

Leonard Rosen

This is an exploratory study designed to present in a systematic way selected aspects in the development of the mother's understanding of her mentally retarded child. This study is limited to observations and reactions of the mothers concerning their mentally retarded children.

An examination of related research studies indicates that most investigators in the past have devoted more attention to the retarded child than to his parents. Most writings in the field of mental retardation have been based upon the opinions and experiences of the authors rather than upon organized study. When the parents are the subject of study, adequate counseling techniques are stressed. To date there has been only one systematic study of parents of retarded children. That study was concerned with the acceptance of the retarded child by his parents. . . .

THE POPULATION

The population used for this study consisted of thirty-six mothers of thirty-six retarded children, including twenty-six boys and ten girls. On the basis of certain criteria, the mothers were selected from eighteen hundred case records of mentally retarded children. All the mothers and children were interviewed at the New Jersey Mental Hygiene Bureau where they voluntarily sought advice to help their children. The purpose in selecting this population was to study a group of mothers who were as similar as possible with respect to their environment and certain personal factors, and which would still provide an adequate population for this study. All the mothers accepted objectively their children's mental retardation on the basis of the following criteria: (1) able to admit that her child was retarded, (2) no longer looking for a miraculous cure, (3) trying to act constructively for the child's present and future welfare. However, they still maintained hope that the child could be helped.

While complete homogeneity was not attained insofar as the children were concerned, all were mentally retarded, ambulatory, devoid of physical characteristics which are readily identifiable with mental retardation, had never been placed in a training school for the mentally retarded, and never presented severe behavior problems.

All parents and children were American-born in families of average social status and income. All cases in which the parents were divorced, separated, or where one was deceased before the time of the interview, were excluded from the study.

THE DESIGN OF THE STUDY

Analysis of the writing of Pearl Buck and John P. Frank indicated a developmental pattern of growing comprehension when parents recognized a child's mental retardation. The trend of developments observed in this pattern bears similarity to the analysis of problem development as set forth by John Dewey. The following five phases represent the adaptations from Dewey's "Steps in Thinking," and are used as the plan of organization for this study. . . .

The phases were expanded further in this study into a pattern of organization called the "Outline of Developmental Phases." (The term *phase* as used in this study implies a dimension of time, having indefinite limits within which certain phenomena occur characteristic of that phase.) A certain amount of overlapping is to be expected between phases. Within each phase, aspects were selected for investigation on the basis of the experience of the author and a pilot study of eight cases. Other determinants of selection were the quality of the aspect to be studied and the degree of familiarity each mother would ordinarily be expected to have had with a particular aspect.

THE STUDY TECHNIQUES

Using the "Outline of Developmental Phases" as a basis, an "Interview Question Guide" composed of fifty-six questions was devised to obtain data from the mothers. These data were recorded on a special answer form from which tabulations were made. All interviewing was done by the writer in private sessions with the mothers. They were told the purpose of the study and were encouraged to discuss their problems freely. The data were analyzed in descriptive rather than statistical terms. This treatment of the data was dictated by the relatively small number of cases and influence of unknown variables. Therefore, when percentages and correlations are presented, they should be interpreted with caution. Validity of information given by the mothers was determined by checking clinic case records with

Adaptation of Dewey's "Steps in Thinking"

Dewey's steps	Writer's phases
1. Felt difficulty	1. Awareness of the problem
2. Location and definition	2. Recognition of the problem
3. Suggestion of possible solution	3. Seeking for the cause
4. Development by reasoning of the bearings of the suggestion	4. Seeking for the solution
5. Further observation and experiment leading to its acceptance or rejection; that is, the conclusion of belief or disbelief.	5. Acceptance of the problem (Combines Dewey's 4th and 5th steps. This phase is never fully attained.)

data obtained in the interviews and through analyzing internal consistency of the mothers' replies in the interview. The reliability of the writer's interview technique was checked by a re-interview of eight cases.

RESULTS

The results are presented here in the form of phases. The phases are *not* to be construed as *sharply delineated* areas, but rather as areas *overlapping* in *varying degrees*. It is possible for awareness and recognition of the problem by the mother to occur almost simultaneously. Also, it is difficult to draw a sharp line of distinction between "Phase of Seeking for the Cause" of mental retardation and "Phase of Seeking for the Solution." In both of these phases, the goal for the mother is to obtain cure or relief for her child's handicap. These two phases run concurrently after awareness of the mental retardation is noted by the mother. They are placed in the following order for purposes of clarity.

Phase of Awareness

The phase of awareness is defined as that phase in which the mother first experiences the feeling that her child is different from other children. The mean chronological age of the child when the mother became aware of his retardation was two years, eight months and the range was from birth to seven years. The mothers themselves, in the majority of the cases, were the first to become aware of the retardation without suggestion by others. At least one-fourth of the mothers

denied having any knowledge that their children were retarded before admission to school. It was indicated by correlation that the intelligence and schooling levels of the mothers have practically no relationship to the estimated ages of children when awareness occurred. Also, there is little reason to assume that the child's level of intelligence is a factor affecting awareness with this selected group of children.

Phase of Recognition

The phase of recognition is defined as the phase in which the mother is cognizant of the child's mental retardation and able to acknowledge it. Recognition may occur abruptly and simultaneously with awareness or it may be a protracted process. There is a suggestion that mothers who become aware of their child's retardation at an early date tend to take longer to recognize it than mothers who become aware of the retardation later in the child's life. The age range of the children at the time recognition occurred to the mother of her child's retardation, is from one to nine years and the mean age for recognition is five years one month. The majority of the mothers recognized the retardation after the child was five years of age. Slowness in developmental aspects of the child's growth was noted earliest, poor behavior next, and school failures last. Most of the mothers felt that the child's slow rate of social and intellectual maturation helped them to recognize the retardation more than any other factor. In over half the cases, teachers were first to offer constructive advice to the mothers. There appears to be very little relationship between the mother's level of intelligence and schooling, and the age of the child when she recognized the retardation. Very little relationship is evident between the child's level of intelligence and the age of the child at the time of recognition of the retardation by the mother.

Phase of Seeking for the Cause

This phase, arbitrarily assigned as the third, is defined as the attempts by the mother to identify the factors or factor making for mental retardation in her child. The age of the child when the mother first sought help could not be determined since the mothers were too indefinite about it. Two aspects were studied: (1) the mother's concept of the cause for her child's retardation; (2) her justification for belief in the cause. Causes of mental retardation were attributed to conditions prior to, during, and subsequent to the birth of the child, hereditary factors, and miscellaneous factors. A majority of the mothers could give no particular reason for belief in their selected cause, but it is suspected that many of them based their beliefs upon superstitions and hearsay. More than half the mothers believed that there was a physical basis for the child's mental retardation, but in only three cases was a sound physical basis found. The majority of the mothers were dissatisfied with their concept of the cause and wished to know more about it.

Phase of Seeking for the Solution

The fourth phase is defined as the mother's attempts to find some measure of cure or relief for her child's

mental retardation, and is concerned with the nature and number of individuals and agencies consulted by the mother, and how these resources influenced her understanding. While no definite point in time could be established when this phase begins, there is evidence that a mother may make her first definite contact for help before the child is one year of age. It is more important to note that the majority of the mothers sought help at or after the time they recognized the retardation. The total number of times the mothers in this study were directed to sources of help was 115. Of this number, the schools ranked first in over half the cases in referring the mothers to sources of help, physicians came second, mothers acting on their initiative third, friends of the parents fourth, and members of the family and miscellaneous agencies and individuals fifth. Concerning the number of agencies or individuals contacted by the mothers, the physicians ranked highest, community clinics second, hospital clinics third, school psychological clinics fourth, and private professional persons (such as psychologists and osteopaths) ranked lowest. Most mothers were more satisfied with a psychological than a physical-medical interpretation of the problem.

Phase of Acceptance

The fifth phase is defined as the attainment by the mother of an objective attitude toward having a retarded child while still maintaining hope that her child could be helped. No definite point in time could be established when the mother accepted her child's retardation because of the complexity of acceptance. Mothers of retarded children generally define mental retardation in terms of "slowness" of behavior. It does not seem necessary for a mother to have an accurate understanding of the cause in order to accept her child's mental retardation. Almost all the mothers admitted feeling reluctant to accept their child's handicap. Most of the mothers estimated their child's mental level with a fair degree of accuracy. However, it is not known how much prior knowledge the mothers brought to bear upon their estimate.

The majority of the mothers felt that they were helped most to accept the problem by having mental retardation explained to them, while several mothers found that comparisons of the retarded child with his siblings were most helpful. Most mothers found that the presence of the retarded child in the home did not create any unusual problems insofar as the siblings were concerned. In this respect, it should be noted that the retarded children in this study appeared physically normal. All the mothers admitted to having resigned themselves to the problem even though they still maintained hope for improvement in the child.

When asked what advice they would give to other mothers of retarded children, these mothers suggested: (1) an immediate psychological examination for the child, (2) full use of all educational facilities available, (3) a need for the parents to be patient and understanding. Despite recognition of the stigma attached to special classes, most mothers considered such classes to be the best method at present for helping the retarded child individually. The mothers seemed to be divided equally concerning placement of the child in an institution in the future. One half of the mothers definitely would not take such action, while the other half would consider placement only with reservations. Most of the mothers were against taking such action at the present time. All but two of the mothers considered an institution as being different from a training school. Considerable confusion is evident concerning the nature and function of a training school for the mentally retarded.

One-half the mothers felt that their own feelings constituted the greatest obstacle impeding their acceptance of the retardation while the other half attributed it to symptoms in the child's behavior which they could not control or understand. The majority of the mothers would not want to have more children for fear that the next child would be mentally retarded. Over one-half of the mothers were more concerned about their child's vocational future and much less concerned about his future social adjustment. Mothers of retarded girls are more concerned over the sexual adjustment of their daughters in the future than are mothers of retarded boys. This concern appeared to heighten when the girls reached puberty. Most mothers felt that the public in general does not understand the slow child and were of the opinion that the public should be educated in the problems of mental retardation. Most of the mothers felt that parents should not try to conceal the fact that their children are retarded but would not like to be pointed out individually as being parents of retarded children.

RELATED EDUCATIONAL ASPECTS

This part of the study is not a phase but is presented here to emphasize the close relationship existing between the mother of the retarded child and the school. All the mothers were of the opinion that the school helped them in understanding their child's condition except for one mother whose child had just entered school and therefore could make no statement. Over one-half the children were five or six years old and were in kindergarten when the teacher informed the mother that her child was retarded. The attitudes of these mothers toward the teachers were very favorable. It was the opinion of the mothers that kind and understanding teachers are considered more desirable than specially trained teachers. However, it should be noted that these are mothers who have been able to accept their child's retardation. The mothers' choices of the "happiest" grade for her child coincided with the choices of the "best" teachers in most cases. No particular grade levels stand out as being the "happiest" or "unhappiest."

Most of the mothers could recall feeling hostile toward the school when recognition of their child's retardation took place because of the lack of special facilities for teaching retarded children. It was found that the teacher, more than any other member of the faculty, is the one who usually takes on the burden of making recommendations to the mothers. Psychological examinations were recommended in almost one-half the cases by the teachers. In the remaining cases, additional homework or exclusion of the child for an appreciable length of time was suggested. On the whole, the present general attitude of the mothers toward the school was favorable with appreciation being expressed for the teacher's efforts.

CONCLUSIONS

The conclusions in this study apply only to this group of mothers or to similar mothers meeting the criteria used in this research project. However, under certain conditions, wider application of these conclusions might be made to mothers of other retarded children.

1. There is a marked similarity among the mothers in their attitudes and opinions toward their child's mental retardation. In the development of understanding, the mothers followed a general pattern but with individual differences. The nature of this pattern is such as to suggest that the development appears to be affected very little by intellectual factors. Among other factors, emotions may be an important influence upon the mothers' understanding. The process involved in the development of mothers' understanding is protracted and painful to them. They seek, and, at the same time, resist acceptance of the fact that their child is mentally retarded.

In this respect, many of the mothers in this study recalled having strong feelings of hostility toward the school which in their opinion failed to carry out its educational obligation to their child. This attitude toward the school appears to prevail when the mother has not attained acceptance. However, it is important to note that the mothers in this study who had accepted their child's retardation felt that the school had been helpful and sympathetic in its attitude. This change of attitude in the mothers points out that the school can provide a beneficial and sustaining influence for the mother during this difficult period. In this respect, it is vital for educators to bear in mind the frustrations of these mothers as they try to help them.

2. On the basis of the data obtained from these mothers, there is much to suggest that the medical profession needs enlightenment in the problem of mental retardation. For example, many mothers were told by the physicians that "The child is lazy," "he would grow out of it," or "he's smart but nervous." The remarks and recommendations made by the majority of the physicians (as reported by the mothers) reflected evasiveness, disregard for the mother's feelings, or lack of knowledge. These findings are all the more important in view of the fact that the physicians constitute the largest group to which the mothers turn first for help. As a result, the attitude of most of the mothers was not favorable toward the medical profession. It is important that the medical profession become aware of its responsibilities in this matter.

3. It is probably true that the public in general lacks an understanding attitude toward the problem of mental retardation. This is evident not only from the reports of the mothers but is generally conceded by those who are familiar with the problem of mental retardation. This attitude probably has its roots in the fact that our culture places a high value upon self-sufficiency and superior intellectual ability. Thus, when parents find that they have a mentally retarded child, they feel a stigma is attached to them and their child because of his inability to meet cultural standards. This accounts for the desire of most parents of retarded children to remain anonymous.

Any program designed to modify public attitudes should originate from the needs of the parents of retarded children. More recently, the parents of retarded children have begun to assume their responsibility in this manner through the formation of parents' groups for retarded children. These groups are now being organized on a state, local and national level by the parents themselves. Thus far, these groups have been successful in bringing parents of retarded children together by affording them an opportunity to enhance their own understanding of the problem through discussions with each other and specialists. Through concerned group action and the medium of interpretive publicity, these groups are attempting to familiarize the public with problems peculiar to mental retardation. At present, the organization of these groups appears to be the most satisfactory way of modifying public attitudes and should be encouraged.

It is the writer's opinion that the

major contribution of this research study lies in its value as a guide for those who work with mothers of retarded children. While the findings and conclusions may not be universally applicable to all mothers of retarded children, prudent use of this study should offer some enlightenment in many instances. It is hoped that this study will be of value to all those concerned with the problem of mental retardation.

24 A First Survey of the Effects of a Subnormal Child on the Family Unit

*Fred J. Schonell
and B. H. Watts*

Systematic research in the field of mentally subnormal children is of comparatively recent origin and even now sporadic in nature and small in volume. Hence, there are many areas of the problem of subnormality which have not been explored. One of these areas relates to the effect the subnormal child has upon his family unit. The hypothesis that a subnormal child tends to have a disrupting effect on family life has often been stated, but there has been little objective analysis of evidence to uphold or disprove this statement or to discover which aspects of family life are most affected by the presence of such a child. The aim of this research was, then, to make some assessment of the extent to which a subnormal child influences the family unit and to discover in what particular ways family life is most affected.

NATURE OF THE SAMPLE

The population used for this study consisted of fifty families resident in Brisbane, Australia. The sample was chosen from those families who had registered their subnormal children with the Queensland Subnormal Children's Welfare Association. Two requirements were set down: (a) The children had to be within the age range five to seventeen years, and (b) the children had to be resident at home and not attending any school or kindergarten at the time of the enquiry.

We define subnormal children as those children whose intellectual development is so seriously retarded as to render them incapable of profiting from instruction given in an ordinary school or in a special or opportunity class. In addition, their social development is, in most cases, seriously retarded. However, some of them, as they mature and as training is provided for them, do improve in respect to social competency.

Further, it is advisable, in the light of practice, to divide subnormal children into two groups: (a) those whose intelligence quotients lie between 35 and 55 and whose social development renders them capable of training in an Occupation Centre, and (b) those with intelligence quotients below 35 whose social development makes them unsuitable even to training in an Occupation Centre and who are better placed in an institution for care and protection. The children in our sample were assessed on intelligence test results, on carefully compiled social and personal schedules and on a careful physical examination.

METHOD OF COLLECTING DATA

A careful analysis of all aspects of family life likely to be affected by the subnormal child was made and an Interview Schedule was prepared. The kinds of items covered by the schedule were as follows: first observations of subnormality, behavior difficulties, kind of assistance desired by the family, understanding the child's subnormality; the effect of subnormal children on family plans, home management and routine, school adjustments, housing, leisure time, and adjustment to work.

The interviews were conducted in the houses of the selected families by research workers from the Faculty of Education, who had had extensive social and psychological training. It was thought that the informal atmosphere of the home would put the parents more at ease. As most of the visiting was done during normal working hours the mother was usually the only parent interviewed.

OBJECTIVE DATA OF THE SAMPLE FAMILIES

The range of the children's ages in the sample is given below:

Age	Number of Children
4 yrs.	1
5 yrs.	1
6 yrs.	5
7 yrs.	10
8 yrs.	4
9 yrs.	6
10 yrs.	11
11 yrs.	8
12 yrs.	2

Continued...

Age	Number of Children
13 yrs.	1
14 yrs.	0
15 yrs.	0
16 yrs.	1

The fact that 43 out of the 50 children fall within the age range 6 to 11 years inclusive is in itself indicative, for obviously the parents of these children for whom there was no assistance whatsoever were seeking help when they became members of the voluntary organization which was shortly to open a center for children aged 7 to 14 years.

It may be interesting to note that in the majority of cases surveyed in this investigation the subnormal child was either the youngest or the eldest in the family. The total number of children in the 50 families was 175. Including the 2 only children in the families sampled, there was a possible number of 98 children who could be either youngest or oldest in the family. Of those, 38 (that is, 39 per cent) were subnormal. Of the remaining 77 children in a mid-position only 12 (that is, 16 per cent) were subnormal. The distribution of subnormal children in the family positions is shown below:

Oldest Child	Mid-Position	Youngest Child	Only Child
15	12	21	2

The number of children—both normal and subnormal—in the families visited range from 1 to 13, the average per family being 3.5 children. In only 8 cases, did the number of children in the family exceed 4.

The speech of the subnormal children was rated as follows: normal, below normal (that is, intelligible but with a certain indistinctness of articulation and pronunciation), very much below normal (that is, extremely difficult to follow; intelligible usually only to the parents), and completely un-intelligible or lacking in speech.

Ages	Norm.	Below	Much Below	Unintell.
4–6	0	2	2	3
7–9	1	8	6	5
10–12	2	8	6	5
13–16	1	0	1	0
Totals	4	18	15	13

The occupations of the fathers were rated in accordance with the socio-economic classifications quoted by Parkyn. As can be seen from the following table, the incidence of subnormality in our sample was not restricted to any narrow range of occupations.

Higher professional and administrative work	1
Lower professional, technical and executive work	3
Clerical and highly skilled work	10
Skilled work	8
Semi-skilled repetitive work	15
Unskilled repetitive work	5
Farm and farm manager, orchardist	2
Deceased	2
Unspecified	4

QUALITATIVE DATA

The answers to the questions asked during the interview are treated below in some detail. There was a considerable variation in the exact times when the mothers claimed that they were first aware of the fact that the particular children were subnormal. Most noticed some symptoms of subnormality

in the child before the age of one year. It would appear all had recognized the condition by the age of five years. . . . The distribution of the age levels at which first indications of subnormality were noticed is shown below:

	At Birth	Brith– 1 Yr.	1–3 Yrs.	3–5 Yrs.
No. Cases	13	22	10	5

In the majority of cases the mothers themselves were the first to recognize signs of retardation. In most cases, retarded physical development gave the first indication of the child's subnormal state. This was often revealed by slowness of development, particularly in contrast to siblings: "He wasn't like the other children; he didn't walk till he was two years old." Mental conditions which aroused anxiety included lack of speech, listlessness and slow mental development. There were, however, some cases where the mother's attention was drawn to the child's state by either medical or outside observers. The number of such cases, together with the subnormal condition first noticeable, is as follows:

Observation	Physical	Mental
Mother's	26	12
Medical	11	0
Outsider's	1	0

In the above classification, recognition of mongolism has been included in physical observations since it was the physical aspect of the case that was first noticed. The sample included sixteen mongoloid children.

It was to the doctors and clinics that the mothers turned initially for explanations and diagnoses. Twenty-eight mothers took their children first to the family doctors; of these, nineteen then sought the aid of specialists. Twenty-one went directly to the child specialists. Eight then sought confirmation of the diagnosis at psychiatric or psychological clinics, while two placed their children for training under quacks. In very few cases did the mothers rest content with the first diagnosis of subnormality or backwardness; nor did they reconcile themselves to the verdict that no treatment was possible. *Twenty-four families reported that they had incurred a great deal of expense* (mainly medical), *in trying to find amelioration for the child's condition. . . .*

25 Early Identification of Mildly Retarded Children

Sonya Oppenheimer

The purpose of this paper is to present the preliminary findings of a longitudinal study entitled, "Early Identification of Mild Retardation in the First Three Years of Life." The importance of early detection is obvious when mental retardation has an organic cause which is amenable to treatment. The value of early recognition is not as clear in instances of mental handicap where there is no physical treatment. Treatment in such instances consists mainly of prevention of superimposed emotional difficulties. This can best be done by parents who are well informed, supported and assisted in rearing their handicapped children.

In order to understand better the developmental difficulties of retarded children and the adjustment that parents must make to handle these differences at an early age, a continuous study of children who showed delayed social, motor, and language development in the first three years of life was undertaken. The study had three aims: (1) to determine at what age and by what developmental signs one can detect mild forms of retardation in the absence of specific physical signs; (2) to collect longitudinal information about these children, and (3) to delineate special problems.

The significance of such a study must be considered in terms of both theoretical and clinical aspects. First, there is a problem of validity of early developmental measures. Many practitioners believe that psychological measures before the age of three years have no predictive value. However, there is evidence that children falling below average in early tests show greater consistency than those in the average or above average range. Recently, several articles have substantiated this viewpoint. Further light on this validity question will rest on longitudinal studies. Secondly, one can assume theoretically that the early recognition of mental retardation in the absence of recognizable medical disease is important in bringing possible cause and effect relationships closer together. In addition, however, one is interested in the purposes served for the specific child in question. It is not sufficient to put the child through various physical and psychological tests and give the conventional brief interpretation of the findings.

Prevalence studies of retardation indicate that less than one per cent of the under-five-years-of-age population are reported to fall in the retarded range. There is a large increase in the percentage of retarded in the school-age population with a peak in the 10-to-14 year range. One would suspect that this small percentage is primarily due to the difficulty of identifying the under-five population as retarded, rather than the fact that retardation does not exist under the age of five. A recent screening project in a pediatric setting showed that with the proper tools the under-five retarded can be detected. Early longitudinal studies have shown the relationship between prenatal complications and subsequent defects of the child. This has been especially true of the numerous papers describing the association of neurological sequelae and retardation of premature infants. These studies describe specific medical abnormalities found in these children and list the I.Q. variations. These studies do not describe these children's emotional development, nor do they describe their function in a home environment. Masland, Sarrason and Gladwin in *Mental Subnormality* state that:

> When it is noted that there has not been a single comprehensive longitudinal study of subnormal individuals mentally retarded or mentally defective, it will probably be understood why throughout this report we have discussed the needs for such studies. It is as if there have been two implicit assumptions about the importance of longitudinal studies. a) The subnormal child is relatively unaffected by his environment and the longitudinal study, therefore, would not be too revealing; b) Odd behavior of the subnormal individual is explainable by his intellectual deficit—he is what he is because of his deficit and all other factors are secondary. There is no evidence for either assumption. From the standpoint of any psychological theory, one would assume that the subnormal individual, even the severely defective one, is influenced by and in turn influences the familial and social milieu into which he is born and in which

he develops. In terms of this assumption the study of the early development of the subnormal individual as a scientific problem needs no justification. In the case of a defective child, for example, there is simply no available scientific basis for the guidance of parents in the rearing of the child.

Disagreement also has been expressed regarding both the possibility of early identification of mild retardation in the absence of clearcut medical diseases and also regarding the value of early identification. Illingsworth has stated an affirmative case on both counts. He reported a follow-up study of 125 children diagnosed as retarded before the age of two years. Five years later repeated evaluations substantiated the early diagnosis in the vast majority of cases. Further, Illingsworth stated his opinion that a mother should be informed as soon as possible so that she does not have to face a long period of anxiety and doubt. The negative case has been stated by Kirman who questioned the purpose of early identification. His study was based on children who had been institutionalized at an early age following the diagnosis. If the diagnosis of mental retardation is assumed to carry with it the recommendation of institutionalization, Kirman's objections would have considerable validity in the face of what is known about retarded children whose infancy was spent in an institution versus those who remain at home.

In general, pediatricians hold the opinion that if there is no cure it serves little purpose to disturb the parent with one's suspicions until the child approaches school age. Another point of view is that the parents themselves recognize that the child is in some way different from others and that this recognition itself is upsetting. This awareness may lead to an estrangement in parent-child relationship or it may lead to actual conflict as the parent strives to force the child into behavior that is normal for his chronological age.

It was our hope in this project to demonstrate positive values of early diagnosis when it is coupled with parental guidance.

METHOD

Obtaining and selecting subjects was a major problem in this study. It is difficult to encourage referrals on the basis of questionable retardation in the first three years of life. Letters were sent to physicians and clinics in the community requesting their assistance in referring young children who fit the project description. Criteria for referral and exclusion included: sitting delayed beyond nine months of age; lack of imitative behavior at one year; walking delayed beyond 18 months; marked lack of interest in the usual toys, and delay in the identification of objects by verbal names. Exclusion criteria included mongolism, structural abnormalities such as microcephaly, etc. Participation in the project involved: (1) initial diagnostic evaluation, including the usual history-taking methods, complete physical measurements, bone-age determinations, developmental diagnostic tests and such special tests as

seemed indicated by the findings; (2) periodic developmental examination of the child using the Cattell Infant Psychological Test, or the Stanford-Binet Intelligence Test (the children and parents were seen at least every three months until the age of three and one-half, and then every six months until the age of give years); (3) parent guidance was an integral part of the visits. As was expected, some parents wanted or needed more assistance than could be provided on a three-month basis. Therefore, these parents were referred to a caseworker assigned to the study-project and intensive parent counseling sessions were arranged. The private physican in no way relinquished his role in the medical care of the patient. In 18 months a total of 97 children was referred. Evaluations have been completed on 66 of these cases. A recent screening project for mental retardation in a pediatric clinic by the same project team showed that 6.5 per cent of the under-three population had I.Q.'s in the 50 to 84 range. This group of 21 children is now being incorporated into the current study, bringing the total number to 118.

RESULTS

I.Q. ranges were as follows: below 50 —20, 50 to 84—34, above 84—12. The following information concerns the 34 subjects included in the 50 to 84 I.Q. group: 26 of the children were male, 8 were female; 25 were white, 9 were Negro. Four of the fathers were professional, 4 were in the managerial, semi-professional category, 14 were skilled workers, 9 were unskilled, and 3 of the children came from foster-home placements. In six cases the etiology was definite or had an associated medical disease (one child had P.K.U., two had mild cerebral palsy, one Delange syndrome, one rare chromosomal abnormality, one albino). Fourteen had a suspicious birth or neonatal history which is sometimes associated with retardation. These cases had no obvious physical stigmata. Fourteen of the children were 20 months of age, 20 were above 20 months of age at the time of referral. In this group study the average age of sitting without support was 9.5 months as compared to a previously determined control group of normals which was 6.8 months, and a more severely retarded group which was 13.5 months. (The normal and severely retarded group was determined from statistical analysis of all cases seen at the Mental Development Center over a five-year period.) The average age of those children who were walking was 18.4 months as compared to a normal control group of 16.3 months and 19.8 months for the severely retarded. Fifteen of the study children had some speech which included words other than "mama, dada." The average age of talking for this group was 20 months as compared to a normal control group whose talking age was 18 months and a more severely retarded group whose talking age was 33 months. There did not appear to be an excess of illnesses in this group, and only a few children had histories of hospitalizations. The most common physical defect was strabismus.

The following case history illustrates some of the common problems found in counseling:

Jimmy (18 months of age) was referred to the study by a private pediatrician because of the parents' anxiety about his slow development. Mrs. R stated she first became concerned when at 15 months of age Jimmy would not put anything into his mouth. About this time the parents were also concerned about the child's delay in walking. They blamed part of this on the fact that his eyes were crossed so that he couldn't orient himself. The physician referred them to an eye specialist who recommended the routine treatment for strabismus. Because of the continued concern of the parents the physician then referred them to the study. At the initial interview the mother said she was specifically interested in determining the child's age level and wanted an I.Q. She recognized that his sister (age three) was more advanced at the same age. Both she and her husband were extremely anxious at the first interview.

Both parents had finished the eighth grade of school and were 32 years of age at the birth of Jimmy. Pregnancy, delivery and neonatal period were normal except for hyperbilirubinemia to 18 mgms %. No exchange transfusion was done. During the first months of life the parents noted nothing unusual about the baby except that he was exceptionally quiet and slow to perform motor tasks (sat at nine months). The first problem involved feeding. The mother felt that the child needed the bottle longer than average because of his slowness in development. At 18 months he could hold a glass but persisted in drinking from the bottle. The mother did not try table foods until age 15 months. He made no attempt to feed himself. They were concerned that their continued feeding of Jimmy would result in his becoming too dependent on them. They had become involved in forcing the child's hand to his mouth to teach him to eat. Jimmy had always been a good sleeper. The parents had made several feeble attempts at toilet training but had given up when he showed no response.

At the time Jimmy was initially seen (18 months) the most remarkable part of his performance was extreme passivity. He had very little speech or speech comprehension and appeared to be slow in all areas of development. He achieved an I.Q. of 56 on the Cattell Infant Intelligence Scale and a Mental Age score of 10 months.

During subsequent counseling sessions the mother asked questions about physical causation and about getting further medical studies. Various medical tests were done. No specific medical etiology for the retardation was found. A mild hip dislocation was the only abnormality. This did involve applications of casts and two short hospitalizations. The hip problem increased the mother's anxiety and tended to focus attention on the medical problem rather than the child's overall development.

Subsequently, Jimmy continued to make progress. Suggestions were made concerning feeding, general development of independence, and speech so that he began feeding himself, developed more motor agility, and began using several words. His retardation was discussed in terms of general child management. As he became more active, the mother wondered how much and what type of discipline would be effective since she was afraid to restrain him too much because she might discourage his curiosity. The mother also wondered if they had not overprotected him because he was slow. She questioned if allowing the sibling her rights and not giving in to Jimmy would slow him up. The current focus of counseling is on toilet training, which the mother was reluctant to start because she thought he might not understand, though he had given many signs of awareness.

Currently at age 34 months Jimmy is much more curious and responsive. He babbles and repeats words. He has made a great deal of progress in self-help and is currently trying to dress himself. On the Cattell Infant Scale he functions in the 60s with a Mental Age between 20–22 months.

There has been an evident change in the mother's attitude. She is no longer fearful and distraught, but is accepting Jimmy's progress and yet understanding the problems of his slow development.

DISCUSSION

As was suspected, some of the children will not be permanently retarded. Some of the children may be showing retarded development because of emotional problems, maternal neglect, and environmental deprivation or parents who are unintentionally infantilizing their children and holding them back. In these instances we hope by intervention to "cure" the retardation. In other cases the developmental slowness may be of no permanent significance or limited to a single aspect of functioning. In still other cases the developmental retardation will presage permanent retardation and here the goal is the avoidance of secondary complications. The period of follow-up is still too short to permit any statement as to the permanence or degree of handicap in these early diagnosed cases of mild retardation.

The results to date would indicate that it is possible to locate mildly retarded children under the age of three years of age, even in the absence of definite medical disease. This can only be done with energetic detection programs which alert the pediatrician to these problems in his private practice and in outpatient pediatric clinics.

The initial phase of this project has served primarily to locate and identify a group of mildly retarded youngsters. We have been able to delineate some of the numerous characteristics that make up this heterogeneous group and to delineate some of the specific behavioral problems that arise in such children. The next immediate problem is what to do after the early detection.

The following patterns of parent guidance are emerging:

1. Diagnostically oriented guidance for parents of children under two years of age who recognize that something is wrong. These parents are usually adequate to the task of rearing a normal child but are confused and bewildered when faced with a child who is conspicuously slower. At this early point the parents need support, reassurance that they are doing all that can be done for the child and that the child will continue to grow and develop albeit at a slow rate. They are concerned about the diagnosis and need someone to whom they can show their realistic anxiety, but they also need someone to relieve their mind of unrealistic worries. The specific questions which they raise have to do with feeding, encouraging motor development, and stimulating interest in the environment. It is important that they work with the child at an appropriate level to avoid frustration both for themselves and for the child. This kind of counseling with the parents of this description in children of this age is perhaps most easily done by the pediatrician.

2. Family-oriented guidance for parents who are not aware of the child's developmental problems because of their own inadequacy (preoccupation, depression, or whatever). These parents usually come from clinic populations and do not seek help on their own accord. In these instances the child's retardation may stem in part from insufficiency of the environment and one may have some hope for primary prevention. This kind of guid-

ance requires the worker to take the initiative lacking in the parent and represents a form of "reaching-out" family casework.

3. Child-oriented guidance for parents of retarded children in the preschool range between two and four years. These children are in the beginning stages of language development, but usually are not ready to profit from group experiences and nursery schools. The questions raised by the parents are concerned with what to expect, how to discipline, questions around toilet training and self-help and the stimulation of speech. Hopefully, the experience with the child and his parents in the first two years provides a relationship with the parents and a basis for understanding the child. At this point, secondary prevention is the aim. That is, the prevention of emotional problems to which these children are particularly vulnerable and reducing the degree of social and intellectual handicaps. One hopes to help the mother empathize with the child and to communicate with him in helping him achieve independence and mastery. The professional person in-

volved may come from any one of a number of professions: pediatrics, psychology, education, social work—whoever has a relationship with the parents on the special understanding of emotional problems of children with this degree of intellectual limitation.

In summary then, this study has accomplished the following: (1) identified a group of mildly retarded youngsters in the absence of specific physical signs; (2) collected longitudinal information about these children, and (3) delineated three specific types of counseling which may aid in the special problems in rearing the slow child.

REFERENCES

Illingsworth, R. 1960. *The Development of the Infant and Young Child, Normal and Abnormal.* Baltimore: Williams and Wilkins.

Kirman, B. H. 1953. The backward baby. *J. of Mental Science.* 99.

Masland, Sarrason and Gladwin. 1955. *Mental Subnormality.* New York: Basic Books.

[Seven references not reprinted.]

26 Parents' Estimates of the Intelligence of Retarded Children

*Jerome L. Schulman
and Sheila Stern*

Many professional persons who deal with retarded children are reluctant to inform the parents as to their child's degree of retardation. This reluctance is partly due to a lack of confidence in the various tests employed to ascertain the degree of retardation. We believe, however, that the main obstacle to a frank discussion is the doctor's fear of the parents' reaction to such news.

In our experience with the parents of retarded children it has been our impression that the parents themselves, when they first seek help, are already aware of the retardation and are frequently capable of making accurate estimations of their child's developmental level. In broaching the subject with parents, we have found it helpful to secure their estimate of the child's mental abilities. This study was undertaken to obtain a statistical evaluation of the accuracy of parents' estimates as compared with psychometric evaluations.

MATERIALS AND METHODS

The parents of 50 retarded children referred to the Children's Psychiatric Service of the Harriet Lane Home [Johns Hopkins Hospital, Baltimore] were asked to give their estimate of the developmental age of their children prior to the actual testing. In 7 cases estimates were obtained from both parents, in 36 cases from the mother alone, in 4 cases from the father alone, and in 1 case each from an aunt, a grandmother, and a sister. Of the 50 cases, 36 were dispensary, 11 were semi-private, and 3 were private patients. These people could best be described as a rather unsophisticated group. Most of the patients were referred from the general pediatric clinic primarily for psychometric evaluations rather than for complete psychiatric evaluations.

The ages of these patients ranged from 3 years and 3 months to 12 years and 10 months. The average age was 5 years and 8 months. There were 24 males and 26 females. Each of the children received a psychometric examination to determine his level of intelligence. In 35 cases the test administered was the Revised Stanford-Binet Intelligence Scale—Form L. In 12 cases the Gesell Developmental Schedule was administered and in 2 cases both the Revised Stanford-Binet Intelligence Scale—Form L and the Gesell Developmental Schedules were given. In 1 case the Vineland Social Maturity Scale was used.

The parents' estimate of the child's mental age was converted into an "I.Q." score by dividing the estimated mental age by the chronological age and multiplying by 100. In this way a basis for comparison with the test-determined I.Q. was obtained.

Estimates were obtained from parents in various ways depending upon the specific situation. The following questions are representative examples of the type of approach employed. "Your child is . . . years old. At what age would you estimate he is functioning?" "You have had a good deal of opportunity to observe and to compare your child with other children. With what age child do you think he compares?" Frequently the parents would respond by saying that it is difficult to give an estimate because their child performs better in some areas than others. In these cases the parents were asked to make an estimate which would be an average of all the child's abilities.

RESULTS

The average test I.Q. obtained was 55.5 with a range of 17 to 82 and a standard deviation of 16.6. The average "I.Q." estimated by parents was 57.2 with a range of 17 to 100 and a standard deviation of 17.4. In 23 cases the parents overestimated their child's mental abilities by an average of 12.6 I.Q. points whereas in 19 cases the parents underestimated by an average of 10.7 I.Q. points. In 8 cases the parents' estimate corresponded exactly with the test result. In the entire 50 cases there were only 4 instances where the parents' estimate exceeded the test I.Q. by more than 20 points and 7 instances where the parents' estimate exceeded the test I.Q. by more than 15 points. In only 1 case did the

parents estimate that their child's mental abilities were normal.

The correlation coefficient between the test I.Q. and the "parent I.Q." was found to be +0.67. The product-moment correlation was positive with a significance. Although it is recognized that the tests employed are not completely comparable with each other, each represented the best effort to secure an objective evaluation of the correct level of functioning.

DISCUSSION

These findings demonstrate a degree of correlation between a child's test performance and his parents' estimate. There was only one parent who felt that her child was functioning in the normal range. Children's abilities were underestimated almost as frequently as they were overestimated.

Since the majority of these patients were referred from the pediatric clinic for psychometric evaluations rather than for full psychiatric consultations, these results are undoubtedly more accurate than would be obtained in a group of retarded children with coexisting psychiatric problems. The relative lack of sophistication in the parents would also tend to influence the results in the same direction.

The method of approaching parents to obtain the estimate is of great importance. One must convey the impression that the estimate offered by the parents will be accepted as a thoughtful judgment.

These results clearly indicate that there is no basis for the widely held belief that the parents are unaware of their child's retardation prior to seeking professional help. However, the awareness they have is sensed rather than clearly understood and, with improper management, can easily be converted into confusion, guilt, and anxiety.

We often employ the parents' estimate of intelligence as a springboard for a discussion of the whole problem. This is done by complimenting their ability to observe the child accurately and to realize his limitations. The rapport that is obtained in this manner aids immeasurably in preparing the parents for the subsequent discussion concerning the implications of these findings for the child's future. . . .

27 Recoil from the Diagnosis of Mental Retardation

*Barbara Keogh
and Camille Legeay*

"We know she is slow, but she is not mentally retarded. She just needs time and love." "You wait. He will grow up to be a great baseball player." "So he is retarded. You leave us alone and we will work out our problems." Such statements are often heard in clinics when parents are told their children are mentally retarded.

It is difficult to conceive of a more anxiety-arousing situation than that surrounding a parent who is being told formally and officially that his child is retarded. Thus, we can almost expect that parents will react with anger, denial, fear, or defeat. Some parents become hostile toward those who make or present such a diagnosis and its interpretation; some become hostile toward each other, or toward the child. At times, they find it impossible to accept the diagnosis or the retarded child. People differ in the ways in which they deal with their own anxieties. Coping techniques may be adaptive or maladaptive, healthy or unhealthy, positive or negative. Sometimes, excessive stress causes real disturbance in behavior.

At the Mental Retardation Community Service Center of Childrens Hospital, Los Angeles, California, the multidisciplinary approach to the diagnostic evaluation of atypical children involves a pediatrician, a public health nurse, a psychologist, a social worker, and a speech and hearing consultant.

All have contact with the patient and his family and are present in the staffing conference when the diagnosis and recommendations are discussed with parents.

Although we try to make parents feel comfortable and accepted, this conference is obviously a stressful situation. Parents come with great apprehension to hear the diagnosis. They often come from some distance and are "dressed up" both physically and emotionally. The indications of overt anxiety in the clinic may be well controlled by the parents and the staff. Consequently, we may not know what parents' real feelings are. Feelings are masked by parents' awareness of the social demands of the setting and by their feelings toward doctors, mental retardation, the child, and themselves.

We may see the more subtle signs of anxiety, however. For example, the parents may misinterpret the professional staff's interest in the clinical indications of retardation as overconcern or preoccupation with the negative. Parents may over-react to casual questions or comments. They may misunderstand and read in significance where none was intended.

Recently, one of us hesitated before picking up a baby and asked the mother if the baby spit up. The mother immediately became more upset and wanted to know why; what did it mean if the baby spit up? When told

167

by the psychologist, a mother of four, that she did not want sour milk on her dress, the mother visibly relaxed and could talk about the baby's eating habits. The questions and emphasis on certain conditions or symptoms may cause a parent with a high anxiety level to see only negative or pathologic indications, or to resent the clinician's seeming lack of recognition of or interest in the child as a person.

It is interesting to note that parents often have few questions after the diagnosis is given and discussed. Unfortunately, this does not necessarily indicate that we have done a good job of interpretation. Rather, it may indicate an extremely high tension level. Recently, after a long and detailed diagnostic interpretation by a competent professional, a mother called the public health nurse the next morning and asked for information and help. She said, "I didn't hear a thing yesterday when we were in the room with everyone. I thought my husband was listening, but he couldn't remember what was said either." Another parent said to the group recently, "I know I will have questions as soon as I get home, but I just can't seem to think now."

Response to the diagnosis sometimes seems to vary with the kind of retardation. That is, parents may react differently to a retarded child with obvious physical anomalies than to one who appears normal. Perhaps it is easier to acknowledge mental retardation in a child who physically looks retarded. Is there more anxiety about retardation that is inherited or that occurs by chance? What about the confusion and guilt of parents who feel responsible for the retardation because of something they did or failed

to do? For example, what of the mother who failed to get adequate prenatal care or who took some questionable medication during pregnancy? What of parents who feel responsible for brain damage resulting from an accident, or complications from measles when vaccine was available but not used? Does a parent have more anxiety about a child whose diagnosis and probable developmental potential are identifiable soon after birth, or one whose development may depend on his responsibility or action? The anxieties parents exhibit in the clinic clearly are bound up in the larger aspects of parent-child interactions, and with the parents' abilities to cope with these tensions.

For illustrative purposes, we should like to describe initial parental reactions to the diagnosis of mental retardation in the clinic, comparing parents of two children with phenylketonuria and parents of two children with Down's syndrome.

REACTIONS TO PKU

A child with phenylketonuria is unable to use certain protein elements in food. This inherited condition is one of a number of similar abnormalities that may lead to mental retardation, unless a modified diet is started during the first few weeks after the child is born. PKU can be discovered by routine blood or urine tests in the first few days or weeks of life. Parents usually have no forewarning that this defect is present, but it places specific and continuing demands on them. The following case reports show parental reactions.

Family One

The patient was a first child, a two-month-old girl, referred by a private physician, who suspected PKU after routine testing in his office. The mother, aged 20, was a high-school graduate. The father, aged 21, had had two years of college and was a part-time student. Both parents evidenced signs of distress during the conference.

They gave some indication of simple denial, in that they found it difficult to understand the diagnosis in view of the obvious signs of alertness and health in their baby. They were inquisitive, however, and interested in learning about the disease process, the hereditary factors, and treatment. They asked for material that they could read and talk over with other members of their family.

The father expressed considerable anxiety and conflict about his own educational aspiration as well as the condition of his daughter. Prior to and during the infant's hospitalization for evaluation and the beginning of treatment, the mother's questions were reality oriented and her requests were reasonable and appropriate.

When the baby was discharged, the parents were given specific directions regarding the infant's special needs and her medical diagnosis. The mother telephoned clinic personnel regularly regarding her child's progress. After the initial shock reaction, these parents mobilized their resources into appropriate, adaptive reactions.

Family Two

The mother, aged 26, was a high-school graduate and a housewife. This was her first marriage and her first child. The father, aged 47, was a high-school graduate. This was his fourth marriage and sixth child.

The infant son was referred at two weeks of age by their private physician. Staff had discussed the diagnosis, hereditary components, and diet with the parents during the infant's hospitalization. They were seen together on the day of discharge in the team setting. The mother held the baby during the staffing and paid almost constant attention to him. Her reactions were confusion, blocking, and dependency on her husband. The father assumed control, minimized any problems or potential problems, and exuded confidence. They asked no questions at that time.

Later, the mother telephoned many times with questions. Some were related to the normal behavior and care of a newborn. She seemed to need much support, as she had many feelings of inadequacy regarding her mothering abilities, particularly in view of her husband's criticisms of her. He was rigid in his treatment of the infant. He let him cry and did not want him picked up. There was also some indication that he attempted to force feedings. The mother said that her husband's "ego" was suffering as he could not accept having an imperfect child.

The reactions of these parents were not necessarily adaptive nor appropriate. The mother said she would never have another baby and projected her anxieties to the future. She wondered and worried about the problems of social adjustment her son might have as an adolescent because of the PKU. In contrast to Family One, these parents denied the diagnosis to relatives and friends and used subterfuge to prevent them from learning about it.

In both cases, the parents have acknowledged the diagnosis and are observing the diet restrictions. Neither pair had heard of phenylketonuria so past experiences with retardation from this disease could not influence their reactions to the diagnosis. Both sets of parents evidenced strong anxiety initially, but the first responded adaptively, more appropriately, and more realistically. The second set has shown indications of continued denial, projections of anxiety in unrealistic ways, and hostility, both direct and displaced.

DOWN'S SYNDROME

The two children referred for confirmation of the diagnosis of Down's syndrome present somewhat different pictures. Down's syndrome, sometimes called mongolism or, perhaps more correctly, trisomy 21, results from a chromosomal abnormality consisting of an extra particle of autosomal chromosome. Certain physical characteristics are associated with this condition. These appear in infants. The condition usually can be diagnosed at birth. There is no known way to correct the abnormality nor to prevent the mental retardation, which generally becomes apparent as the child develops. Parents, however, can do a great deal to help their child develop to his fullest potential.

Family One

The 39-year-old mother was a high-school graduate and a housewife. The father, aged 45, was a high-school graduate and a welder. They had two normal, older children. The patient was a three-and-a-half-year-old girl referred for differential diagnosis and planning around possible Down's syndrome.

The parents expressed some anger toward the referring physician, who, they said, called their child "mongoloid." They reported that they had gone to him for a medical diagnosis of the child's heart condition and were shocked with the additional diagnosis. This was compounded by the doctor's alleged statement that "The taxpayers do not want to waste their money on repair of a heart condition for a retarded child."

A routine check with the health department revealed that a diagnosis of Down's syndrome had been made by a physician there in the first few months of the baby's life. The parents had denied the diagnosis and never returned to the agency. Despite their maladaptive responses, the parents provided optimum physical and emotional care for their daughter.

By the time of the conference at the center, the parents had reached the point of acknowledging that the child was retarded in her growth and development and that she had some of the symptoms of Down's syndrome. They still were not interested in joining a parents' group, nor were they particularly interested in learning more about the condition. They thought they did not need further help at the time but wished to continue their contact with the clinic.

Family Two

The mother, aged 29, a high-school graduate, was a housewife. The father,

30, had a degree in engineering. They had three normal, older children. The four-day-old son was referred by a community agency the parents had called for help. When they called the agency, they had not seen their new baby, as their physicians had recommended immediate placement from the hospital. Although they initially accepted the diagnosis, they questioned it after they took their son home and looked at him closely.

When they came to our clinic, the parents evidenced mixed reactions. They showed considerable direct hostility toward the physicians who made the diagnosis. They denied the meaning of some of the signs. We saw considerable projection of anxiety into future considerations, and, for the father, controlled intellectualization of his feelings. The mother interpreted the obstetrician's recommendation of institutionalization as a reflection on her mothering abilities and expressed anger toward him.

Both parents, however, showed interest in learning more about the condition, its signs and symptoms. They asked for literature on the associated characteristics of hands and feet and studies that might help them project the intellectual achievement of their son. They delayed considering future plans and joined the study group at Childrens Hospital. They expressed their intent to carry out any recommended treatment.

COUNSELING NEEDS

What implications can we draw from these cases? With all the parents, we observed immediate and often intense anxiety reactions during the team conference. Other reactions were, for the most part, successful in that they effectively reduced or at least controlled parental anxiety. They were not always adaptive nor positive in a larger sense, as the reactions frequently consisted of denial, hostility, confusion, and blocking. In some cases, parents replaced these reactions with more adaptive, realistic, and appropriate ways of coping with their tension.

For the parents of the children with PKU, an intellectual acceptance of the reality of the diagnosis was implied by their cooperation with the initial hospitalization, tests, dietary management, and the repeated inconveniences in ongoing care. We can give such parents some assurance that their children will develop normally if they can maintain the prescribed diet. Such parents can be given something specific related to the diagnosis of the disease. This in itself may help them direct the energy generated by the stress of the diagnosis toward realistic measures that offer hope.

For a child with Down's syndrome, there is little so specific that a parent can do. We see them tending to focus on the Down's signs, on the physical indications of the condition, with specific concerns about retardation. These parents often come to the clinic with already well-developed negative attitudes and fear about the diagnosis. They tend to think of "mongolian idiot" and project into the future a fatalistic outlook of no hope for their child.

From our experience in the clinic conferences, we believe that parents require two particular kinds of counseling. The first has to do with immediate follow-up, which allows the parents to pull themselves together and talk about what they have just heard. This implies emotional support and reassurance from the staff, and an acceptance of the parents' initial anxiety reactions even when they are negative. The second counseling need is concerned with long-term help that is ongoing and related to the child and his family. This involves continued emotional support of the family. It also suggests the need for practical help with day-to-day management problems and with progressive family stresses related to the retarded child.

REFERENCES

[Two references not reprinted.]

28 Parents of the Mentally Retarded: An Operational Approach to Diagnosis and Management

Frank J. Menolascino

It has become clear to workers in the area of mental retardation that the proper management of parents of the mentally retarded is the cornerstone for the facilitation of optimal developmental progression for these children. I shall review our experiences in a diagnostic and evaluation clinic which suggest a need for an operational reconceptualization of the issues in counseling parents of the retarded. The three most common differential patterns of family interactions that we have observed will be reviewed, and an operational approach (Wolfensberger, 1967) which focuses on specific treatment implications is presented and discussed.

EVOLUTION OF A CRISIS ORIENTATION TO PARENTS OF THE RETARDED

In reviewing the early literature on parents of the retarded, Wolfensberger (1967) has noted: "In the mid-1940's through the early 1950's a trickle of armchair papers began to discuss the relevant parent dynamics, to be followed by almost a flood of such papers in the more recent past. It is also curious to note that the parents discussed in the literature are rarely representative of parents of the retarded in general. Instead, they often tend to be: 1) mothers of middle and upper class status; 2) white; 3) consumers of outpatient diagnostic clinic services; and 4) parents of young and low functioning retardates. Nevertheless, generalizations are only too readily drawn about parents of the retarded. Failure to include fathers in research, overreliance on maternal information and an assumption that such maternal information, particularly regarding the father, is valid are very common" (p. 314). . . .

The early theoretical conceptualizations (and resultant treatment approaches) strongly focused on guilt. The guilt motif was employed as the universal construct in viewing parents of the blind, cerebral palsied, and mentally retarded. These parents were commonly viewed as in conflict, and guilt, projection, and reaction formation mechanisms were emphasized. Since the prototypic parental response, "I love him more now that I know he is retarded," can be viewed positively as well as negatively, these constructs literally lead nowhere in regard to their clinical utility value. The psychoanalytic contribution of viewing the parental response to a mentally retarded child as object loss with attendant grief and mourning was extended to encompass the concept of the "grief work" in this area. . . . A further refinement was the focus on

173

the realistic demands and burdens which such parents experience, and the disputing of the previous unitary neurotic interpretation approach. . . Some empirical approaches have focused on stages of parental acceptance . . . [Other] descriptive studies emphasize what parents of the retarded experience with reference to the previously noted universal constructs (e.g., guilt, object loss, etc.). There is also an increasing number of studies that explore parental knowledge about and attitudes to mental retardation and how these may directly relate to family role identification problems.

I have briefly reviewed, in historical order, some of the key theoretical constructs specifically applied to parents of the mentally retarded: (a) guilt has been the classic *standby* and the universal explanatory construct; (b) child-object loss as equated with sorrow and grief, recently refined with emphasis on the realistic family demands and burdens which the retarded child so often presents; and (c) recent descriptive studies which have discussed some types of parental crisis in relation to their mentally retarded child. None of the above formulations is unique, but they are the key representatives of past trends in the literature.

AN OPERATIONAL DIAGNOSTIC MANAGEMENT APPROACH TO PARENTS OF THE RETARDED

Wolfensberger (1967) has recently formulated a novel theory of parental reaction patterns to mental retardation which embodies some of the former conceptualizations in this area. In this overview I would like to describe this operational refinement and underscore its major meritorious feature: a direct relationship between types of family responses and specific treatment needs. I shall review the three most common differential patterns which we have observed of family reaction and interaction to their knowledge and awareness of mental retardation in their child. Some parents experience all of these, others one or none. The crises may occur simultaneously, but to some degree they will tend to correlate with the age of the child. It is also conceivable that some of the crises can be of rather long-term nature. These three patterns are: (1) The Novelty Shock Crisis; (2) The Crisis of Personal Values; and (3) The Reality Crisis.

Our clinic has had extensive experience in assessing parents of the mentally retarded. The type of parental crises reported herein is based on our experiences with a sample of 946 parental pairs seen from 1958 to mid-1966. The clinic setting, multidisciplinary approach, and population served have previously been reviewed (Menolascino, 1965).

The Novelty Shock Crisis

This crisis is noted when the diagnosis of mental retardation is presented to unsuspecting parents: it frequently occurs shortly after birth in such instances as mongolism. Even a normal birth tends to be an occasion for stress, emotionality, and regression. The parents are usually very expectant and looking forward to the birth of a normal child. They have many notions concerning the future occupation, marital status, and other attributes of their unborn child. Accordingly, the birth of any baby which markedly upsets these expectancies may precipitate a *novelty shock crisis*. Such an unexpected event can disorganize the parents' adjustment, since it occurs at a point of great parental vulnerability.

In such a crisis situation it often happens that the parents, having little knowledge of the nature of their baby's disorder, may relinquish the baby shortly after birth. Thus the novelty shock crisis may be precipitated when they are told that their baby is a "mongoloid idiot." Though these parents may realize that their previous expectancies have to be radically revised, they commonly know little or nothing concerning realistic expectancies for their new baby. Other examples of this particular crisis are noted in clinical conditions such as Apert-Park-Powers and Sturge-Weber-Dimitri syndromes. The parents in these two instances are faced with the unknowns of "What is wrong—and how bad is it?" in conjunction with the associated problem of their previous expectations of normality. *The crucial element here is not mental retardation at all: it is the demolition of expectancies.*

The above-noted features of this particular pattern of family response to mental retardation suggest the need for the following treatment consideration: (1) immediate supportive counseling measures; (2) information initially aimed at explanations that help erase the unknown aura from the child's condition; (3) outline of expectations for immediate developmental course; (4) underscoring the usual lack of urgency as to long-range fears or plans; and (5) preparing the parents for a mutual adventure in "life planning" . . . for their child.

The Crisis of Personal Values

The parental reaction pattern subsequent to chronic sorrow (stemming from the destruction of their overdetermined expectation of the child) represents the second differential pattern of family interaction in parents of mentally retarded children. Mental retardation and its manifestations are unacceptable to many people, even though the reaction is to an expectancy "set" in their own minds rather than to objective reality. It may be totally unacceptable to some parents that though a son may not have the potential to become a successful merchant or professional man, he may ultimately become self-supporting at unskilled or semiskilled work. Expected censure from the extended family, overconcern about social ostracism, and feelings of guilt or failure may contribute to the personal anguish of those parents who experience crises of personal values.

This personal value crisis may lead to various degrees of parental emotional rejection of the retardate. In mild instances this may be manifested by ambivalence and overprotection. In its severest form, it usually leads to early institutional placement and complete denial of the retardate's existence. Unlike the other two crises, the personal value crisis is more likely to last a lifetime and may coincide with any of the others.

Relevant to this crisis are the studies that indicate that a retarded child may have a deep unconscious meaning to a parent (which may only come to awareness in depth psychotherapy). . . . This meaning may satisfy pre-existing neurotic needs of a parent, or the child is viewed as a symbol of past transgressions, of religious retribution, etc. . . . Further, the parent may symbolically re-enact with the retarded child the relationship with his or her own parents . . . or the parents may view the child as a sign of underlying failure of their marriage. . . .

Clinical examples of this value crisis were most commonly noted, in our experience, in the upwardly mobile families who also have strong achievement orientations. Here we noted clear references to the loss of an object, and the associated concept of "grief work" was most appropriate. Also frequently noted were instances of lifelong sadness, anguish, and sorrow, with structured parental psychopathology in the realm of the depressive reactions. In this group were parents who attempted to alleviate their quandary by tutoring the child excessively (with associated denial of the physically obvious), or who had "rescue fantasies," wishing and seeking for magical cures. Some of the books published by parents of retarded children eloquently point out the crises of personal values which they have experienced.

In considering the treatment needs of these parents, we have found that if neurotic or characterological features are in the foreground (usually noted in instances where one or both parents had had personality difficulties prior to the birth of their retarded child),

then formal psychotherapeutic intervention is needed. Another group frequently requiring specific treatment intervention consists of those who have strong existential quandaries concerning their child's problems. These individuals usually seem quite normal except for this particular existential dimension. Treatment approaches must therefore aim at clarification of their values and how these relate to their child. Thus, one goal of treatment here is the exploration of the possibility that the child possesses certain attributes (e.g., appearance, behavioral passivity, etc.) which these parents can appreciate within their value systems.

The Reality Crisis

This particular pattern of family interaction has been most frequently encountered in our own clinical experience. It appears that the nature, frequency, and treatment requirements of this pattern have only recently received specific appreciation. By this term I am referring to those situations in which forces external to and only partially controllable by the parents result in crises which make it impossible, exceedingly difficult, or inadvisable for the retardate to remain integrated into the family or the community. A mother with a very hyperactive child, in a family with several young children, may not be able to meet these physical demands, and unless effective community help is forthcoming, the situational demands may overwhelm her. Sexual behavior on the part of a young adult retardate may be judged either dangerous to others or unacceptable to the community. While such a situation may represent more of a value crisis for the community, the social pressures may constitute a reality crisis for the family. Death of a parent is a very straightforward reality crisis, especially for a surviving father. The reality crisis rarely occurs at birth unless the baby requires unusual amounts or types of medical care (e.g., spina bifida).

The reality crisis occurs frequently and tends to correlate with the severity and multiplicity of the child's handicaps and resources in the family (e.g., size, emotional climate, socio-economic, geographic proximity to available service, etc.). Unlike the parents demonstrating the previously noted two patterns of family interaction, this group of parents have all too well accepted the fact of their child's chronic handicaps, from initial interpretation to intellectual and emotional acceptance. Where then is the problem? In brief, the two major factors appear to be: (1) a relative lack of professional awareness of the reality-based nature of their requests; and (2) the paucity of available services for mentally retarded individuals in our country. Since both of these issues relate to the problems of treatment in this particular pattern of family interaction, I shall elaborate on them.

It seems to me that a major professional blindspot in this area is the one-sided and at times distorted view of parents of the mentally retarded. As previously indicated, there are unique aspects and problems in counseling parents of the retarded. In sharp contrast to the emotionally disturbed child (who has been viewed by most theorists as the end product of a dis-turbed family interactional system), the mentally retarded child is introduced *into* the family unit and can become disturbing *to* it. This essential difference is unfortunately often overlooked by professionals who view the parents with reality crises (e.g., seeking medical or special educational guidelines) as being in need of psychotherapy, focus on an exploration of their feelings and defenses, and search for their "real" reason for seeking help. Other problems are: (a) counter-transference reactions in the counselor who may view mental retardation as "a neurologically hopeless" condition and sternly tell parents to stop "shopping" and institutionalize their child, or emit professional jargon that mystifies rather than clarifies (at times with the unspoken wish that the parents will "just go away"...); (b) the traditional action orientation of the physician may be frustrated by the relative lack of "direct action" medical services that are available for the retarded, and he may displace this frustration into seemingly endless consultations at the expense of formulating long-range plans of action; and (c) many individuals who handle parents of the retarded, even if free of detrimental attitudes and backgrounds, have had little training or experience in mental retardation or even in normal child development. They may feel inadequate in managing practical problems and therefore often restrict counseling to stereotyped discussions of parental feelings.

The *second* major need of parents in the reality crisis is the quick availability of a continuum of services for their child. Though I have previously noted that such services are not abundant at the present time, one must at least know *what* the child needs before a search can be made for it. According to the age and severity of the child's problems, the necessary services may encompass homemaker services, public health nurse visits (e.g., special instructions in toilet training the retarded child), nursery school placement (at times for mother's relief), gadgetry (e.g., special chairs and standing tables), etc.

Thus, professional understanding and support, in conjunction with the judicious use of available services, can effectively quell these reality crises. The suggested realignment of approaches to this particular family interactional pattern can possibly alter the current frequency of seemingly unnecessary institutionalization of retarded children at the time of this crisis. It is also necessary to stress to these families that similar reality problems will arise as subsequent life stages present different demands upon them, and thus intermittent and ongoing contact with professionals will be necessary (and welcomed!). . . .

DISCUSSION

I have reviewed some of the older theoretical and treatment approaches to parents of the mentally retarded in an effort to illustrate some of the present practices. Early theoretical concepts embraced guilt as the common dynamic in these parents; an increasing level of theoretical and clinical sophistication has expanded the construct of guilt into mourning, and then into grief with its accompanying reality referents. These theoretical transformations have occurred in the last ten years and have ushered in a veritable revolution in both the nature and extent of treatment and management modes.

From a strictly psychiatric emphasis on all parents of the retarded as "atypical" patients, the therapeutic pendulum has swung far enough over to encompass differential patterns of family interaction and their specific treatment and management needs. For example, it has become apparent that there is a need for reviewing the current concepts of denial, rejection, value system, and identity problem in parents of the mentally retarded. Denial may not be pathological, since we must also stress its integrative and adaptive features; every parent should not be expected to accept fully the chronic handicap of mental retardation in his child, as this might destroy parental adjustment. In this regard, Begab (1964) noted, "The pervasive or life-long character of certain forms of retardation is an unending burden to many parents which few can carry unaided." Hope may be necessary for certain parents who are overcome by adversity, and this hope may sometimes only be tenable if the retardation is denied. . . . Thus parental regression (via denial of the obvious) may actually help the parents adjust to a very terrible reality. One form of parental denial of retardation consists of "rescue fantasies" usually of a magical nature with a persistent search for sudden "cures" . . . if parents believe in such magical "cures," it is probable that these fantasies are essential to their ability to continue functioning as an intact family, and family counseling may break down if these beliefs are dispelled too abruptly (before parental acceptance of more realistic forms of expectancies and hope). Thus, premature professional emphasis on reality determinants can negate successful family management attempts. . . . just by coming to a clinic at all, parents indicate that they are perplexed and want clarification. Accordingly, the initial rejection of a diagnosis of mental retardation may represent not solely denial of the interpretation findings, but rather indicate a slow acceptance of the reality.

The crisis orientation to parents of the mentally retarded proposed by Wolfensberger (1967) strongly indicates the need for a re-evaluation of the recurrent professional themes that focus unduly on parental denial and rejection of the child's problems. These professional themes tend to equate parental awareness of the child's problems with almost automatic acceptance of them. Olshansky (1962) and Roos (1963) question whether this conceptual judgment is correct. For example, Olshansky (1962) commented: "The helping professions have somewhat belabored the tendency of the parent to deny the reality of this child's mental deficiency. Few workers have reported what is probably a more frequent occurrence: the parent's tendency to deny his chronic sorrow. This tendency often is reinforced by the professional helper's habit of viewing chronic sorrow as a neurotic manifestation rather than as a natural and understandable response to a tragic

fact" (p. 193). Similarly Roos (1963) noted: "The drama of experiencing retardation in one's child may precipitate serious existential conflicts. Concern with religion, the meaning of life, the tragedy of death, the inescapability of aloneness and the relative insignificance and helplessness of man may preoccupy the parents. Although these concerns are less obvious than other reactions, their significance should not be underestimated." In this regard, Wolfensberger, Olshansky, and Roos all point out the need for re-evaluating the traditional psychiatric clinic view toward parents of the mentally retarded.

In this paper I have presented an operational approach to parents of the mentally retarded which attempts to encompass three of the most frequently noted patterns of family crisis and their specific treatment-management considerations. It attempts to be both explanatory as to the dynamics the clinician may encounter in each crisis, and prognostic in its overriding concern of relating family diagnosis to specific treatment needs.

It is worthwhile to reconsider the rationale of the basic parameters in the counseling of parents of the retarded because one must remember that it benefits the parent, the retarded member of the family, the family as a unit, and society as a whole. The parent benefits by achieving a higher level of understanding and acceptance of the problem, by recognizing and overcoming his conflicts, and by subsequently leading a better adjusted life. The retardee benefits by experiencing better parental acceptance and management. The family benefits because the better adjustment of the retardee and the parents is expressed in more harmonious interaction between all family members. Society benefits because the likelihood of family dissolution, emotional problems, and institutionalization is diminished. Thus, it is imperative that we review any clinical considerations which may help increase both the direct and indirect positive effects of parent counseling.

I would stress that professional workers must continue to attempt to reconceptualize this and similar problems in such a manner that testable hypotheses can be properly evaluated and shared with colleagues in the field of mental retardation . . . Such considerations are pertinent in regard to "old" and current theories and treatment approaches. For example, our own previously reviewed schemata may indeed soon be remiss in their scant attention and relevance to the apparent shift in the availability and usage of mental retardation services (diagnostic, counseling, and otherwise) from the upper and middle socioeconomic classes to the lower socioeconomic classes. In the lower socioeconomic class, in contrast to the other two socioeconomic classes, the retardate is often not viewed as a deviant. He has been termed the "invisible retardate," and undoubtedly encompasses a different spectrum of social and family forces of expectancy.

Our operational approach to these frequently occurring patterns of family responses and specific crisis situations also suggests possible modifications in the presently available spectrum of services. The psychiatrist who is attempting to help parents with a crisis of personal values can profit greatly from a close collaborative relationship with their minister. Similarly, perhaps treatment programming for parents with reality crises can be more efficiently managed by (a) the N.A.R.C. [National Association for Retarded Children] information service centers; (b) the outpatient staff of a local institution for the retarded; or (c) the newly evolving university-affiliated mental retardation centers. Such reconsiderations truly embrace the challenge of the President's Panel (1962) for both changing and enlarging the scope of available services for the mentally retarded.

Such considerations strongly suggest that continuing attention to delineating the differential patterns of family crises in the mentally retarded would be most fruitful to the retardee, his family, and the professional workers who seek to help. . . .

REFERENCES

Begab, M. J. 1964. *Canada's Ment. Health* 12 (3): 2–5.

Menolascino, F. J. 1965. *Amer. J. Orthopsychiat.* 35:852–61.

Olshansky, S. 1962. *Soc. Casewk.* 43:190–93.

Roos, P. 1963. *Ment. Ret.* 1:345–50.

Wolfensberger, W. 1967. Counseling the parents of the retarded. In: *Mental Retardation,* ed. A. A. Baumeister, pp. 329–400. Chicago: Aldine.

[Twenty-three references not reprinted.]

29 *Embarrassments in the Diagnostic Process*

Wolf Wolfensberger

I propose that the diagnostic process as currently conducted in mental retardation is ridden with contradictions and inefficiencies, thoughtless cliches and bankrupt practices. Specifically, I wish to identify five problems or practices which I believe to constitute embarrassments to the field.

EMBARRASSMENT NO. 1

Diagnosis is quite often a dead end for the family. Instead of leading to a meaningful service assignment it frequently results only in a frustrating series of fruitless cross-referrals. A typical case in my experience is that of a mildly retarded, homosexually inclined, moderately disturbed teenager who was referred back and forth between the following agencies: regular and special school programs, a child guidance and residential treatment center, a state hospital, two state institutions for the retarded, and the state vocational rehabilitation service. He was judged to be too retarded for the regular grades, too disturbing in special class, too retarded for the outpatient and too old for the inpatient service of the disturbed children's center, too homosexual for the children's ward of the state hospital and too young for its adult wards, too high functioning for the first state retardation institution, not quite enough of a number of things for the special treatment unit of the second, and too effeminate for the programs vocational rehabilitation offered.

This cross-referring took place within a relatively short time span and three or four agencies ran him through their standard diagnostic mill. In the end, the boy somehow did not quite fit in anywhere and lived at home without any service whatever. On paper, however, he was a great success as far as the agencies were concerned. Since he was referred in each instance to what was considered to be an appropriate service by the agency one step ahead in the referral chain, he constituted at least six successful close-outs and will thus enter our national mental health, mental retardation and education statistics. A similar case has been recorded in the literature ... where a boy was handed on among 18 physicians, 4 teachers, 1 chiropractor, 2 clinics, 2 hospitals, and 7 schools. After this, the boy became "uncooperative, untidy, disturbed," and the mother stated that "not even the worst prognosis he had received in all our long years of searching for help had prepared us for this." Many a parent has questioned bitterly what good the diagnostic evaluation did if it failed to lead to assignation to a service, or, even worse, if it actually resulted in the child's exclusion from a program previously enrolled in.

EMBARRASSMENT NO. 2

Many diagnostic centers do not provide adequate feedback counseling, considering their duty done the moment the diagnostic process is completed *to their satisfaction.* Once the professional staff involved has reached a conclusion, the case is closed except for one, often hurried, impatient, and perhaps patronizing, feedback session with the parents. They are given the facts as seen by the professional and told to "accept" them.

More than one feedback session may be felt to be beyond the scope of diagnosis, and a series of sessions is sometimes already considered psychotherapy which, being a "service," the parent is supposed to get elsewhere. Parents who are dissatisfied with this type of management are considered maladjusted, difficult, and "nonaccepting."

Professionals look askance at the parent who does not "accept" their diagnosis and who keeps looking elsewhere for confirmation or disconfirmation. It is undoubtedly true that many a child has been subjected to redundant diagnostics because of the parents' emotional maladjustments and feelings of guilt and hostility. At the same time I believe strongly that a good deal of diagnosis shopping has been due to inadequate feedback counseling. I am convinced that it takes a series of sessions, spread out over several months, before most parents come somewhat to grips with the nature and, particularly, the implications of the diagnosis.

Time and again, one finds that neither parents with professional and mental health backgrounds nor those who profess a verbal understanding during the first feedback session have even made a good start in working through their conflicts. For this reason, spaced and repeated feedback counseling should be viewed not as a luxury but as an integral part of the function of a diagnostic service. Such counseling should be offered even if it necessitates case load reduction since, in the long run, it will probably conserve professional manpower.

It is penny-wise and pound-foolish to invest up to several hundred dollars worth of professional man-hours into the diagnostic process only to begrudge a few additional hours of counseling. If the parents are not adequately counseled, they may either go shopping and/or their defenses may harden, and in the end this may cost ten, a hundred and even a thousandfold what a few hours of counseling would have cost.

EMBARRASSMENT NO. 3

Diagnostic services are often overdeveloped in comparison to other available resources. Indeed, of the services in the field, diagnosis is probably the most readily available. A large number of retardates undergo repeated and redundant evaluations and which parents can obtain at relatively little cost if they are willing to expend time and effort. In the writer's experience, the record was held by a boy who, within five years, was subjected to eight evaluations, most of these by a typical clinical team, and several at well-known clinics. Obtaining needed services, however, was another matter.

I have heard program planners in the field talk about "services" when they meant nothing more than diagnosis. Often the diagnostic center is the first and for years the only resource to be developed. Considerable manpower is channeled to it and away from other services. It appears legitimate to question this practice and ask why it is adhered to so determinedly.

Diagnosis is an intellectual exercise which calls upon basic skills the professional has learned in his training and which *can be carried out in his office.* It gives him a deceptive feeling of accomplishment and can do so several times a week. In diagnosis, the professional can find many rewards and a good deal of security—just the opposite of what the parent typically finds in it. However, when it comes to other services, the professional finds neither security nor easy satisfaction. Traditional approaches used in mental health (and of questionable success even there) have not been very successful in mental retardation. For many new services desperately needed in this country we have little precedence, experience, or training, and many mental health and retardation professionals do not feel secure in relatively untried and new services. Furthermore, the rewards of most services in mental retardation come very, very slowly as treatment is a long, drawn-out, difficult, and laborious process. Reinforcement in the form of visible progress in an individual case may be apparent sporadically through the years rather than several times a week as in diagnosis. Finally, most effective services simply cannot be rendered in an office. All of this may keep professionals clinging to diagnosis and shying away from other services.

EMBARRASSMENT NO. 4

According to theory and cliche, it is of utmost importance that diagnosis take place as early as possible. In practice, however, early diagnosis can be a disaster. When a child is born into a family it is usually accepted and loved with little reservation. Should the child later turn out to be retarded, the problem may be worked out within the family because of the strong bonds that have been formed. However, a child diagnosed as retarded at or near birth may never find the crucial initial acceptance and may be viewed with conflicted attitudes which prevent the formation of deep parental love. This can lead to early and quite unnecessary institutionalization or other consequences detrimental to the child.

I have encountered many instances, numbering in the hundreds, where early diagnosis such as in mongolism exposed the family to professional management which appeared contrary to the welfare of child, family, and society. The most common counsel seems to be the stereotyped "put the child in the institution right away," often accompanied by the sincere admonition to "forget you ever had him" and perhaps the consolation to "have another one instead." This sort of advice is, by no means, the most inappropriate or callous readily encountered and repeatedly documented in the literature. The dictum that early diagnosis is always optimal may thus need to be qualified. Early diagnosis is desirable when it leads to prevention, early treatment, or constructive counseling; it is irrelevant if it is purely academic and does not change the course of events; it is harmful if, in balance, child or family reaps more disadvantages than benefits.

EMBARRASSMENT NO. 5

I contend that we really have no strong empirical basis for claiming even a fraction of the benefits attributed to the team evaluation in mental retardation. For example, one of its most spectacular failures has been in vocational prediction. On the other hand, to my shock and amazement, I observed programs in England where outstanding services were offered even though the majority of clients had never undergone the type of comprehensive evaluation which is readily available to us ... In fact, many clients had never even had an intelligence test!

I have concluded that even the best team evaluation is often wasted either because the presenting question could have been answered without it, because it did not concern itself with the underlying problems of the case, or because the data typically collected are not relevant to the prediction to be made. At this point, it seems time to ask: Is it at all possible that we have lost perspective?

In many cases where the main object of diagnosis is the identification of service needs, a brief interview with the family can sometimes even be sufficient. While the case itself may be complex, the *need* may be very simple. Thus, the need for a mother's helper, day care, trainable classes, public health nurse visits, etc., is often so blatant that an intelligent layman could render a good judgment, especially when the existence of retardation is no longer in question and when previously obtained diagnostic data are already available. Yet many agencies will blindly administer a mammoth and stereotyped dose of diagnostics to all comers, even where the needs are as obvious as the total lack of means to satisfy them. This may well be due to feelings of inadequacy and helplessness. If the family's situational needs cannot be met, the staff can at least rid itself of its feelings of futility by engaging in complicated diagnostics instead of turning the family away categorically.

Considering the costs involved, diagnosis should be rendered only in terms of the question: *"Diagnosis for what?"* Often detailed pre-diagnostic questionnaires and letters to previous contact agencies will reveal that the family only needs counseling, selective evaluation, or a referral instead of "the works." Yet, in my experience, pre-diagnostic screening is often very cursory and inadequate. Even when diagnosis could be rendered in a meaningful context it is only too often of low utility. Many diagnostic teams are new to the field and are still learning, and even skilled diagnosticians do not always render reports of practical utility to those who are often the only ones actually doing anything meaningful for the retardate, namely the family and the teaching and habilitative professions.

What is needed is a fresh look at practices and needs in the much hailed but often rather stereotyped team approach to mental retardation diagnosis. Above all, a family-centered attitude must replace the staff-centered traditionalism of the typical diagnostic team. The family's needs must be placed above the needs of the professional, and the question should be asked if all the money invested in diagnostic centers and staffs is as well spent as it could be, or whether some of it would not be better spent on other services in the field.

REFERENCES

[Three references not reprinted.]

Part V

TREATMENT

30 Introduction to Part V

Treatment is the natural sequel to diagnosis, but treatment here is not a self-evident term. Since mental retardation in this book does not refer to a functional disorder, there really is no treatment leading to a cure. Rather, *treatment* refers to all that is done to maximize the growth potential of the retarded child. Some of this is done by the service system as in providing special education, and some is done by the parents as in modifying usual and natural child rearing techniques to suit the needs of the retarded child. Thus there is a natural division of labor between service system and parents in maximizing the growth potential of the retarded child, and the service system's responsibility is to contribute formally to the division of labor.

Although the overall conceptualization of this book is unique, there is a time-honored concept of treatment in terms of the consumer-provider division of labor. In his book on *Child Welfare Services* (1967), Kadushin classified all services relative to the parents as *supportive, supplementary,* or *substitutive. Supportive* services are those rendered to the parents; all benefit to the child is indirect. *Supplementary* services are direct professional services to the child. For example, advising parents on helping the child learn to play with other children is a supportive service; the parent retains all contacts with the child. However, if the service system enrolls the child in a day-care program for the same purpose, the service is *supplementary.* In *substitute* services, the service system absorbs all parental functions. If the supportive and supplementary services described above prove ineffectual, the child may be placed in a residential treatment facility where the duties of parents are performed by the service system alone.

This manner of conceptualizing treatment implicitly assumes that the child belongs to the parents, not to the service system. The service system classifies its work by how much of the parental role it assumes. Second, it has an explicit sense of priority, generally described in the literature as "lines of defense." The first line of defense is supportive service. It may be necessary to proceed to the second line of defense, supplementary services, or even to the third line of defense, substitutive services.

Supportive services include individual counseling, group counseling, parent education, and parent instruction in therapy. Individual counseling (in contrast to counseling groups of parents) dominates the literature in this book more than any other topic, yet counseling is generally discussed from the perspective of the profession of the author. (Part III on professional roles deals mainly with counseling.) Also, counseling is frequently only one consideration. The Oppenheimer article (Part IV, Detection and Diagnosis), for instance, considers counseling as the end point of a process beginning with detection.

In this Part, Beck (1959) describes the casework perspective on counseling and illustrates how variable counseling may be depending on the circumstance.

In other articles not reprinted, Milligan (1965) considers counseling a process unto itself without regard to which profession is carrying it out; Dalton (1963) distinguishes between counseling parents of mildly retarded and severely retarded children. Those who are interested should consult the book by Noland (1970) which contains thirty-one readings on the subject.

Group counseling commands a prominent place in the literature. Coleman (1953) was one of the earliest writers on the subject and includes more details of operation than later authors. (The recent literature is more concerned with the effect of group counseling than with the procedure. Lewis—1972, not reprinted—provides interesting evidence of the effectiveness of the process.)

Articles on counseling and professional roles suggest that many parents are so emotionally disoriented by the introduction of a retarded child into their lives that adequate care of the child becomes improbable. Such an orientation tends to ignore problems unrelated to the psychodynamics of the situation. Cianci (1955), Frey (1965), and Wildman (1965)—not reprinted—all focus on education of the parent. The implication is that parents are *not* so emotionally disoriented that they are unable to understand or use information wisely.

The recent and growing literature on parent instruction in therapy is principally a literature on operant conditioning. The article on chewing by Butterfield in Part II is a case example of *operant conditioning*. It is based on simple principles and can be taught to parents. In this Part, Terdal and Buell (1969) provide a straightforward, nontechnical description of a program which teaches operant conditioning techniques to parents.

Needless to say, more than one type of treatment is frequently required. Smith et al. (1972, not reprinted) tell how supportive and substitutive services are combined sequentially into a treatment plan. Retarded children with behavioral problems are institutionalized (substitute services) and a behavior modification plan is tested. The parents are taught the techniques and gradually reassume total care, with supervision, of the child in the home (supportive services). At that point the authors consider the parents "paraprofessionals in the use of behavior modification."

The supportive services described above leave parental roles to the parents. By establishing emotional equilibrium, imparting information, and teaching home management techniques, parents are expected to be better able to discharge their responsibilities and, consequently, retarded children are more likely to attain their maximum potential.

The needs of retarded children vary from child to child and the needs of each retarded child vary from time to time. The capacity to meet needs also varies from parent to parent and the capacity of each parent varies from time to time. In the ideal world, the service community would offer essentially two supportive services: continuing supportive services for those parents who are in continuous need of them and sporadic supportive services for those parents who only need them occasionally. In either case, supportive services alone may not be adequate, and the service system may have to *supplement* parental roles, i.e., assume a direct part of the labor of caring for the child.

Frequently the use of supplementary services is an individualized decision, and Arnold (1966) gives two examples of the use of homemakers as supplementary services to stabilize an explosive situation while the family uses the supportive service of counseling.

However, individualized appraisal of the need for supplementary services is time consuming, and many supplementary services are, therefore, routinely offered because experience has shown that most families need them. Jubenville (1962) describes the early experience of a state-wide network of day care centers for severely retarded children, a supplementary service offered because of *presumed* need. The Jubenville article reveals an enormous array of developmental problems among the children. Some of them could be corrected by operant conditioning as described above. The difference is that operant conditioning requires an individualized appraisal of need and day care assumes the need because a population of severely retarded children usually contains it.

As supportive services alone may be insufficient, so may supplementary services, and the service system may have to assume all parental roles. The substitute service of institutionalization has inspired an enormous literature and has an interesting history. Not long ago, many retarded children, especially those so diagnosed at birth, were automatically institutionalized on the basis of presumed need. However, there has been a continuing trend to individualized appraisal of the need for institutionalization, and it is increasingly seen as a stop-gap measure rather than life-long. Dittman (1962) describes this trend and the process of institutionalization and reacceptance from the parents' point of view, and does so most poignantly.

Other substitute services are adoption and foster care, foster care being more common. Garrett (1970) examines foster care as an alternative to institutionalization or to home care with supportive and/or supplementary services. Foster care is described here, as in all places, as a service which is offered after a highly individualized appraisal of need.

Some services are generally associated with a profession. For instance, usually a psychologist teaches parents operant conditioning, and a social worker generally arranges for foster care. Counseling and parent education fall within the purview of many professions, while institutional and day care services generally require a set of skills no one profession has. About two decades ago it was realized that parents who had needs associated with more than one discipline had to go from program to program. Professionals began to refer to this type of organization of services as "fragmented," and "compartmentalized." They urged pulling all the professions together under one administrative roof, a "comprehensive" program to meet the total needs of the family.

The Allen (1966) article covers interdisciplinary processes and comprehensive care. It describes a program which treats many handicaps of which mental retardation is one. The authors consider comprehensive care necessary for all chronic conditions and treatment as only one phase of comprehensive care. They also stress continuity of care as a major objective of comprehensive care. Scheerenberger (1970) examines services on the community level and tablulates opinions of parents and service system personnel alike.

Since services for parents of retarded children have been changing constantly and have not yet reached an acceptable state, an historical perspective is necessary. Journal articles are useful since they are written about *contemporary* practice. The dates of publication of the articles in all sections of this book show two trends. First, absolving parents of all responsibility for care of their retarded children (institutionalization or other forms of substitute service) is less and less acceptable. More and more, parents must participate in the care of their children. Second, individual professions seem to have arrived at acceptable role definitions in this division of labor and have recently focused more on the organization of services in the community, with "comprehensive" care the current ideal. And comprehensive care is defended mainly as a convenience for the consumer, not as an economy for the provider.

All trends in service follow trends in conceptualization. The Rodriquez and Lombardi article in Part I described the extent to which legal considerations had permeated educational thinking. But as Dybwad (1973) has pointed out, the legal rights of the retarded and their families are further being specified in the areas of employment, living conditions, citizenship, medical care, and guardianship. (Dybwad includes in his article the "Declaration on the Rights of Mentally Retarded Persons" which was passed by the General Assembly of the United Nations in January 1972.) Suits by individuals and class action suits also appear to be increasing in frequency.

Scandinavian countries have long approached services to the retarded from the concept of normalization—enabling the retarded to function in ways considered to be within the acceptable norms of his society. Wolfensberger (1970) was the first to introduce this term and concept to the American literature and has recently expanded the concept to include all human services for all conditions and to include other concepts such as advocacy (*The Principle of Normalization in Human Services,* 1972). This idea, however, appears to be riding the trend from institutions to halfway houses to community placement rather than leading it.

31 Counseling Parents of Retarded Children

Helen L. Beck

In all services directed at helping children, treatment necessarily includes, besides the child, another person who is directly responsible for the child and closely affected by his condition. This person is usually the mother, and though not a patient, is always a client of the agency. This is particularly true in clinics concerned with mental retardation. Treatment of mentally retarded children has to be primarily aimed at reduction of secondary difficulties and improvement in tolerance of the condition and in ability to handle it on the part of the persons carrying responsibility for the child. The problem of retardation is always a family problem, and diagnosis has therefore to be a family diagnosis focused on the total situation. Thus, parent counseling becomes one of the most effective treatment tools.

"Parent counseling" is used here primarily to describe a process of casework treatment, based on diagnostic findings and aimed at ego support and adjustment to reality. It is an enabling and helping process based on the understanding of the dynamics of personality and it uses relationships as a vehicle. "Diagnosis" as used here will include medical, social, and psychological diagnosis of the child's condition, of the needs of the family, as a unit, of the parents' personalities, and of their ability to use available services.

Many of the problems that occur in connection with mental retardation are common to families of handicapped children in general. The parents have to understand the nature and extent of the child's condition, face their own feelings of guilt and rebellion, and learn adequate modes of handling the afflicted child. In such families other children may be neglected and normal life experiences curtailed for either the healthy or the handicapped members, or both. Family breakdown may result from the parents' own withdrawal from normal activities. In the family with a mentally retarded child additional factors of social shame, embarrassment over the child's behavior, and bafflement over the child's uneven capacities, often must be dealt with.

In contrast to other medical conditions, treatment of the retarded child's condition rests primarily with the parents rather than with a professional worker, even if the youngster attends school or a day care center. It usually consists of helping the child to achieve optimal development and maximum use of his capacities. To do this effectively parents need help in working through their own feelings and adjustments as well as practical advice in regard to their everyday problems.

RELATIONSHIP AND TIMING

Development of a good professional relationship is one of the main prerequisites for successful work with parents. Parents tend to reject painful information that comes from a seemingly uninterested or unfeeling source. If the diagnostic process in the clinic is an unhurried one, parents have time to understand step by step what the clinic personnel are attempting to do, to prepare themselves to accept the diagnosis and a treatment plan, and to develop a workable two-way relationship with the clinic personnel based on trust and respect. Much of the frantic "shopping around" in connection with chronic conditions may be caused by attempts on the part of clinicians to shortcut the diagnostic processes. The team approach in diagnosis gives the parent an opportunity to work through negative feelings that emerge in one or the other contact and to clarify interpretations. "Shopping around" can often be avoided by permitting parents to use the various team members for comparison of opinions.

Parents' previous experience with other facilities has to be dealt with directly at the time of first contact. If the new clinic does not want to be just one of a growing list of clinics in the parents' experience, client and workers must clearly understand the reasons for dissatisfaction with the previous agencies and what the client's present expectations are.

At the Mental Retardation Unit of St. Christopher's Hospital for Children [Philadelphia] the diagnosis may extend over several weeks. The clinic is staffed by a team representing a variety of professional disciplines. Cases are screened for admission by the pediatrician, and most of the team members are involved in the diagnostic work-up. This is terminated by a team conference in which plans are worked out with full consideration of the child's needs, family wishes, and avail-able facilities. The team delegates discussion of such plans with the family to the person who has developed the most workable relationship with the family and who will have to carry the main responsibility for helping them carry out or modify the suggested plans. This is frequently the social caseworker.

In regard to mental retardation there is sometimes a strange notion that establishing diagnosis is identical with giving treatment. Diagnosis is an essential step toward understanding treatment needs, but it is not treatment. The parents' expectancy and readiness for help are necessarily being aroused during the diagnostic process. If this is not followed up promptly with an actual treatment plan, their readiness to involve themselves in a treatment process may be lost.

The parents' most crucial need for service occurs at the time when they first learn of the diagnosis. It is then that they need support in handling their emotions, help in clearly understanding the diagnosis and its implications, and assistance in planning for their child.

Considerable anxiety is usually aroused by a diagnosis of mental retardation. If this is not handled promptly, parents may develop rigid defenses which are not easily amenable to change. A caseworker can help parents set up the kind of defenses that will cushion reality adjustment rather than paralyze functioning. Even the most stable parents have to cope with a certain amount of personality disorganization in reaction to severe stress and shock. Professional casework services at this point work as a "catalyst" for helping parents to recognize their thoughts and reestablish ability to function.

CASEWORK APPROACH

The parents who come to a mental retardation clinic are as a rule quite aware of the fact that they have a problem. They may, however, deny its nature. Parents should clearly understand the findings of the clinicians in regard to their child's difficulty. However, they need not accept these findings immediately and fully in order to work toward relief of their problem. Diagnosis of mental retardation is not likely to change, and the parents' acceptance may come gradually as a result of treatment.

If a parent persists in calling his child "slow" instead of retarded, the worker may do the same. If the parent continues to express conviction that the child will eventually "catch up," or does not belong in this "terrible" special class, the worker need not contradict him but can patiently help him face the truth. Parents can be helped gradually to see the diagnosis not as a "dead end" verdict, but as a starting point from which to approach much of the problem.

Parents often spend considerable effort in trying to prove to the worker that the child is normal. If they really believed this, they would not continue with the clinic. They often try to push the worker into an argument in order to convince themselves. The worker does well not to be drawn into such an argument. In time the parents draw their own conclusions.

We found most of the parents seen at our clinic very eager to find and use services. Many cooperate far beyond their own need and show good grasp of the value of their contributions to the understanding of the problem. However, as in any clinic setting, some parents withhold information or try to manipulate clinic personnel and time. Such behavior has to be discussed quite directly with the clients and limits should be set.

Service cannot be effective without the full and voluntary participation of parents. The parent who cannot respond to efforts to help him and who continues to try to manipulate the clinic will manipulate treatment goals. Neither he nor the child will in the end profit from treatment. However, the amount of responsibility for initiation and continuation of contact that can and should be put on the client should be determined on the basis of the psychosocial diagnosis rather than on rigidly established clinic procedures.

Through social-casework counseling, parents of retarded children can be helped to develop:

1. Some understanding of the meaning of the term "retarded" as it applies to their child.

2. Understanding of the degree of their child's handicap and what this will mean in the future.

3. Ability to understand their child's assets, his needs, and his difficulties.

4. Appreciation of the effect the presence of a handicapped child has on family life in general, on their other children, and on themselves as parents, and on adjustment of the family within the neighborhood.

5. Understanding of the fact that the child's retardation and his behavior are separate entities and that behavior can

be influenced at least to a degree by educational approaches.

6. Ability to judge whether neighborhood reactions are caused by the child's behavior, appearance, or mental ability.

7. Techniques to use such understanding constructively in order to help the handicapped child, the entire family, and the community.

8. Knowledge of available resources relating to their own situation and to the problem of retardation in general.

While needs differ, time for consideration of these areas has to be provided in planning. The "one shot" approach is rarely helpful.

PATTERNS IN COUNSELING

In spite of the uniqueness of each case, definite patterns emerge that may serve to guide program planning. Contacts fall roughly into four phases: (1) the initial period, encompassing the diagnostic process, clarification of the situation and needs, establishment of treatment goals, and selection of treatment methods; (2) treatment, consisting of more or less intensive counseling, individually or in groups; (3) tapering off, a time when, goals being achieved, contact becomes less frequent and is eventually stopped; (4) follow-up, consisting of occasional contact either as needs arise or as children are brought to the clinic for other appointments.

Initial Period

It is neither feasible nor necessary to offer counseling services to all parents who come to a clinic for diagnosis of their child. By the end of the diagnostic period it should be possible to estimate fairly accurately the parents' need for counseling services, their amenability to this type of service, and the feasibility of intermediate as well as long-range goals.

Selection of appropriate treatment methods should be made after consideration of a number of factors:

1. Ego strength—the parents' maturity; emotional stability; capacity to accept their roles as parents, as marital partners, as members of their community; their intellectual endowment and the use they make of it.

2. Family strength—the quality of interrelationships between the different members of the family, and the kind of emotional and practical support parents can count on from other family members.

3. Environmental and cultural influences—the presence or absence of other irritants in the home or in the neighborhood and the influence of cultural and religious factors on the family's acceptance or rejection of the problem.

4. Degree of handicap and the parents' understanding of it. It is considerably more difficult for the parents of a moderately retarded child who is physically healthy and attractive to accept the diagnosis than to see him as plain stubborn, lazy, or spoiled. The parent of a severely retarded child with external stigmata is less able to avoid the problem.

Treatment Goals

In mental retardation, treatment is aimed at increased comfort of all people concerned with a trying situation.

Problems have to be analyzed so that partial solutions can be found as the need arises. Tension and frustration in parent and child may be reduced by cathartic experiences for the parents, and by help with practical problems such as learning ways of handling unacceptable behavior, and planning for school or other types of placement. If problems are met as they occur, many retarded children can live happily within their own family groups and make their contributions to family living, at least during their childhood years. Where placement away from home is indicated, the parents can be helped to see that this has advantages for the handicapped child as well as for the rest of the family.

Level of Treatment

In general, the level of treatment remains in the area of reality adjustment, ego reintegration, and development of techniques for daily living. Intensity and depth of treatment vary greatly within the range of clinic function. If the parents have prominent personality disturbances or many problems in addition to their child's retardation, they may have to be referred to more appropriate agencies.

Treatment Techniques

Treatment techniques most often used are clarification, supportive counseling, and environmental reorganization. This does not preclude the use of insight therapy, but where such therapy is of paramount importance, referral becomes necessary. Though the counseling focuses on the problem of mental retardation, parents may be enabled by treatment to translate the help they get for one problem to others as needed. This happened in the case of the A family.

The A's were referred by their family physician, who was struck by the intensity of the negative parent-child relationships. The oldest child, Tim, retarded because of an organic condition, was extremely hyperactive and lacked concentration. The parents' severity in trying to control his behavior had led to violent negativism on his part. The younger brother, Don, considerably brighter than Tim, got vicarious enjoyment out of teasing his older brother into temper outbursts resulting in actions for which Tim eventually was punished.

During the contact here, explanation as to the organic basis of some of Tim's behavior was given to both parents. They were helped to evaluate their own approach to the children, to consider the differences of their children's needs, and to try new ways of meeting these needs.

The parents became aware of the teasing of the younger child and of the effect on both children of their own impatience and high standards. They also became aware of their own strained relationships and how these resulted in their undercutting each other's effectiveness with the children. Gradually the whole family situation calmed down. When a new baby was born, both parents were able to avoid many of the mistakes they had made at Don's birth which had created such intense jealousy and difficulties between the boys.

Treatment Methods

The caseworker may counsel either in individual contact or in groups. It has been hoped that the development of group techniques might prove more economical of the worker's time than individual contacts. This has hardly been the case as far as economics of time and professional efforts are concerned. The economy lies in the fact that the more appropriate treatment is the more effective one.

INDIVIDUAL COUNSELING

At the St. Christopher's clinic individual counseling has been offered to the parent with highly individualized needs, strong emotional dependency, intense masochism with certain types of passive-aggressive adjustment, or clearly psychotic tendencies. We found such parents poor group risks, since they tend to be disruptive to group processes because of their urgent need for attention, the intensity of their relationships, or their need to act out. In individual contact the worker can adjust the process to the individual and can control the gratification of his particular needs. This was the method used in the B case.

The B's had accepted the diagnosis of their only child's retardation before coming to the clinic, but they felt strongly resentful of the doctor who had given the diagnosis. They interpreted his state-ments as meaning that no limits could be set for the boy's behavior. They joined a parents' organization and used the group to project their anxiety about their own problem.

In individual contact, the B's were brought back again and again to their own problem of handling their child's behavior. They were helped to face their misinterpretations of what they had been told. They also came to realize how much they acted out their own discouragement by proving time and again that they were not able to set limits for their child, while other people were able to do so. As it became necessary, the caseworker allowed them to forgo discussion of the child and his problem and focus on their general discouragement and disappointment, of which the child was only one factor.

The caseworker saw the parents in separate interviews and helped them work through some of their rivalry in their positions within the family so that a common approach could be established.

GROUP COUNSELING

In group counseling we are not concerned with intensive group therapy, but with casework counseling in groups. Goals are: personality reintegration and adjustment to reality. Group processes and teaching methods are combined to afford the individual relief from tension, understanding of children's behavior, and techniques for handling specific problems.

Group processes are helpful to basically mature parents whose functioning is temporarily impaired by the overwhelming nature of their problem; to parents with a tendency toward projection and intellectualization; to parents with pronounced though well-controlled feelings of hostility, who can find relief through limited acting out; and to parents with dependency needs which may be met through group identification and support.

In selecting members for groups at St. Christopher's we have not found it particularly necessary to strive toward homogeneity of social strata, intellectual capacity, personality makeup, or degree of defect in the members' children. Groups soon develop a homogeneity of their own, the members becoming quite supportive of one another. The case of Mrs. C illustrates several of these points.

Mrs. C was unable to make effective use of individual contact when it was offered. She covered up her intense feelings of hostility by complete denial and adopted an attitude of submissiveness. In the group she quickly assumed a certain amount of leadership, which the group kept from going beyond bounds. She used the group constructively to gain better understanding of her own problems, to learn from other parents techniques of handling situations, and to get gratification for her need to dominate.

After the series of group sessions ended, a second attempt at individual counseling, made at Mrs. C's request, was no more effective than the first. But in another series of group sessions she again used the group experience constructively.

LENGTH OF CONTACT

Length of time necessary to achieve intermediary or long-range goals varies greatly, depending on the kind of emotional or reality problems to be worked out and the complications encountered in the process. Length of contact may be in inverse ratio to the severity of the actual handicap. An obviously severe handicap often allows for clearer diagnosis, less parental resistance, and fewer alternatives. On the other hand, parents of a more salvageable child may be in need of longer periods of service to achieve an acceptance of the retardation and evaluate a variety of possibilities for the child.

At the St. Christopher's clinic cases that receive *short-term services* only fall roughly into three groups.

Group 1 includes parents who during the diagnostic process or previously have learned to understand and ·accept their problem and are basically able to handle it on their own. Usually only one interview following the diagnostic period is needed to clarify that the clinic stands ready to help them whenever necessary. Such parents use the clinic as needs arise.

Group 2 includes parents who are not accessible to continued treatment even if they are in need of it. They either have not accepted the diagnosis or are unable to mobilize themselves sufficiently to involve themselves in treatment. The caseworker alerts other team members to these problems so that the parents may receive some help when they bring the child in for follow-up visits to the physician or the psychologist and may be referred to the caseworker at a later date if feasible. In the interim the caseworker seeks opportunities for casual contact with the parents in the clinics.

Group 3 includes parents already known to community agencies, which usually continue service to the family, often in collaboration with clinic personnel.

Intensive casework treatment over a longer period is offered parents with complex problems either of their own personalities, environmental situations, or difficulties with the child. We have found it most economical and helpful to offer intensive, frequent interviews at the very beginning of the treatment period and then to gradually decrease contacts as parents become able to manage on their own.

Recently we have begun to experiment with a more extensive than intensive approach consisting of a cooperative effort between the public health nurse and the social worker. Two groups of parents have been included in this program: (1) basically stable parents whose problems of child management are caused by the child's severe handicap; (2) immature, anxious parents who have management problems with their children caused at least in part by their own insecurity. No attempts are being made with either group toward too strong involvement in the parents' own problems. Explanations are given for the

child's behavior and new approaches to handling are suggested. The public health nurse visits the more immature parents to demonstrate ways of handling the child. It is too early to say how helpful such an approach may be. However, considerable relief of upset has been achieved in a few of the families in this experiment.

All tapering off of long-term treatment should be on a planned basis. Unplanned "fizzling out" devaluates the treatment received and may leave the parents with a feeling of dissatisfaction. As treatment goals are gradually realized, parents themselves usually begin to express a lessened need for contact. Increase in problems and anxiety may occur as wider spacing of interviews begins. If the caseworker permits the parents to set their own pace, the frequency of contacts will decrease.

One advantage of casework at a clinic is that cases can be followed over extended periods of time without maintaining intensive or regular contact. Parents often use scheduled follow-up visits to the pediatrician, psychologist, or speech pathologist as opportunity to bring the caseworker up to date with their present stage of affairs. The caseworker also may schedule follow-up interviews at certain stages in the child's life, for example when he is getting ready for a nursery school experience, camp experience, or school placement.

PARENTS' ORGANIZATIONS

Parents' organizations such as the Association for Retarded Children should be used as a resource in planning with parents of mentally retarded children. These organizations provide such parents with strong emotional support and valuable outlets for the constructive channeling of their anxieties, frustrations, and tensions. However, referrals to such groups should be made on the basis of diagnostic considerations, and should include preparation of the client and the organization as in any agency referral.

The timing of such a referral is important. These organizations properly expect their members to promote understanding of the problem of mental retardation. To do this effectively and without harm to themselves parents have really to understand and accept the nature of their own problem and they have to be ready to identify with a large group. Otherwise they may use activity in the organization to avoid facing their own problems and working through their own anxieties

and difficulties. We have found that parents who have joined large organizations of parents without preparation often accept mental retardation as a community problem, but do not really acknowledge their own problems in relation to their own mentally retarded child.

Parents who are well prepared for group membership can offer a great deal to these organizations in their work to spread understanding of the needs of the mentally retarded. However, this type of activity cannot substitute for the emotional and practical help needed by parents at crucial points to maintain their own and family stability in facing the problems presented by the fact of their child's retardation. In offering such help, the goal of casework counseling, whether to individuals or groups, is to help parents achieve their optimum functioning to meet their own responsibility for the treatment of their child.

32 Group Therapy with Parents of Mentally Deficient Children

James C. Coleman

The present study represents an attempt to evaluate the use of group therapy in working with the parents of mentally deficient children. It grew out of: (1) the need for a better coordination of activities between a private school for mentally deficient children and the home situation of these children, (2) the continual demand of parents for counseling time concerning their children which placed excessive demands upon the time of school personnel, and (3) the many common problems which these parents revealed in counseling which seemed amenable to a group approach.

In recruitment no attempt was made to actually select from among the parents those who needed group therapy or would be likely to profit from it most. Rather an opportunity was provided for all parents to participate in bi-monthly evening meetings. Although the parents were sent postcards indicating the time and place of the meeting, the topic for discussion that evening, and an expressed wish that they would find the meeting of value, no direct appeal or pressure was put upon them to attend.

The parents in general were of lower middle class socioeconomic status, although they ranged from skilled tradesmen to business men, writers, lawyers, and other professionally trained persons. The average education of the parents was comple-tion of the 10th grade. Approximately one-fourth had attended college. At the first meeting some 30, or about one-third of the total parents of children in the school, attended. Attendance at subsequent meetings varied between 20 and 35 with some shift in personnel each time due to new additions and unavoidable absences of those parents who had attended preceding meetings. However, most of those attending the first two meetings continued through the six-month trial period with only occasional absences. Fourteen of the parents attended each of the 12 meetings.

PHYSICAL ARRANGEMENTS

The group meetings were held on the 2nd and 4th Tuesday evening of each month from 8:00 until approximately 9:30 p.m. No attempt was made to set up a definite closing time for the meetings although 9:30 was usually considered the maximum length. The meetings actually varied from about 1 hour to 1¾ hours with the average approximating 1¼ hours. The group meetings were held in a large room of the school made possible by combining two of the regular school classrooms via a movable partition. Regular classroom desks were removed and straight-backed folding chairs were substituted and placed in two semi-circular rows around the periphery of the room. Ashtrays and necessary materials were made available for those who wished to smoke. A screen and projection equipment were provided for showing slides and movies. One of the regular school teachers acted as secretary-recorder for the sessions.

The group sessions were terminated at the end of a six-month period, and this fact was made known to the parents during the first meeting when the objectives of the meetings and other structuring were undertaken.

PROCEDURE IN THERAPY

In structuring the meetings to the parents, emphasis was placed on the coordination of home and school activities in the best interests of the children and upon freedom to discuss any and all problems which might have some bearing upon this basic objective. The term group therapy was not used and no attempt was made to structure the situation as therapy in any form.

Each meeting was initiated with an educational motion picture or talk by local authorities, e.g., psychiatrists, pediatricians, dentists, school principals, on the problems of mental deficiency. The films and talks were limited to 30 minutes followed by a question and answer period and general group discussion presided over by the group leader (author). The group leader made every attempt to promote a permissive, mutually supportive atmosphere in which the participants would feel free to bring up their problems and express their true feelings

concerning them. The general approach to the group discussion was a flexible one, although an attempt was made to remain as non-directive as the situation seemed to permit. No attempt was made by the group leader to direct the discussion into certain channels or toward preconceived topics. The major emphasis was placed on bringing out the commonality of problems, in supporting individual discussants when this was necessary, and in pointing up group formulations of insights into (and coping techniques for dealing with) various problems worked on. This general orientation proved highly effective in eliciting group discussion and in making the parents feel that this was their meeting and their responsibility to get as much out of it as possible.

In a sense the interaction was maintained on a relatively surface level since the group discussion was restricted to parent child relations and did not take up various personal problems in other life areas. However, many of these parent child problems went relatively deep in terms of personality conflicts centering around guilt, sex, and attitudes toward spouses.

GROUP INTERACTION

During the first three meetings the group discussion was highly intellectualized, focusing primarily on the formal topic which was scheduled for that particular meeting or the general activities of the school. However, now and again more personal problems came to the fore in the form of personal experience or specific questions of what to do in this or that particular situation. After the third meeting the discussion became less and less restricted by the particular topic scheduled for that evening and directed more and more toward specific parent-child-relations problems.

Among the major problems which were brought to the fore and actively worked on by the group were the following:

1. Acceptance of themselves as parents of mentally deficient children without feeling guilty or devaluated. A large number of the parents expressed feelings of guilt concerning their possible role in the bearing of a mentally deficient child. Their guilt feelings were in the main engendered by false ideas of heredity, alcoholic consumption, and "immoral" sexual practices which they felt were largely their individual responsibility. The dispelling of these misconceptions as well as the mutual support gained by group identification with other parents having this problem were considered two of the most important values of the group sessions.

2. Acceptance of their mentally deficient child. Parental reactions to the realization that their child was mentally deficient seemed to vary from rejecting the child at one extreme to denying reality and refusing to believe that the child was really below normal in his intellectual potentialities. Several parents pointed to the tendency toward wishful thinking in the form of believing that some new method of treatment would soon be forthcoming or that some miracle would occur and bring their child up to normal. It was

brought out also that the frustration of parental ambitions for their children undoubtedly was related to their tendency toward rejection of their child. Most of the parents agreed that it was a serious problem to view their children realistically and still accept them as worthwhile human beings.

3. Adjusting parental level of aspiration for child to his actual abilities. Closely related to viewing their children realistically in the light of their actual abilities and potentialities was the problem of adjusting parental levels of aspiration to this realistic view. Many parents admitted that they had had such high hopes for their child and found it very difficult to face reality and accept his limitations, especially without rejecting the child or feeling differently toward him than toward their other children of normal intelligence. As noted previously it was admitted that this in part resulted from the frustration of the parent's own ambition and aspirations.

4. Avoiding pampering the child and giving him all sorts of special privileges. It was pointed out that guilt feelings and feelings that their child was sick often contributed to a tendency to overindulge the child and to overprotect and baby him. This tended to inhibit the development of his potentialities toward actualization and independence.

5. Problems centering around normal siblings. A variety of problems were brought up by the parents centering around the mental deficient's relations to other siblings. Parents pointed out that punishment for misbehavior was particularly difficult since their mentally deficient children did not fully

understand the probable consequences of their misbehavior and hence were in a sense not morally responsible agents. This frequently led to the dilemma of punishing one or more of the siblings while excusing the same misbehavior on the part of the mental deficient. Since the other children often could not understand the justice of this procedure, problems in parent-child relations were automatically created. Other sibling problems centered around the intellectual effect on other siblings of having to play and work with a mentally deficient sibling, and emotional adjustments of siblings necessitated by children in the neighborhood making derogatory remarks about their mentally deficient brother or sister. This problem was sometimes accentuated by other parents in the neighborhood who would permit their children to play with the normal siblings but not with the mental deficient.

6. Sexual problems of the mentally deficient child. Here parents discussed the handling of masturbation and other specific problems faced by the mentally deficient child. Many of these children had been found out in sexual behavior of various natures with other children. In large part this was thought to result from their lack of normal inhibitions and understanding of sexual mores. Due to the prevalence of misconceptions concerning the harmfulness of masturbation and other sexual misinformation, a good deal of didactic therapy was undertaken at this point by the group leader. Topics related to the mentally deficient child's sexual adjustment which came up for discussion included sterilization, marriage and parenthood, and permissible sexual outlets.

7. Problems relating to keeping the child in the home or placing him in an institution. Parents pointed out the strain placed upon the home relationships by the various special problems introduced by the mentally deficient child and discussed the desirability of placing such children in an institution where they would receive some training and unburden the immediate family situation. Difficulties in resolving this problem were raised such as the fact that the higher level mentally deficient child is capable of loving and wanting to be with his family just like other children, by the over-crowded conditions of public institutions for the mentally deficient which made any adequate education training difficult to obtain, and by the financial problems created by maintaining him in a private school.

8. Providing for child's future. Realizing that these children would never be able to function in the community without someone to supervise and care for them, the problem of their future was often a difficult one for the parents. Here matters relating to trust funds, community supervision for mentally deficients, and general methods of enabling them to live as adequate a life as possible were discussed.

9. Things the parents can do in the home to help the child. Many of the parents had tried out on their children special educational techniques such as tracing in learning to read. A whole series of questions came up relating to the educational procedures and other

activities the parents might undertake in order to better coordinate their activities with those of the school and to be of maximum assistance to the mentally deficient child. Here the importance of a practical, reality oriented program to enrich the child's everyday experiences and related activities was discussed.

10. Things the parents might do to help the school. Toward the closing phases of the group sessions the discussion often centered around deficiencies in the school program such as lack of desirable equipment which the parents might assist in rectifying. Plans were undertaken on the initiative of the parents for school dinners and semi-social events to raise money for special equipment and other needed materials which the finances of the school did not permit.

It is interesting to note that the group interaction paralleled very closely that found in more typical group therapy groups, starting with a rather intellectual level of discussion, progressing to personal specific problems, and terminating in a more generalized and socially oriented approach to their problems. It was felt that most of the parents participated effectively in the group discussions. Some were of course more active than others, but even the most diffident seemed to be drawn into the discussion when problems closely affecting them were brought to light.

Three of the parents were particularly active in the group in raising problems, supporting other participants, and enthusiastically backing the group sessions. They were considered most helpful by the group leader. In general, little conflict among members of the group was noted, although occasionally one participant would interrupt another to inject a comment of his own or to rather violently disagree with the opinions expressed. More characteristic were patterns of mutual support, group identification, assistance with problems raised, and immersion in the atmosphere of group understanding and acceptance.

Evaluation of the group sessions. It is a difficult problem to evaluate group therapy results with the best available experimental controls, and in the present study such controls were lacking. However, there were a number of favorable indications: the range and importance of the discussion content, the parallel course of the group interaction to that in more typical groups, the continued high attendance, the accepting and understanding group atmosphere created, and the almost unanimous verbal testimonials to the value of the group sessions.

Undoubtedly much of the enthusiasm generated in the group members grew directly out of the supportive group identification with accepting and understanding fellows. For many this was a new and most welcome experience. This rather favorable view of the outcome of the group sessions was augmented by the requests of six of the participants for referrals to qualified psychologists or psychiatrists who might help them with personal problems not directly related to their mentally deficient children. This was interpreted as an expression of confidence in the value of bringing their problems out into the open and attempting with professional assistance to deal with them more realistically and effectively.

The findings of the present study indicate the possibility of utilizing group therapy with the parents of mentally deficient children for promoting better coordination between educational institutions and the home, as well as helping the parents themselves in developing understanding and healthier attitudes toward the various problems centering around the rearing of mentally deficient children.

33 Parent Education in Managing Retarded Children with Behavior Deficits and Inappropriate Behaviors

Leif Terdal
and Joan Buell

In January 1967 a behavioral program was initiated at the Crippled Children's Division of the University of Oregon Medical School as part of a medical-behavioral-educational pilot project in mental retardation. The behavioral aspect of the program is designed to train parents of retarded children in methods of: (1) accurately observing their child's behavior and their own behavior; (2) eliminating problem behaviors at home; (3) building up in their child appropriate behaviors in areas such as self-help, verbal communication, social interaction and emotional reactions to stress situations. Additional aims are: (1) to determine whether any generalities can be valid as to types of problems and extent of deficiencies relative to parent repertoires in handling retarded children; (2) to train personnel of various disciplines in observational techniques and behavior therapy. The present paper describes a program in which trainees were involved in all phases of operation, data analysis, and treatment planning and implementation.

At present the staff consists of psychologist, speech pathologist, social worker, public health nurse, occupational therapist, physical therapist, re-search assistant and special achievement teacher—all either trained or receiving training in the use of operant techniques. The facility includes an observation room, a playroom with a one-way window, two office rooms for interviewing parents, a physical therapy room, and an occupational therapy room. Observation is also done in the child's home.

The child, to be accepted in this behavioral-educational phase of the program, must have first undergone an intensive multiple-disciplinary diagnostic program. Children previously diagnosed as retarded attend the medical diagnostic program in groups of ten for two hours each day for four weeks. During the four weeks, they are observed by a pediatric nurse and other staff as they engage in group activities structured by a special achievement teacher. They are taken from the observation room to undergo neurological, pediatric, orthopedic and dental diagnoses and treatment for any physical problems such as seizures, dental problems, nutritional problems, and visual and hearing problems. They are also evaluated by standard psychological, speech, occupational therapy and physical therapy evaluation procedures. At the end of this period the staff confers with parents to inform them of the findings and to make recommendations for the child's schooling and continuing medical and dental care. The goal is to assure that each child is functioning in an optimal health state. Selected children with the most severe behavioral deficits or the most markedly disruptive behaviors are seen in the behavioral phase of the program.

Behaviors explored in the clinic include deficiencies in self-help skills such as dressing, grooming, feeding, toilet care, and deficiencies in speech and language such as vocalizing in jargon rather than in already acquired speech, echolalia, and low rate of speech. Inappropriate behaviors are varied but have included tantruming, hitting children, and even such extremes as putting eyeglasses in garbage disposal units, smearing food on walls, etc.

In each case the therapists observe the child closely, pinpointing exact behaviors, the context in which they occur, the current social consequences, and the possible competing responses. Potency and variety of available reinforcers are assessed independently. The procedure is based on operant principles. . . .

ENLISTING PARENTS AS COOPERATIVE, EFFECTIVE THERAPISTS

The parents have come in with a plea for help. They find that they cannot handle their child in certain situations. Discipline may be a problem. Specif-

ically, when they see that their child is lacking in many areas of performance, they become worried and seek help. Their child's behavioral problem and/ or deficiencies may have either excluded the child from school programs or seriously interfered with the child's progress in school. For some families a major portion of activity and time is spent in attempts to cope with their child's behavior. They may even have curtailed normal social activities because of embarrassment over their child's behavior and their inability to cope with it.

The clinic requires parental participation since changes in the child's behavior are directly related to changes in parental management of the child. Improvement in the child's behavior will in turn reinforce the parents' attempt to try new approaches and responses to their child.

Parental participation in the program begins with the initial interview. They are encouraged to report to the staff their concern about their child and they are asked to report situations in which problem behaviors occur and to describe how they handle them. The first interview also provides an opportunity to explain to the parents the need for clinic and home observation of the child's behavior.

The parents' report of their child's behavior serves as one basis for the development of the parents' own observational skills; i.e., staff observation and their own observations later in the program can be compared with their initial report. Their verbal report does not serve as a basis for giving guidance on child care and management.

More specifically, when first seeking help, parents may be able to see quite clearly what their children are doing part of the time, but they do not have a clear over-all picture. They are generally so concerned about specific nuisance behaviors that they frequently fail to recognize significant gains in adaptive skills that are possible for their child. For instance, a child who at the age of four continues to be spoon-fed by his mother, may occasionally put some food in his mouth. The parent, *never having broken down the process of learning to eat* into small steps, does not see this as an approximation but only as a messy habit of an uncooperative child. Also, few parents recognize a relationship between the child's behavior and their response to it.

CLINIC OBSERVATIONS

The setting event or context in which behavior problems occur can be replicated in a lab session, so that the child's behaviors can be observed as well as the parent's responses to the child. For example, a child may scream or cry when his mother gives him a command or fall on the floor and bang his head when asked a question; he may hit the parent, or knock over furniture as the parent reads alone, but not while the child plays with her. Or, he may poke another child who is receiving parental attention. These behaviors can be replicated by instructing the parent to give a command, ask a question, read to the child, play with the child, or read alone and not respond to the child,

etc. In this way, observations can be made as to the specific context in which certain behaviors occur, as well as to the reinforcers that maintain those behaviors.

A lab session also provides an opportunity to evaluate the potency of parental attention as a reinforcer for the child. This is accomplished by observing the play behavior of a child and mother and recording data regarding frequency and/or duration of a particular response class. It could be time spent playing with a particular toy, time spent in one section of the room as opposed to another, etc. The mother is then instructed to respond to the child whenever a specified behavior occurs and to withhold responding when any other behavior occurs. The parent is also told that when she does respond she should try to encourage the child by joining him in his activity, commenting on what he is doing, and avoiding criticizing the child or giving him verbal directions. After about five minutes a reversal technique is employed in which the originally reinforced behavior is put on extinction (the mother is instructed not to respond to the child when the behavior appears), and a different play behavior receives attention from the mother.

In this way it becomes clear whether the parent's attention is reinforcing to a child; i.e., whether, when the parent attended verbally or by smile or touch to one behavior, this behavior continued or increased in frequency. In most cases a mother's talking to a child while he is doing a puzzle, for instance, is enough to insure that he will stay with the puzzle. If he shifts and she does not, he will, if her attention is reinforcing, return to the puzzle. In some cases this is not true. A child's responses may be reinforced by termination of the mother's attention. In one case when the mother followed instructions and expressed interest to the child, her child hit her, used abusive language, and at other times simply left what he was doing and went to something else. This information was put together with: (a) the fact that in group activities when a teacher had said, "My, you're doing a good job," the same child hit her and went into a tantrum, and (b) the fact that during home observations both the father and mother, while the child was slumped over, tears on his face, refusing to eat, used such sarcasm as, "Well look at that handsome boy we've got. Isn't he fine, mother?" The conclusion was that verbalization from adults, which to most children would be reinforcing, was to this child aversive.

In another case, the mother and father stated that their child knew how to walk for three months before he would walk in their presence. (Friends and relatives informed them that the child walked but would stop whenever his parents entered). They also indicated that if their child vocalized something which sounded like a word, he would not repeat it if either parent expressed an interest. In a separate lab session both parents were instructed (individually) to join their child while he was engaged in an ongoing activity (playing with a toy telephone) and to show interest and respond to him. The child's response in each case was to stop playing, suck his thumb and stare into space. In these cases giving the parents advice, without taking into account that their parental attention was aversive to the child, would have been expected to worsen the situation.

In the majority of cases, parental attention is a strong reinforcer, and the lab session serves to demonstrate to the parents the effects of positive reinforcement for a desired behavior and withholding positive reinforcement for an undesired behavior.

HOME OBSERVATIONS

Although time consuming, home observations provide an invaluable source of information about environmental factors that relate to a child and his behavioral problems. Home observations are based on interview information about what situations seem to be most troublesome for the family in dealing with the problem child. The time before, during, and after dinner frequently is relevant for a wide range of behavioral problems.

To prepare for home observations, parents are told that the staff wants to observe their child in situations which are as natural as possible, with all members of the family behaving toward the child as they normally do.

During a home observation, the observer takes either a running record of exact verbalizations and actions or, in a later visit, a count of certain behaviors. In each case he is recording not impressions and vague descriptions but actual occurrences: verbalizations, movements from room to room, screams, hits, laughs, hugs, directions, requests, statements, etc. and in exact temporal sequence. During the time that he is recording, he in no way interacts with the parents or the child, nor does he conduct any interview during the home observation.

The observer has asked to be completely ignored. If, at first, the child approaches him he may say, "I'm working now," and from then on he makes no response whatever. After a few minutes the child ignores him also. The parents frequently report that "this is just about the way it always is." Two or three different observers return with very similar data from separate visits.

EVALUATION OF DATA, TREATMENT PLAN

The observations provide highly specific information which gives a context in which to view the child's problem. For example, one child who reportedly never did as he was told was observed to have received 35 commands during a 20-minute play session. When the child ignored commands and went on playing, the mother dropped her request and continued playing with him. When the child began following through on a command, the mother turned away from the child. In this way she was actually putting "following commands" on extinction. Another child who yelled frequently was found to be ignored when he spoke in a normal voice and responded to when he yelled. A third child, whose mother complained, "He will not sit still when I read to him," was observed as his mother "read" to him.

The mother gave her child a series of questions about words that were too difficult for him and then severely criticized him for his incorrect answers. When his squirms escalated to jumping in the air and shrieking, he was told, "O.K. I won't read to you anymore." Apparently "reading" had become highly aversive to him and he had learned ways to terminate it.

Children with serious delays with self-help skills were typically confronted with situations in which parents criticized the child as he was attempting to dress or feed himself, and, when the child gave up, the parents dressed or fed the child. One nine-year-old mildly retarded child was spoon-fed by his mother; a four-year-old was not allowed to touch food even at meal time and thus never went through the finger-feeding and spoon-feeding stages.

Speech and language difficulties were similarly analyzed. A child who seldom initiated speech but who echoed was observed at three home sessions. Over half of his utterances were echoed back to him; *e.g.*, when he said, "I want a truck," rather than bringing him a toy, his mother replied, "You want a truck." A four-year-old girl, who in speech evaluations showed no recognizable speech, and who had a pattern of biazarre hand movements, was observed in her home. She was an only child. She had no toys. Both mother and father mimicked her hand movements and smiled when she imitated. In three one-to-two-hour sessions, not one utterance made by either parent to the child was recognizable as a word by either of two observers. Without a series of home observations, the therapists would not have known how strongly the child's environment supported the behavior deficits.

By the time three to four clinic and home observations have been completed, the parents have observed the effect of their attention on the behavior of their child, and have discussed these observations with therapists. It is at this stage, as all the small parts are put together into a whole, that the parents can help choose what problem they want to work on first, to what extent they want to include siblings in the treatment plan, and whether they want to start with clinic sessions or whether they want to start at home.

When the parent decides to work on a certain problem behavior or to try to build in a needed behavior, the first question to be answered must be "What behavior on the part of the parent will we help him change in order to alter a behavior in the child?" Whether or not the parents will withhold attention, contingent on a problem behavior, and give it only contingent on behaviors that are incompatible with the problem behavior, depends on whether we have found the parents' attention to be a reinforcer for this child.

In cases where parental attention is a strong reinforcer, teaching the parent to withhold attention contingent on a problem behavior is only part of the solution. In some cases the mother has found it difficult to give warm, loving attention when the child is doing well. The patterns of response which involve "leaving him alone when he's not getting into trouble," are so strong that it has taken several sessions to teach the mother to respond to the child as he is behaving appropriately. Occasionally a therapist has taken the child into the playroom and worked on shaping a small behavior using social reinforcers, while the mother and another therapist watch and discuss what is going on. As the mother sees the therapist at work, she is encouraged to try different ways of motivating her child. It is as she uses these patterns and as they begin to show results, and only then, that she begins to find the child himself more reinforcing to her, and begins to find more confidence in working on problems and building in new behaviors. It is at this point that the parent can usually begin to see small approximations toward other useful, desirable behaviors to which she could respond in her child.

The situation is more difficult in cases where parental attention is not a reinforcer. For one thing, when parental attention is not reinforcing to a child, the pattern of parent-child interaction will be unusual because many behaviors of the parent will have been extinguished by a lack of response on the part of the child. Play between parent and child will be absent, and the parents will generally interact by punishing a child and attempting to suppress an ongoing behavior. When the child is not actively causing a disturbance, the parents will not intervene. In these cases the parents must first be taught to use potent extrinsic reinforcers and to pair them with a class of verbal and gestural responses on their part that can eventually be used as reinforcers. They must also be taught when to reinforce approximations toward useful behaviors in areas of grooming, dressing, feeding, playing, and talking.

TYPES OF TREATMENT SESSIONS

In beginning treatment, the most successful method has been to give the mother a chance to try out suggestions while in the clinic. She and the child play together in the playroom under observation, and she practices, for example, reading to a child while he is sitting still next to her and not attending to him while he wiggles around or leaves her to go and play with something else in the room. This gives her experience in making her attention contingent on a desired behavior. As soon as she has accomplished a marked change in the child's rate of sitting and listening, she can discuss with staff the methods she used and the ways to use them at home. A following session then might be on a more marked problem behavior such as whining, tantruming when given a direction, or distracting the mother from a task at hand.

Concurrent with clinic sessions, the staff has conducted home treatment sessions. The therapist, having helped the family decide what problem to work on, goes to the home and observes them as they put the changes into effect. These visits are much like the early observations except that now, with definite behavioral contingencies planned, discussions will hinge on the ways in which the parents are succeeding and on elements that deserve further consideration or possible change. . . . The program under discussion here was developed to assist a large number of parents, each dealing with a retarded child.

It is obvious that parents constitute a large portion of a child's social environment and that they have control over a variety of potent reinforcers. Behaviors which are followed either inadvertently or intentionally by one or more of these reinforcers will increase in frequency whether they are adaptive or disruptive. Teaching parents to observe carefully and to respond at times when adaptive behaviors appear in their child's repertoire will increase the child's chances of learning a significant number of skills. Only when a child has been observed interacting with his family can specific help be given. Following the isolation and treatment of one or more specific problems, the parents can begin to apply their skills in other areas of the child's behavior.

As we learn more about the repertoires of parents who have retarded children, though each case still must be treated as an individual instance, some broad patterns may appear. Systematic study of common pitfalls should aid in planning that will help parents avoid these typical problems.

REFERENCES

[Five references not reprinted.]

34 Homemaker Services to Families with Young Retarded Children

Irene L. Arnold
and Lawrence Goodman

In an effort to bring together two social trends which have been slow to meet—the growing concern for the retarded in our population and the increasing recognition of homemaker services in helping families cope with situations of stress—two voluntary agencies in New York City recently carried out a three-year project to demonstrate the potential contribution of homemakers and other home helpers toward preserving families of the retarded. Its results may suggest guidelines for the most effective, economical, and efficient utilization of such services in community plans for the retarded.

Established to examine systematically the effectiveness of homemaker and other home-help services to families with retarded children under five years old, the project was cooperatively conducted by the Retarded Infants Services, Inc. (R.I.S.), and the Association for Homemaker Service, Inc. (A.H.S.), with support from the Federal Children's Bureau. Behind its establishment was the conviction that such services, perhaps with various levels of integration with casework services, have an important place in the chain of services required by families of the retarded at the various times in the retarded person's life.

How parents respond initially to the fact of their child's retardation will determine to a great degree the quality of their lifelong reaction to their child, whether or not he remains with the family. The shock of learning that their child will not develop normally may cause them so much inner turmoil—characterized by ambivalent feelings of guilt, sorrow, and disappointment—that they may want to cut themselves off from the offending object by immediately placing the child in an institution or by withdrawing from him emotionally. New and more lasting problems can be created in such a futile effort to regain a semblance of normality. If the child is to be placed away from home, the effect of an insufficiently considered decision can result in later self-blame and other manifestations of unresolved inner conflict. Providing the parents with help at the crucial period following their confrontation with the fact of their child's retardation must be the first phase of any broad program for the retarded.

In planning to help families at such a time, the first concern, of course, must be with the accessibility of comprehensive medical and psychological evaluation of the child and of whatever treatment may be indicated. At the same time the provision of skilled casework counseling to the parents can mean for many of them the difference between workable solutions and destructive ones. But also of vital importance are the associated services which may be able to relieve parents of the

overwhelming sense of burden sufficiently to permit utilization of other
kinds of help. Here is where homemaker services may play a key role.
Our purpose was to demonstrate how.

PROCEDURES

The project focused on 35 families. All
were drawn from new referrals to
R.I.S.; 24 had been referred from general hospital clinics, 6 from the New
York State Department of Mental Hygiene, 3 from clinics for the retarded,
2 from private physicians. The intake
social worker's determination that the
family needed homemaker service was
the basis for selecting the family for
participation in the project. The only
criteria were that the family have a
mentally retarded child under five
years of age and appear able to benefit
from the presence of a helper in the
home.

Of the 35 families, 9 were referred
to A.H.S. for a conventional homemaker service in which a caseworker
and a homemaker, both on the staff of
the agency, work closely together as a
team; and 20 remained with R.I.S. for
service, which included the help of domestic workers called home aides re-
cruited for the family by the agency
and some limited casework treatment.
A control group of six families received no service but were put on the
waiting list for future service.

A clarification of the two terms,
"homemaker" and "home aide,"
seems pertinent. According to the
standards suggested by the Child Welfare League of America: "The distinc-
tive elements of homemaker service

are (a) placement in the home of a
trained homemaker employed as an
agency staff member, who works together with a caseworker in carrying
out a casework plan to help restore
and strengthen parental functioning,
or otherwise assure that the child has
the care he needs; and (b) use of casework as an integral part of the service." Homemaker service, as thus described, is closely interwoven with
casework.

Home aides, as used by R.I.S., also
are assigned and supervised by caseworkers, but the emphasis is placed on
their ability to do light cleaning and
cooking and their experience in caring
for children, rather than on working
consciously with the caseworker to
help restore parental functioning. The
family may concurrently receive some
casework treatment focused on helping the parents reach the best plan for
the child's care.

Experienced homemakers from the
staff of A.H.S. who were selected for
the project participated with the casework staff in a seven-session orientation program These sessions focused
on the condition of mental retardation; the differences and similarities
between retarded children and normal
children; and the kinds of parental responses they could expect. Most of the
home aides who took part in the project had had previous experience with
R.I.S. Each was carefully prepared by
the caseworker to be aware of the general dynamics of each case situation.
In each case the particular homemakers and home aides assigned to the
families were selected on the basis of
the caseworker's professional judgment.

The two treatment conditions were not set up for the purpose of measuring the efficacy of one service over the other, but rather to seek further understanding of the impact on families of direct assistance in meeting the burdens of the family's daily routines, whether or not this assistance is interwoven with continuing casework treatment. If improvement were possible without the close caseworker-homemaker teamwork, this would seem to suggest that homemaker services for families of the retarded might be offered at different levels of casework involvement, depending on the families' need, capacity, and readiness to use total services.

Instruments created for the study included a "family rating form" for measuring the quality of interaction within the family; and a "decision-making form" for evaluating the character and adequacy of the parent's decision about the retarded child at the close of treatment. At the end of the period of service, all participating families were seen by a social worker in a follow-up interview. In this the interviewer attempted to view objectively the carry-over effect of the treatment received.

FINDINGS

Both the data secured from testing the case material with the measuring instruments and the data from the clinical follow-up showed improved functioning in the families served by either homemakers or home aides, in contrast to the families which received no service. The family rating forms indi-cated that, in contrast to the control group, families served by A.H.S. made important gains in their intrafamily relations as did families served by R.I.S., though there were some subtle differences between the two groups in the types of changes which occurred. For example, the A.H.S. group showed a greater increase in friendliness among family members than the R.I.S. group, but the R.I.S. group showed greater development in rationality of conduct. The decision-making forms indicated that families in both serviced groups rated much higher than those in the nontreatment control group in the quality of plans made for the retarded child. Little difference existed between the A.H.S. and R.I.S. groups.

Similarly, the clinical follow-up of cases indicated a high degree of sustained gain in families which had received service, regardless of which agency had served them. Some parents who had become involved in relatively intensive casework were able to face openly some of their basic conflicts about their child. However, even families in which the parents regarded the casework they had received as superfluous, but who had a high regard for the help they had received from the homemaker or home aide, improved in intrafamily interaction. Also, the families who had had only occasional encounters with a caseworker focused on specific problems showed sustained improvement.

Thus the findings suggest that, in families confronted with the reality of retardation, help from a homemaker or home aide, selected and supported by a casework agency, can in itself be salutary. The following two cases illustrate how this may be so at different levels of casework involvement.

The A Family

Mr. and Mrs. A were referred to R.I.S. by a diagnostic clinic. At the time of referral, their retarded child Amy was four years of age. Her brother James, age nine, had normal intelligence. Mr. A was unemployed because of a strike. Mrs. A said she was at the breaking point because Amy was completely unmanageable, could not be left alone at any time, and had proved to be a tremendous burden to James, who was charged with some of her care.

Both parents seemed immature, demanding, and manipulative. A severe marital problem had developed out of conflict around Amy. The mother was particularly anxious, describing herself as confused, forgetful, and fearful of harming Amy. Mr. A and his parents were pressing her to send Amy to an institution; Mrs. A was not yet ready to do so.

R.I.S. referred the case to A.H.S., which sent a homemaker into the home. She was trained not only to assist the mother in carrying the burden of household management and child care, but also to observe changes in behavior and attitudes. Part of her role was to help find out whether or not Amy was educable.

Under the regular supervision of the A.H.S. caseworker, the homemaker assumed a nurturing, maternal role with both the children and the parents, but she was careful not to encourage lingering dependency. Amy responded well to her special attention and soon began to show remarkable improvement. Mrs. A apparently had been too tense to handle her in a way that could bring out her potentials.

James, too, showed improvement. He had not only been relieved of Amy's care, but was also getting more attention from his parents. Soon he seemed less withdrawn and behaved in a more forthright and appropriately aggressive manner.

Mrs. A seemed more relaxed, since for the first time in years she had some time for her own needs. The tension between the parents also relaxed a little, and both seemed to have less need to reject Amy.

The A.H.S. caseworker kept in regular touch with the staff of the referring diagnostic clinic who soon reported that the homemaker services had helped clarify the condition of the child and the dynamics of the family situation. It was then agreed that the A.H.S. caseworker would take over the family counseling role from the clinic and would attempt to bring about better relations between the parents by helping them both to a better understanding of the needs of their retarded child, of their normal child, and of each other. As a result, it became possible to enter Amy into a special day class for the retarded instead of into an institution.

This case exemplifies homemaker service in its complete sense. The steadying influence of the homemaker, working in close partnership with the caseworker, expanded the understanding on which a diagnosis could be made, thus making possible more appropriate recommendations for the child's management and care.

As is common with organically damaged children, Amy had responded negatively and with hyperactivity to the anxiety-ridden, erratic handling she had been getting from her parents, and thus her true functioning ability had been obscured. The consistent, well-planned approach of the homemaker helped the child function less destructively and on a higher intellectual level. The resulting decrease of tension in the home increased the parents' ability to make use of casework help. Thus, an institutionalization, likely to be harmful to both the child and the parents, was avoided.

The M Family

The following case illustrates the provision of home help chiefly to relieve harried parents while they are mobilizing themselves to adjust to a severe emotional blow.

Mr. and Mrs. M were first known to R.I.S. in 1962 after they learned that their two-year-old daughter Ruth was severely brain damaged and hopelessly retarded. With the assistance of the agency the child had been placed in an institution. Recently the tragedy was re-enacted. R.I.S. received a call from Mr. M, who was crying hysterically. His wife was in a hos-

pital having an operation and he had just been informed by the family's pediatrician that his seven-month-old son John was also severely retarded. Mr. M seemed to be at the breaking point.

The R.I.S. social caseworker made a home visit the next morning and immediately arranged for a home aide to go into the home to assist Mr. M in the care of both the retarded baby and the family's five-year-old normal child. Within a few days, Mr. M had recovered sufficiently to go back to work.

After Mrs. M returned from the hospital, the home aide, a person of much warmth and sensitivity, remained in the home to help out while Mrs. M recovered from her physical weakness as well as from the emotional shock of the baby's retardation. At the same time, the social worker and the family pediatrician worked closely together to help both parents accept the diagnosis and again prepare for placing a child in an institution. Mrs. M also received help from the social worker in explaining the baby's condition to the five-year-old.

Throughout our analysis of the project cases, the effectiveness of the help given by the homemakers appeared most clearly when, as in this case, it was extended to families in the early stages of their response to a crisis. By providing instant help with the burdens of daily existence, the home helper often made it possible for parents to begin to regain enough psychic balance to be able to use casework counseling and help with planning for their child's future.

SOME CONCLUSIONS

The nature of parents' early reaction to their child's retardation—often with the need to deny reality and to isolate all feeling—can block parents from entering into a therapeutic relationship with a social caseworker, as well as from being able to encourage their child's progress or create the kind of emotional atmosphere that can stimulate development. While not all parents respond to a crisis in the same way or experience trauma with the same intensity or duration, many do remain fixed in a state of emotional turmoil for long periods of time. Suppressed anger toward the retarded child, and toward fate in general, becomes internalized and thrust upon the self.

When such psychic turmoil is taking place, the introduction of a homemaker or home aide, who offers warmth and support and provides direct evidence of the community's desire to share their misfortune, can cut through some of the sense of hopelessness. Freed sufficiently to deal with the needs of other family members and to resume activity outside the home, the parents may then be able to perceive the retarded child with sufficient objectivity to consider alternatives in planning and to participate in the kind of continuing casework treatment that can build up the strength in the family. Thus the dynamic potentials of homemaker services go far beyond the practical assistance offered.

We found in the project that most families were enabled to maintain the child at home until a reasoned, reality-based decision about his future had been made. But even when parents proceeded with inadequate planning, the home helper's assumption of many of the responsibilities of the retarded child's care tended to mitigate their guilt and anxiety regarding their child.

Because existing homemaker agencies can obviously play a major role in helping retarded children and their families to a better life, community plans for comprehensive care for the retarded should incorporate such agencies into the overall design and goals of their programming. Ideally, these agencies should be able to provide home help flexibly, according to the varying needs of families of the retarded. Some families can benefit by home help which is not so closely interwoven with casework treatment as is required to help other families. Where such flexibility is not possible, home aide services might appropriately be offered by specialized agencies for the retarded.

While the project described here focused on the needs of families with young children, homemaker service should not be regarded solely as an emergency resource. Actually it is badly needed by many families on a long-range basis. The demands of a severely or moderately retarded child can be so consuming that at least part-time help may be needed as long as the child remains in the home.

The complex needs of retarded children and their families require bold new planning that includes the creative use and adaptation of existing approaches to families in trouble. Agencies which specialize in service to the retarded must provide the direction that will encourage others to open up a variety of previously unobtainable services to families of the retarded.

35 A State Program of Day Care Centers for Severely Retarded

Charles P. Jubenville

A state-wide, state-supported program of community centers for daytime care and training of severely retarded persons was inaugurated in Delaware in 1958 and is, so far as we know, the first of its kind. It was promulgated to meet the needs of a specific group of mentally handicapped people at no cost to their families.

EVOLUTION OF PROGRAM

Several years prior to the establishment of the Day Care Center program, two groups of parents of mentally handicapped children had been operating day classes for their children. These two associations had taxed themselves and had raised monies in various ways to conduct these facilities for children not acceptable in public schools. Their resolute efforts were recognized by the legislature in the summer of 1957 when it concerned itself, among other interests, with mental retardation. Two bills were introduced and passed. One bill provided that classes for "trainables" could be established in public schools. Only classes for "educables" had existed through prior legislation.

The companion bill authorized the State Board of Trustees of the Delaware State Hospital at Farnhurst to establish and operate centers for the daytime care of severely mentally retarded persons at appropriate locations within the state and provide transportation to and from such centers. Severely mentally retarded persons were defined as those of any age deemed to be neither educable nor trainable in the public schools. In addition, the law appropriated monies for the next biennium for the organization and operation of the centers. It did not specify any chronological age restrictions whatever in contrast to the age limitations set at four and 21 years for public schools.

BASIC PHILOSOPHY

A dual philosophy was evolved by the authorities responsible for initiating, operating, and expanding the program. It is both child-centered and parent-centered. It follows the recommendations ... that a program should provide the greatest possible help to the child and also give to the parents the comfort so needed by them.

For the child, it is believed that he can be helped to reach his highest potential of functioning through a program designed to meet his special needs and one which will help him become a more self-efficient and effective functioning individual. ... the problem is to devise the most effective means of meeting the individual pupil's stage of development, conditions, needs, and potentialities so that he may realize maximum development and adjustment. The child's worth as an individual, his human rights and dignity are recognized.

It is believed that parents of severely retarded children should have assistance similar to that given parents of other types of retarded children. This point of view has been said to be inherent in the philosophy of democracy in that all children are, according to the limit of their capacities, entitled to education. . . .

The program helps parents several hours of the day, especially mothers who often face a tremendous burden of caring for such a person. Help and relief offered by the program contribute often to better mental health of the family as a whole and to its individual components. . . . Parental guidance and counseling are integral parts of this program. Through the program, opportunities are provided the family to re-evaluate the impact of the retarded person on its structure, especially upon the growth and development of normal siblings. Families are assisted in these re-evaluations and in planning for subsequent changes in home management of the retarded individual.

It is known that most mentally retarded persons begin and live out their lives in the community and that their care presents many and often grave problems. Many families do not want to institutionalize their severely retarded children. Delaware's program believes in keeping such children in communities and offers assistance which enables families to avoid institutionalization.

OPERATIONAL STAFF

Personnel needed for the organization and administration of the program are classified in two categories—central and field staffs. The central staff is comprised of the supervisor, two registered nurses, one of whom is a half-time worker, and a secretary. Duties of the supervisor include locating individuals to be served by the program, arranging for screening procedures for admission, locating suitable community facilities as needed, scheduling parent conferences and counseling, promoting public relations, and, generally, organizing and supervising community centers.

Field staff or community center staff members are designated as "training aides." This title was chosen to differentiate them from teachers in public schools and attendants in institutions for retarded. Qualifications for this position include high school graduation or equivalence, emotional stability, and social adequacy. Experience with children is desired, although not necessarily with retarded children. Applicants are screened through pre-employment interviews, medical and psychological examinations, and careful checking of references.

Upon acceptance, these women are given an intensive training course of four to six weeks at the Hospital for the Mentally Retarded at Stockley. They work an eight-hour day, forty-hour week, in the wards with individuals similar to those with whom they will be dealing in a community situation. They are supervised in the wards by the day care center nurse and the hospital nursing staff during this period.

Approximately two hours of each working day are devoted to lectures in the various disciplines allied with the field of mental retardation. Included are such subjects as nursing care, psychology, training and habit formation, recreation, and dietetics. A training manual is provided each trainee. At the close of the training period, the trainee must pass a final examination on the lecture work as well as having maintained satisfactory ward performance. Then, the training aide is assigned to a community center to work with a maximum of six children in her group.

Day Care Center staff currently [May 1961] totals 20 persons. Included are the supervisor, two nurses, a secretary, 13 training aides, and three bus drivers on part-time. Drivers, incidentally, must meet State Board of Education requirements for public school bus drivers.

ADMISSION POLICIES

An open intake policy on referral for admission is maintained since referrals are accepted from all sources. The greatest number is made by school and private consulting psychologists. Other referrals, in descending order of numbers, are made by parents and relatives, Delaware Association for Retarded Children, school officials, day care center personnel, and State Board of Health personnel.

As soon as possible after a referral has been received, the supervisor contacts the family and makes an appointment for a conference in his office or preferably in the home. The program is explained to the family and the necessary admission procedures are outlined. Usually, the nurse of the county of residence is present during the conference. If the family is interested, an appointment is made for the nurse to make a home visit at a later date to obtain signatures on the application blank, authorization for publicity, and to obtain the social history. Following this, all medical sources as listed by the family are contacted for pertinent information. When all such data are completed, an appointment is then made with the County Mental Hygiene Clinic for psychological and psychiatric including neurological evaluations. A final decision is made upon the basis of all data to accept or reject for admission to the program. The family is notified in either case. If the child is accepted, parents are notified of the date of admission to a center and the time of morning pick-up by the bus at the child's home.

Admission criteria are few. Generally, the individual must be evaluated psychologically as I.Q. 35 or below. He must be ambulatory except for C.P. cases needing wheel chairs or relaxing chairs. He need not be toilet trained. Social maturation and adequacy as well as self-help and self-care levels are considered and those who do not meet the standards in these areas for public school trainable classes are accepted in the day care center program as severely retarded or "dependent" children.

When a person has been accepted for admission, a case conference is held before the child is admitted to a community center. The supervisor, the nurse, and the training aide meet to discuss the pertinent information. The aide is informed of the diagnosis and prognosis and the particular problems the child presents. She is given the objectives of a care and training program for the child which have been drawn up by the supervisor with the assistance of the nurse. Objectives of two kinds are discussed—short range and long range. It may be that toilet training, or socialization, or self-feeding is urgent as a first and short range objective and that other problems presented may be secondary or long range objectives. In any event, suggestions are offered the training aide for management of the child in individual and small group situations.

COMMUNITY CENTER

A center is located in a community where generally there are six or more retarded persons within a reasonable commuting radius. This radius has been determined to be between 12 to 15 miles. Criteria for selection are important. Center facilities are rented with heat, light, and janitorial services provided. They must have adequate operating space for the daily program. Toilet facilities and cooking facilities must be immediately adjacent to the main room. Also, the quarters must be close to the ground with few steps to the main floor because many severely retarded also have crippling physical conditions.

All equipment is program-furnished. Each child has a stacking desk and chair of the proper size. Numerous educational and recreational toys, puzzles, games, and supplies are furnished. A record player and well-chosen sets of records are furnished for each unit. Storage cabinets, sand tables, easels, and other equipment are also furnished. Complete kitchen equipment and unbreakable plastic dishes, cups, and glasses are purchased in the amounts needed for a one-unit or more center. The rental facility furnishes the stove, refrigerator, and sink.

Before a center is opened, arrangements are made with local merchants for deliveries (daily, if necessary) of milk and perishable food items. Laundry pick-up and delivery also are arranged for the sheets which are placed on the kindergarten cots at rest periods, bibs, towels, and wash cloths. Diapers or soiled clothing are sent home daily in bags or cases provided by the parents who do the personal laundry. A telephone is installed and maintained by the program for emergency calls and for ordering of daily food supplies. Much of the food supply is purchased wholesale by the program and delivered periodically to the various centers. Where feasible, outdoor playground equipment is program purchased and installed, with permission, close to an entrance to the center.

Transportation of the children is accomplished through program owned vehicles, leased vehicles, and contract transportation. In two areas, the program owns and operates a total of three buses. These are small and are officially listed as sixteen-child passenger buses. In one of these areas, a leased nine-passenger station wagon also is used. For three areas, contract transportation is more economical. Contracts are made with private individuals who are interested in a part-time job using their cars or station wagons to transport the children. This is done on a daily mileage basis and each owner carries ample insurance. Training aides also ride in the vehicles for safety reasons.

OPERATING CENTERS

Currently, there are five community centers of various sizes operating a daily program in the state. The first center was opened in January 1958 in the southern part. It opened in an American Legion Post building with eight children and two training aides and since has reached its full quota of 12 children. This center was the first two-unit center—a unit being comprised of six children in charge of one training aide.

Three other centers opened within the next six months. A one-unit center was opened in the central part of the state and subsequently became a two-unit center. The third center opened as a four-unit facility in Wilmington (in northern Delaware) and since has become a seven-unit center. Fourth to open was another one-unit center, a church in the southwestern part of the state. A year later, in the summer of 1959, a one-unit center was opened in one of the buildings of the Hospital for the Mentally Retarded in the middle of the southern county.

In 36 months, the program has grown from one two-unit facility to include 5 locations with 13 units and 77 children enrolled. Centers operate on a school week basis, Monday through Friday, five and one-half hours a day for eleven and one-half months per year. Further growth is indicated with 22 referrals pending. Two more community centers are planned as well as expansion of one center by two more units.

DAILY PROGRAM

In all of the centers the same general type of program is in operation. It is, in many ways, similar to that which operates in trainable classes in public schools except that it is slower moving and geared to a lower level of individual functioning. The daily program is a highly structured one with fairly rigid schedules. Structuring is necessary for achieving habit formation. Consistency and persistency are necessary to promote proper self-care habits and to reinforce those in the process of being formed.

Children arrive by bus or auto about 9:30 a.m. and begin a daily program of alternating individual and small group activities. Activities also alternate between physically active and sedentary types. Upon arrival, children participate in a short and simply opening exercise, begin the daily program and follow the prescribed routines until dismissal time. Buses leave the centers between 3:00 p.m. and 3:30 p.m. depending upon the centers and distances involved to the home.

Included in the day's schedule are

a mid-morning snack, usually of juice and crackers, a hot lunch at noon which is followed by a rest period on kindergarten cots, and a mid-afternoon snack similar to the morning one. Noon meals follow a basic weekly menu drawn up by a dietitian to assure a well-balanced diet and eye-appeal for the children. Volunteers often prepare and bring the lunches on trays to the rooms in order to give training aides more time for teaching children proper self-feeding skills and habits.

Excellent relations with state and private agencies have been developed and maintained. Children from the Hospital for the Mentally Retarded have been placed on trial visits in homes in communities where day care centers are located and could admit the children. Institutionalization, when necessary, was readily effected by a transfer from the center to the Hospital.

Programs of help given children by other state agencies are continued for the child after admission to a day care center. Several C.P. children receiving physical therapy through services of the State Board of Health have continued to receive therapy in the day care center by this agency. In several instances, the therapist instructed the training aides in techniques to be used between his visits to the child.

Volunteer and private agencies have offered cooperation and assistance. Services important to the functioning of the center have been rendered and items not available through budgeted funds have been donated. In two centers, parents have organized themselves into P.T.A. type groups for services to the program.

One of the general hospitals in Wilmington sends its student nurses while taking the pediatric training block to the center. Students usually spend two days observing the seven units in operation, discussing their observations with training aides and the nurse, and reading records and related literature. Our center staff cooperates very willingly in this affiliation.

POPULATION CHARACTERISTICS

Since the beginning of the program, 196 referrals have been made; 94 children were accepted into the program and 15 others were acceptable but the parents rejected the program for various reasons. The program itself rejected 68 children as being above the limits set by law, except for two out-of-state residents. These individuals were referred to the proper source for help.

Chronologically, the current population ranges from 4 years and 2 months to 21 years with a median of 9 years. Mental ages range from 3 months to 5 years and 6 months with a median of 2 years. I.Q.'s ranged from 10 to 35, with the exception of two special cases, with a median of 25. Twelve children were untestable by any psychometric technique but were classified as dependent upon the bases of competent clinical observations and social-developmental histories.

Of the 94 children admitted to the program, only 38 were diagnosed as merely severely retarded and were approximately equally divided between the sexes. The others were diagnosed as follows: 16 were mongoloids; 10

were brain-damaged hyperactive; 12 were seizure cases; seven were C.P. cases; five were blind; four were emotionally disturbed; and twin girls were afflicted with phenylketonuria. There was a slight preponderance of males noted among these diagnoses.

Problems presented by these children upon admission were classified in three main categories: behavior, habit, and physical problems. Sixteen types of behavior problems were listed. For example, some were listed as aggressive, destructive, fearful, negativistic, antisocial, and temper tantrums. Habit problems were those represented by the need for establishing proper self-help and self-care habits such as feeding, dressing, toileting, as well as need for socialization. Physical conditions were represented by a number of items such as poor balance or coordination, seizures, speech and hearing difficulties, hyperactivity, and difficulties in vision. In the speech area, 49 had no speech, 11 were defective in speech, 23 showed limited speech, and 11 demonstrated good speech. Many had not acquired any form of nonverbal communication. In all, there were 34 kinds of problems listed. Attempts were made to correct these conditions in the daily program of care and training in the centers with, we believe, a large measure of success.

ACHIEVEMENTS

Results of the program were evaluated at the end of the period under discussion by means of the case conference method. The supervisor, the nurse, and the training aide involved reviewed all data from the time of the child's admission. Data included the monthly narrative progress reports written by the aides, special reports and progress noted by the nurse or supervisor, and all other known and observed facts. These were evaluated and contrasted with the diagnosis and list of problems presented upon admission to determine the child's level of achievement and rate of development. Four adjectives were used to describe individual progress—"poor," "fair," "good," and "excellent."

Completed evaluations discovered that 12 children rated as "poor"—seven males to five females; 18 were rated as "fair" with sexes evenly divided; 53 rated as "good"—31 males and 22 females; and 11 as "excellent"—seven males to four females. Similar evaluations had been accomplished twice before at approximately 12-month periods, and for those children who had been rated once or twice previously, ratings remained the same except for one child who dropped one level.

Some specific illustrations of progress follow. Of 53 incontinent children, 22 have become completely toilet trained and 17 partially trained. Seven children who were drinking only from a bottle now drink from a glass unassisted. Forty-five were unable to feed themselves; now 27 are competent self-feeders and 9 are partially so. Eleven of the 13 who would not tolerate solid foods now eat everything. Twenty-three children were admitted who displayed severe temper tantrums but, with training, 19 no longer display this trait and 4 do only occasionally. Of 16 negativistic children, 12 demonstrate a willingness to cooperate within their groups. Forty-five of the 58 unsocialized children no longer show this problem in their behavior. With many of the other problems, success has been met in various degrees. Many problems, of course, have not been eliminated yet.

OPERATIONAL COSTS

The costs of operating the program include salaries of personnel, rental of community facilities, transportation, food, education and recreational equipment and supplies, laundry, telephone, and office operational costs. Currently, with all costs included, the per capita cost amounts to slightly more than $1,000 yearly. This amount is considerably less than the yearly per capita cost of maintaining an individual in the state residential custodial institution for the mentally retarded.

Financial costs do not show the benefits of the program given children and their parents. Parents have written notes and letters voluntarily on many occasions and have made verbal statements to the staff indicating their feelings towards the day care center program. Generally, these statements reflect the gratitude parents feel for the assistance given them and their children by the daily program, by parent-staff meetings, and by conferences. In the words of one mother, "Last year Charles was intolerable but now he is livable. If the center should close, I shall now know how and be able to handle him. . . ."

REFERENCES

[Five references not reprinted.]

36 The Family of the Child in an Institution

Laura L. Dittmann

Little attention has been given to the factors which may make it difficult for parents to maintain or develop meaningful ties with their retarded child who is in an institution. By contrast, considerable study has been made of the impact on the family when a retarded child lives at home ... Meanwhile the primary role of the family is being emphasized currently in all manner of research, and is reasserted daily in publications which range from the most to the least technical. Surely, out of the renewed allegiance to the family as a vital force in determining the child's sense of identity—of who he is and where he comes from—there must be a growing dilemma for parents who have severed this tie.

Persons who work with children agree that the family is so vitally important that any substitute for the child's own home must be viewed cautiously. When circumstances make it necessary to take a child out of his own home, it is accepted as a second-best arrangement. Whenever a child is placed in an institution, it usually means, therefore, that an overwhelming reason to place the child away from home has confronted his family. The implications of this decision—to the parents, to others in the family, and to the child himself—are profound. The assumption is usually made that the family will continue to think of itself as the continuing and primary

touchstone for the child, yet this does not occur automatically. The purpose of this paper is to explore, in an impressionistic way, some of the inhibiting factors which seem to be present on both sides, within the family and within the institution itself.

Parents usually make the decision to place a child in a residential institution with mixed feelings. Reluctance is present, that is, if it is a decision at all, rather than compliance with advice given by a physician or someone else. Placement may be undertaken shortly after the birth of a child when the parents are in a state of numbness and ignorance about the true nature of the child's condition. If the baby is placed at that time, most parents have to arrive at the decision, independently, at a later time. Many, who do, feel they would have acted differently had they been helped to consider all the factors. Those who are never able to review their actions, after hastily placing a child in the first days or weeks of his life, probably are never able to develop true parental feelings about that child at all.

Before a conclusion is reached, even post hoc, the parents argue it pro and con, individually and together. Frequently the question is explored at length with a physician, pastor, or social worker. Generally, relatives become involved in the discussion. Grandparents who have a "hands off" attitude about the other children, or other matters pertaining to the family, almost always become actively involved. The extended family—kin on both sides—recognize placement as such a fundamental decision they feel entitled to put in their "two cents" worth. Usually, they regard their contribution as worth a lot more.

Finally, somehow, the decision is made. The course is set, application papers are filled out. Then the waiting period begins. During this interval, the question may remain unresolved in the minds of the parents. One day the child seems more manageable and the parents wonder if they should withdraw the application. Possibly, the child reflects the let-up of pressures and expectations as the family realizes that the trouble can end. Everyone relaxes a little with the prospect of relief, however distant.

As time goes by, however, and the wait for a court hearing or an empty bed is extended, all interest becomes focused on *when,* no longer *if.* And when the day for admission finally arrives, all energies become caught up in the physical details of arranging for the move. In the weeks following the departure of the child, there comes a letdown, a period of release and relief alternated with nagging doubts about the necessity of placing the child after all. "We could have managed, somehow. I must have been exaggerating the problem." Round and round; back and forth. When this ambivalence exists, and persists, it is difficult for the parent to behave consistently and spontaneously toward others, toward the child, toward his brothers and sisters still at home, and toward the staff of the training school.

This basic story is affirmed by most parents who have placed a child. Almost without exception, there is a note of apology in their voices when they reveal that their son or daughter is away at a school or home. There is a hesitancy lest they be judged, and found wanting in faith or patience.

One would expect that parents who have placed a child would be able to get support for their decision from other parents of retarded children. Yet within local organized groups of parents this ambivalence can be observed. Most of the meetings are concerned with interpreting the needs of retarded children to the public and to the development of community programs for the retarded. Of course, parent groups are dedicated to improving care for the retarded wherever they are, but this refinement may be lost, at times anyhow, as the members see and work with parents who have kept their child at home. The parent whose child is away must realize that the day school, camps and workshops which the organization is working toward won't profit his child at all.

Even if things go well in the absence of the child, an illogical, but nonetheless real, doubt may be felt which might be something like "We shouldn't have it so good. We don't deserve this relief." Before the placement, the tune went "We don't deserve to have him at home, he might spoil chances for the other children." A double-bind of this type, when either course selected brings misgivings, is not an enviable position to be in.

Things may not go well at home, however. Other problems, submerged by the demands which the presence of the retarded child placed on the emotional reserves of the members of the family, are revealed glaringly when the shield is removed. Once hidden or shadowed, these problems may be disclosed with clarity. The other children may quarrel still; the older daughter, whose lack of popularity was blamed on the retarded child, may still be unpopular and need sympathetic help in learning how to get along with others. The relationship between the parents, tried by the retarded child, still isn't good, and recriminations and resentments continue. New questions confront everyone.

The brothers and sisters of the child who is placed may have doubts. If young, they may secretly wonder if they, too, will be sent away from home if they misbehave. They may wonder if they contributed to the decision by complaining about their retarded sibling, by flareups of hate, by not helping enough. Students of child development recognize that children frequently feel to blame when events around them go wrong, and reproach themselves silently, although the casual adult observer may feel them to be blissfully carefree.

When these ambivalences, misconceptions, and conflicts are present, they are bound to influence behavior. Such feelings may make it hard for the parents and children to visit the training school. A parent might make promises, which he would be unable to keep or would forget to keep. He might make promises which he knows he couldn't keep, and blame the rules of the institution, the staff, the physician, or social worker, for his own failure to follow through.

It might happen that no one would remember the child's bad points—how destructive he was, how hard to feed, how difficult the sleepless nights. The family may idealize him. No one would dare to speak of his shortcomings. The tendency to eulogize the absent one is not confined to retarded children, of course. The absent parent, when there is divorce, may become the ideal loving, Santa Claus type of parent in the mind of the child. The tyrannical, irascible, selfish old lady, once she dies, may, in the minds of her relieved children, be transformed into a loving, dear little grandmother.

It might work in another way. The parents would not dare to speak up about the defects and inadequacies of the institution, let alone critically examine the place, lest in some way the child's situation there be affected adversely or the staff would retaliate or neglect the child. Parents might not dare to become thoroughly acquainted with the institution, lest they find it so clearly undesirable that they would have to face the fact that placement there was unsuitable. Parents could not admit its weaknesses to themselves.

The foregoing statements relate primarily to the attitude of parents toward placement. Today another factor is often present. Current emphasis on the role of the institution as a training center, not a terminal placement, has complicated the picture, rather than simplified it for parents. Placing a child in an institution is no longer considered a lifetime decision. In the last decade, recognition that retarded children do grow and can be taught ("can be helped" in the words of the National Association for Retarded Children) has become axiomatic. This implies that the needs of the retarded, like those of all other children, are not fixed and static. As they change over the years, new demands on both the family and the institution emerge. At one time in a child's life, one thing is needed. At another, an entirely different plan is indicated. For the first few years, family life may be desirable; at a later time, schooling available only in the institution may be needed, after which the young adult will return home.

The family, therefore, has to be ready to let the child go, and at the same time, be willing to assume a receiving posture again. Unlike the severing of dependent ties through normal adolescence, these parents may have to take the young adult back again. The normal young adult son or daughter may return to his parents in a new role, as friend and more-or-less equal; the retarded may return in the role of a dependent child still needing them to guide and protect.

We have said that placement in an institution, as a way of answering lifetime problems, has changed for many retarded children today. There will continue to be those so severely damaged that they will need hospital or custodial care all their lives. But for many others, the institution itself must change to become a dynamic place, with a program which can grow as the resident changes and grows. If

this is to come about, the institution must develop a different relationship with the community. The institution no longer can attempt to answer everything, since certain necessary services may be available on a more skilled or efficient basis outside its gates. Instead of attempting to reproduce within the plant all of the varied services a child may need throughout his life, the institution, too, will have to reach out. Perhaps better diagnostic facilities can be obtained outside; speech clinics, vocational opportunities, recreation may be sought. Possibly the community will turn to the institution for some services on an out-patient basis.

These factors influence the thinking of the family, and pose new problems for the staff of the institution as well. We must recognize their existence before we can answer such questions as: What can parents do for the child in an institution? What do parents expect from the institution? What does the institution expect from them?

Parents and institution staff profess that they want a closer relationship. Parents, daring now for the first time to assume that they have rights—and duties—and that their children have rights, want to know the truth about the institution—its problems, its strong points, its "skeletons," its triumphs. The parents want to know the reasons behind its policies and procedures. Some are traditions, hoary with age. These need review in the light of modern practices and philosophy. Some are for the convenience of staff, not necessarily for the good of child or parent. Some suit one kind of child and not another.

The policy regulating visiting may be one area where tradition has interfered with, not cemented, closer relationships. It may be appropriate to compare institution practices with those of hospitals which plan for young patients with acute or chronic illness.

Formerly hospitals found visits upsetting to their routines, and pointed out that they upset the child as well. So visiting hours were infrequent, and brief. Now hospital staffs no longer regard parents as a necessary evil, but recognize that the presence of the mother, and father, may determine to a large degree the value of the treatment being administered. A child's sense of continued closeness to his family is regarded as good medicine.

A great deal of thoughtful attention has been given to the meaning of hospitalization to a young child. Robertson (1959) took movies of a two-year-old in the hospital, which show the process by which a child, initially resistant and negative, refusing the attention of nurses and staff, finally, "settles in" and becomes docile and manageable. The child stops crying and accepts the attentions of the staff. Everyone felt this to be a desirable state of affairs. In fact, hospital staffs pointed out that when the child's parents came to visit, the patient might pull away or withdraw from them, or act as if they weren't there. This behavior had successfully fooled everybody, and was used by the staff for their own convenience to keep parents out from underfoot. Nurses observed that when the parents left, the child was upset all over again, and at first glance it seemed to everybody, parents as well, that it might have been better if they hadn't come.

A closer look revealed that the child's docile and withdrawn behavior wasn't a good sign at all. If it continued for any length of time, without the frequent and regular appearance of the parents, the child could be seriously damaged by the deprivation. This could result in profound personality changes which would mean that the child would make but superficial contacts with others, not daring to invest himself closely in another, that is, to love. His good behavior in the absence of his parents might be partly to prove that he is good enough to go home, and partly to hide from himself how desperate he feels. He would protect himself from further painful departures by appearing not to care. Frequent, regular visits not only assure him that he still has a mother and a father, but help him release his anxious feelings which otherwise can remain frozen within him too long, causing real disturbance. Continued reassurance from his parents gives the child a knowledge of who he is, the will to grow and live.

In the light of such studies, institutions might well review their visiting policies. Most restrict visiting hours stringently. Many forbid visits at all for the first six weeks or more, until the child "settles in" and becomes, in some instances, potentially unreachable.

Absurdly little thought has been given to the importance of preparing a child for his new residence. For a long time, we have been convinced that children profit from an explanation of what is going to happen to them. Even if they are too immature to understand the real meaning of what they are told, any effort to prepare a child for a major change pays off, whether it be the coming of a new baby, the need for him to have his tonsils out, the departure of mother to go to work, or any other forthcoming crisis.

Preparation of a retarded child would rarely be accomplished by talking about the school. Doubtless institution staffs and parents could come up with simple and creative suggestions—more often than not, of things they wish they had done. One easily accomplished step could be that of asking the child's assistance in packing a suitcase, with pointed omissions of possessions, too. In this way the child might know that some of his belongings were being kept at home for his return. It would seem that if parents were able to attempt any kind of advance preparation for their child, or through counseling were helped to find words and ways to use, they would be in a better position to help other children in the family understand what was involved also.

The behavior of children who leave the institution to come home for a visit is frequently puzzling to parents. Again, a parallel might be found in the behavior of children who return home from a long hospital stay. When the sick child is dismissed and returns home, everyone expects a brief letdown. Fond parents are indulgent for a few hours or a day, but then they expect things to right themselves rather quickly. Interviews reveal that events seldom warrant this expectation, however. The child often lets down completely, after his bravery

through the separation, and may become extremely difficult to handle. He may wish to be fed, start to wet himself again, be wildly upset when his mother leaves the room, or appear to be angry at his parents for what has happened to him (what they've done to him). He may throw temper tantrums or become destructive. It requires extreme patience to deal with a child who shows these effects of a hospital stay and it is very important to see him through this trying period by giving him what he shows he needs—loving reassurance.

It is often not easy for parents to see that loving reassurance is not the same as licensed indulgence. They frequently need understanding help to see that when they stop teasing or naughty behavior, they assure him in a concrete way that he is important to them. They demonstrate that they care enough to stop him and expect him to assume responsibility for his behavior in keeping with his abilities and age.

Frequently a retarded child, home for a visit, tests out his parents with behavior which is demanding and requires the greatest ingenuity to handle. It is difficult to keep the retarded child in line, and at the same time give him reassurance that he belongs and is valued for himself alone, especially when the visit is apt to be a short one. Their uncertainty about what it is reasonable to expect is compounded by the fact that parents frequently have a poor day-to-day notion of the capabilities of a child who has been separated from them for a considerable length of time. It would be easy, after a few disheartening experiences, to decide it wasn't worth it to bring the child home at all, yet such a decision would add to the child's deprivation in a real way. The institution could assist parents by devoting time to preparing and interpreting to them the behavior they might be likely to experience.

The mother of a retarded adolescent mongoloid boy described graphically her growth in ability to handle both her boy, and her own feelings, on visits home. At first, she felt she must assure him of her love by permitting him to raid the icebox at all times. As a result, the effort to help him lose weight at the institution was sabotaged. Even more troubling to her was her son's refusal to return to the training school. When she began to limit him to three meals a day, plus occasional special treats as they traveled about the city, she found the boy less reluctant to return to school when his holiday ended. She was proud of herself, too, as she was able to see how her wish to indulge the boy had been more a reflection of her own needs than his.

Visits are but one way of keeping in close touch. Most institutions have a desperate shortage of help, and can use volunteers, either parents or other friends, in creative and stimulating ways. This requires that a parent be willing to give of him or herself to other children, and represents a stage of maturity which many parents can be helped to reach if they have been made to feel, all along, as adequate—not inadequate—to the job of parenthood.

If contact is to be on a close basis, a lot of things must be faced honestly.

It's relatively easy to put something away and hide all the unresolved doubts and feelings along with the hidden package. If you are going to get the package out frequently, figuratively speaking, ambivalences, rivalries, and doubts must be faced.

The condition of the child must be talked over honestly, and continuously, with the other children in the family who will know of visits, and may be included themselves from time to time. As the placement is faced, and brought to the surface again and again by close contact with the child in his new home, chances are the parents can grow in their assurance that the decision was a correct one. As a result, they can become more positive in their discussions with their other children and associates.

With close contact, parents themselves can undertake the role of public relations and interpretation to the community. As they identify themselves with the institution, they will become informed members of the larger family, the institutional family. And as such, they can be the most effective people to interpret the institution to their friends and neighbors, to the legislators and committeemen. Through an active, informed parent who considers his own child still a part of his immediate family, institutional doors can be thrown wide open with tremendous improvement for his, and all other children.

REFERENCES

[Four references not reprinted.]

37 Foster Family Services for Mentally Retarded Children

Beatrice L. Garrett

A year ago the President's Committee On Mental Retardation issued a report that challenges community planners, persons in the helping professions, and lay citizens alike to develop a more adequate range of resources for mentally retarded children than presently exists. Such a range of services the committee saw as necessary for achieving the "programming goals" of integrating the child into normal community living and enabling him "to develop his ability and potential to the fullest possible extent."

The most important resource for achieving such goals is services to enable mentally retarded children to develop within their own families. However, some children cannot be cared for at home, and for them a major resource is foster family care. Foster family service can provide the child with an opportunity to become a part of the community. It can also provide him the kind of individual, loving attention that in many cases has helped mentally retarded children realize unsuspected potential. Whether a child who cannot be kept at home is placed in foster family care or an alternative resource must, of course, be based on the individual needs of the child and his family. Experience has shown, however, that most children, especially younger children, thrive better in a family setting, provided the family has an understanding of their needs and how to meet these needs.

Foster family care is distinguished from group care and institutional care by its smaller size (six or fewer children in the home unless they are all siblings), by being community based, by age differences in the children, and by the family living pattern. In states that require foster families to meet standards for licensing, the use of overcrowded foster homes—or what amounts to small institutions labeled as foster homes—can be avoided.

Used appropriately, foster family service often results in more progress and less misery for the mentally retarded child. It may also save money, but how much can desirably be saved is questionable. One study has indicated that foster family placement of 24 children saved a state $200,000 in one year. The question is, however, whether the program *should* have saved that much money. Were the foster families not sufficiently reimbursed or the children's special needs not met?

Because of the many advantages of foster care for children who must be away from their parents, many institutions and child welfare agencies today are attempting to increase and improve foster family services for mentally retarded children. In doing so they are often confronted with many difficult problems.

CONCEPTS FOR PROGRAMMING

The President's Committee on Mental Retardation has identified two concepts for working with the mentally retarded that can be valuable as guides in evaluating, improving, and developing foster family service for mentally retarded children. These concepts have been called "normalization" and "human management." Normalization refers to designing programs for mentally retarded children so that they will—

1. Enable the child to behave in a way that will lead others to perceive him as not too different from other children—or at least as little different as possible.

2. Help others see the child's strengths and similarities to other children so that his differences from others will be minimized.

3. Help people in general gain a broader perspective of what is normal and acceptable in child development.

Four interrelated and inseparable principles, derived from the normalization concept, apply to foster family service:

Integration—promoting opportunities for the child to interact with others in the community. This goal can best be achieved for the child who can adjust outside of a group situation when he lives in a normal community with a family that uses the community's resources in the usual ways.

Dispersal—placing no more foster children in each community than can be absorbed and integrated into community life.

Specialization—developing a team of social caseworkers, mental retarda-

tion specialists, and foster parents with knowledge and skill in fostering the potentials of children who have problems of development and acceptability.

Continuity—ensuring the continuing involvement of the child's own family in his life through opportunities for interplay between the parents and the child as long as this is useful for the child.

The human management concept applies to the parents of the mentally retarded child as well as to the child himself. It has three main requirements:

That the child's parents be regarded by the helping staff as normal persons under unusual stress, and not be "denormalized" by being regarded as different from other parents.

That, with rare exceptions, the foster family be used only to supplement and not supplant the role of the child's own family. Next in importance to maintenance of life for the child is maintenance of his place within his family.

That decisions regarding structure, policy, and individual problems be measured by whether they best meet the individual needs of the parents and child, not by whether they promote medical, institutional, or program "efficiency."

PROVISION OF SERVICE

Today foster family services for mentally retarded children are provided under various auspices—specialized institutions, state and local child welfare agencies, voluntary child welfare agencies, and different combinations of these. In a recent study of intake of public and voluntary child welfare services in seven cities, 5.2 percent of the children served had I.Q.'s below 75. Seventy-nine percent of these children were served by public agencies.

If medical, psychiatric, psychological, or other specialized services the child needs are available for diagnosis and treatment, the retarded child is usually better served through the existing community-based child welfare agency than through an institution or clinic far from his home. The community-based agency that has a comprehensive service for children and their families can help parents decide whether they can keep the child at home or whether the child should be placed in an institution in another community or in a nearby group home or foster home. An agency can improve its services to mentally retarded children by assigning a staff worker as an ombudsman (or advocate) for such children. The ombudsman will consistently hold the agency to its commitment to meet these children's needs.

Regardless of whether the service to mentally retarded children is provided through a community-based agency or an institution that develops a foster family service, the quality of the service is dependent on clearly spelled-out plans for coordination with other resources. The expertise, knowledge, and resources of both the institution or agency specializing in service to the retarded and the agency specializing in foster family services are required. For instance, a state institution for mentally retarded children may, after an interagency planning conference, enter into a written agreement with a county child welfare agency to provide diagnostic evaluations for a mentally retarded child while the county agency works with the parents and provides foster family services.

Coordination between community resources is also important for staff training. The concepts, knowledge, and skill that social workers have developed to help other children and their families are, of course, basic to foster family service to the mentally retarded. But work with the retarded requires additional knowledge about the meaning of mental retardation to children and their families as well as special skill in dealing with their problems. Agencies need to plan ways of helping their workers achieve the necessary knowledge and skill. The specialized institution or clinic may be the best resource for teaching social workers the unique aspects of such work. Child-caring agencies sometimes arrange for an exchange of workers to achieve such training. Some agencies also assign all cases involving mental retardation to workers who handle only this type of case and who thus have an opportunity to sharpen their insight and skill in helping the mentally retarded.

INDICATIONS FOR USE

Foster family care has several advantages over institutional care for a child, especially one whose retardation stems from emotional deprivation or lack of stimulation rather than from organic causes, for such functional retardates are likely to thrive in a normal family environment: (1) it does not set the child apart; (2) it provides social, emotional, and developmental experiences through close, continuing relationships with parent substitutes; (3) it provides a greater chance for development along socially normal lines through day-to-day interaction within a family and community; and (4) when the child is placed in his home community, it makes it easier for the members of his own family to keep in touch with him. Placing the child near his own home is especially important when the plan calls for his eventual return to his family.

Foster family care is not suitable for the child who, because of severe behavior disturbances, may be dangerous to himself or others when not in a controlled environment. Children who require specialized medical treatment not available in the community may also need institutionalization. Some institutions have developed satellite foster family programs so that children can have the advantages both of family life and specialized medical care.

Retarded children may be placed with foster families for various reasons: (1) to give parents time to deal with the psychological impact of learning of their child's retardation and to come to a considered decision about care of the child; (2) to give a family temporary respite from the strain of caring for the child; (3) to learn through observation whether the child has hidden potentials; (4) to provide the child with a family experience pre-liminary to eventual institutionalization; and (5) to provide part-time care (for example, 5 days a week) or care during the family's vacation.

To be of real value for a child, foster family placement should be selected specifically to meet the child's needs. It should not be just a holding action to serve until institutional space becomes available. Careful selection of the right home, continuing supervision of the child, and support for the foster family tend to prevent the harmful experience of replacement. Placement is effected preferably through a voluntary agreement signed by the parents, but in many instances it results from a temporary or permanent court commitment.

WORK WITH PARENTS

Foster family service has four main components: the provision of social service for the child's own parent; the provision of social service to the child; recruitment, supervision, and education of the foster families; and development of cooperative working arrangements with community resources.

Parents of mentally retarded children needing foster family service come from all socioeconomic levels. The service to parents begins when the possibility of placement is first brought to the agency's attention, whether directly by the parents or through a referral from an individual, a court, or another agency. The service is focused on helping the parents make and follow through with the kind of decision that is most likely to be helpful to their child and one which they can live with comfortably. In helping parents come to a decision, the medical practice of using the least drastic treatment applies. This leads to the following order of priorities for consideration: (1) maintenance of the child in his own home; (2) placement in an adoptive home; (3) placement in a foster family; (4) placement in a group home; (5) placement in an institution.

The decision on treatment is most appropriately made on the basis of careful multidisciplinary study and diagnosis of the specific persons involved and the specific situation, rather than on a general statement of priorities or rules and regulations. For example, consider a five-year-old child whose mother will never be able to make a home for her because of a chronic illness. The accepted priority would be to plan adoption for the child, but the social study establishes the fact that there are strong ties between mother and child. Therefore, the decision is to place the child in a permanent foster family and arrange for regular visiting between mother and child.

Parents have a right to service both as persons in need of help and as parents of a mentally retarded child. All parents who are considering placing their child away from home are experiencing a crisis in their lives. However, parents of a mentally retarded child must deal with a crisis of special severity. In recognizing their child's retardation, they have sustained an angonizing blow to the ego. They are often torn by ambivalence and are dreadfully confused. They cannot help but feel depressed and devaluated. They

may feel guilty. Their defense may lead to rigid denial and "shopping around," to masochistic commitment to the child, or to complete inability to cope.

Such parents need a reliable relationship with someone who is competent to help them, who can give them—whenever they feel the need—personal acceptance, warmth, emotional support, information, guidance, and practical methods for dealing with their problems. They need continuing help in working through their grief before, during, and after the child is placed. A social worker can provide this service through one-to-one conferences, interviews with the whole family, group meetings for education or treatment, and referral to other resources. The social worker must be alert to the often contradictory feelings of parents in order to help them arrive at a sense of security in their decisions and decide how they can handle the spoken and unspoken questions of their other children, neighbors, and relatives.

The development of a careful social diagnosis, tentative prognosis, and recommended treatment, and provision of supportive services are the work of a multidisciplinary team. Besides the social worker, this team may include pediatricians, psychiatrists, psychologists, child development specialists, nurses, speech therapists, nutritionists, physical therapists, and others. To secure the services of such a variety of disciplines, many agencies have to depend on special clinics and institutional staff.

When the time is right, the social worker uses the team's recommendations, as well as its findings concerning both feeling and tangible facts, to involve the parents in weighing alternatives. The parents need time in making their peace with the chronic problem facing them. After the initial crisis that brought them to the agency, they need to feel that an agency, preferably the same one that made the placement, is available to help them when new problems arise. Many parents are more able to accept institutional care than foster family care. They and their neighbors see the institution as a medical facility that provides special services not available to them at home. They can more easily justify this to themselves and others than they can justify placing their child with a family unrelated to them.

THE CHILD

Mentally retarded children for whom foster family care is considered vary greatly. They may be in early infancy or in late adolescence; passive in temperament or hyperactive and hostile; in good physical condition or handicapped by complicated physical defects or medical problems. Their retardation may be regarded as profound, severe, moderate, or borderline. They may look strange or be normal in appearance. In many children the retardation may stem from deprivation rather than organic impairment. In all mentally retarded children there are both similarities to, and differences from, other children. In many of these children the differences result in problems that place extra demands on community resources, on parents, and on foster parents. These problems require

different degrees of care and service, ranging from total physical care to specialized vocational training.

Of significance in foster family placement is the likelihood that the mentally retarded child will be slower than other children to adjust to new people and new places. He needs more preplacement preparation—more retelling of the what and why of placement, and more preplacement visits to the foster family's home. If at all possible, he should be accompanied by his parents on the preplacement visits and at the time of placement. If the child is living in an institution, he may need to be visited by the foster parents several times and then to be taken home with them for a number of overnight stays before being placed in their home.

In working with the foster parents, the social worker can use the child's reactions to the preplacement visits to help the child express his feelings and to answer his spoken and unspoken questions. How the parents, the caseworkers, and the foster parents handle the actual placement and the child's feeling of loss at being separated from his parents will greatly affect the child's future sense of identity. For example, the child whose sense of time is limited and who has difficulty in understanding where his parents are if they are not present, may lose all conception of who he belongs to unless the verbal explanation is reinforced by visits.

Mentally retarded children have certain characteristics in different degrees, for which foster parents need preparation and continuing help. These include: lack of interest in the environment, lack of affectionate response, slowness to learn, inability to communicate feelings or relieve anxiety through verbal expression, rocking and head banging, repetitive behavior, pica, resistance to change, resistance to routine and habit training, slow development of independence and self-help, flightiness or short attention span, hyperactivity, unevenness in ability, memory problems, and apparent immunity to pain. Such characteristics are often sources of frustration and confusion for foster parents.

FOSTER PARENTING

Foster parents of mentally retarded children need the same qualities as foster parents of other children, but they need some of these qualities in an unusual degree. All foster parents need to be in basic marital agreement and to have physical and emotional stamina, the ability to love the child as he is, and the ability to work with the agency and to grow in their vocation. But foster parents of mentally retarded children need some qualities in an unusual degree—patience, confidence, readiness to set up expectations that are tailored to fit the child's individual needs, optimism and an ability to receive satisfaction from small gains, to tolerate frustration and "endless" repetition and to allow the child to be dependent as long as needed without losing sight of ways to help him grow toward self-dependence. They also need a secure feeling of acceptance by their neighbors and by others who are important to them.

The agency can support foster parents through one-to-one supervision and through educational group meetings at which various types of specialists in mental retardation can help them achieve greater understanding and skill in working with the child. The agency can also help foster parents recognize and deal with the child's feelings and capacities; know how much to expect from the child; use toys to encourage motor activities; and help the child understand feelings aroused by objects and people and prepare him for things to come.

The agency may also help foster parents examine their own feelings about the child's own parents and recognize the child's need to express his feeling of loss and separation from his family; learn how to help the child develop a self-image through the use of everyday devices, such as mirrors and pictures; set up and consistently enforce a few rules and routines in accordance with the child's needs; and find ways for the child to do some things successfully, praising him for his effort as well as for his successes. But even more important than developing those techniques, foster parents need to know how to help the child feel loved, enjoyed, and valued.

Of great importance in foster family service is the availability of the special resources the child may need at different stages in his development. What about medical facilities offering expertise in problems of mental retardation? Do the schools provide suitable instruction for mentally retarded children with a minimum of separation from other children? Are there facilities for vocational training and a sheltered workshop for the teenage youth? Are there camps, day camps, "Y's" and other recreation facilities that make provision for these children? Is there a day-care center or nursery school that may be used to stimulate the child and to give relief to the foster parents? What is the neighborhood attitude likely to be toward the child who has a different way of developing? Can the foster parents be helped to handle negative reactions and teach neighborhood children to play with the child? Foster parents need to know about such resources and how to use them.

The process of recruiting and selecting foster parents for mentally retarded children begins the preparation for the important job of foster care. It is a teaching process that must continue on a planned basis throughout the period of service. If mentally retarded children are to be provided with foster care, the community needs to know about their need for foster parents. This requires a year round recruitment program presented in a down-to-earth way that points up the contribution foster parents can make without glossing over the difficulties of caring for a mentally retarded child.

In spite of the difficulties, foster parents can be found for children of all levels of retardation. For example, of 36 foster parents interested in caring for retarded children, 44 percent said the level of retardation did not matter to them; 25 percent said their interest stemmed from previous close contact with a mentally retarded person; and 25 percent said they had accepted retarded children because they were asked to meet a pressing need. Fifty percent said fostering of men-

tally retarded children was a job for which they should be paid.

Many more foster parents are likely to become available and to continue in service when agencies institute certain modern administrative practices for all but permanent foster families. These practices include: full reimbursement for the actual costs of keeping the child; provision when needed of agency-owned or rented houses, in some instances especially equipped for children with handicaps; regular relief help; homemaker service; and a reasonable salary for the foster parents plus the same fringe benefits available to other agency employees.

SOME PROPOSITIONS

In summary, I present the following propositions arising from the concepts of normalization and human management for consideration by persons who have a responsibility to plan for or serve mentally retarded children:

1. When a child cannot be cared for at home or placed for adoption, foster family service should be the preferred method of care unless the child obviously requires another form of care.

2. At the time the child is diagnosed as being mentally retarded, especially a child from a disorganized family, the diagnosis should be tested by providing him with an emotionally enriching and stimulating family and community living experience.

3. A community-based comprehensive child welfare service is the best means for providing a foster family service for mentally retarded children *if* it ac-

cepts this responsibility and makes administrative provision for such a program.

4. Foster family service for mentally retarded children of all socioeconomic levels, as for other children, must include counseling for the child's parents as well as service for the child.

5. The foster parents should be employed by the child-serving agency, be paid a reasonable salary with fringe benefits in addition to the costs of foster care, and be provided with sequential educational opportunities for increasing their competence in serving the child.

REFERENCES

[Eleven references not reprinted.]

38 A Comprehensive Care Program for Children with Handicaps

John E. Allen
and Louis Lelchuck

During the past ten years, the health professions have become increasingly concerned with meeting the multiple needs of the child with handicaps. Recent publications have emphasized the apparent increase of incidence in the occurrence of single and multiple handicaps in children. The development of treatment programs which are comprehensive in scope has not kept pace with the needs presented by these patients.

A definition of the patient population under discussion is essential for a clear understanding of the program presented. The child with a handicap is one with physical or intellectual deficits which result in deviations from the norm of expected growth and development. The deficiencies observed in the management of these patients have been encountered in the practices of both the generalists and the highly trained specialists. In the past, the generalist through his continuing contact with the patient and the family was able to provide much of the support and encouragement which are a necessary part of management. His role diminished as the need for the application of newer areas of knowledge became available. The specialist's skills led to the patient receiving the benefits of new knowledge, but also resulted in a narrowness of approach to the patient's total needs. For example, a great deal of attention was paid to the surgical procedures a child required for improved ambulation, diverting the entire energies of the family to an expectation of a cure and the eventual production of a normal child. This failed to meet the multiple needs of this youngster with a resultant inadequacy in his social adjustment and disappointment to the family and to the child in terms of the expectations they structured along the way.

Over the last quarter of a century, an important factor in preventing the application of a unified and comprehensive approach to the multiple needs of these children has been the development of an ever greater number of private and public agencies designed to meet the specific needs of a particular condition or disease entity. This fragmentation of effort has led to an overemphasis in some areas and inadequacy in others. These agencies have made significant contributions over the years in promoting interest in the specialized areas, in educating both professional and lay people about the special condition, and in carry out research. An outstanding example was the intensive program of the National Foundation—March of Dimes in supporting a wide variety of clinical and laboratory research which culminated in the eradication of paralytic poliomyelitis.

Fragmentation and compartmentalization of the care of the child with handicaps also results in duplication of services and frequently excessive expense. The well meaning but restricted tunnel-vision of the special disease agency frequently precludes the wider view of the total needs of the patient and his family. The last decade has seen a changing response by governmental agencies, such as the Children's Bureau, National Institutes of Health, Maternal and Child Welfare Programs, and a few voluntary agencies in the direction of a unified approach to the needs of the handicapped child. Many individual practitioners and agencies have recognized the needs of this patient population and have attempted to serve them, but have done so by referral to individuals and agencies, resulting frequently in the families being subjected to the problems of poor communication, inconsistency in interpretation, and conflicting prescriptions for future action.

It is this integrative lack which often results in "shopping" phenomena and in a dilution of the effectiveness of the total effort. Also, the fragmented efforts we have described frequently result in a process which lacks focus, one in which there may be a disparate investment of energy in correctional procedures which may have little relevancy to realistic goals.

There have been other contributing factors in the past which precluded the mobilization of energy directed towards the care of chronic and disabling conditions. Until the advent of the antibiotic era, the overwhelming need was for the control of infectious diseases. With the increasing sophistication of the scientific and health fields, these problems were largely resolved. The energies of investigators, laboratories, and sources of financial support were then freed to be reinvested in new areas of endeavor. Another aspect of the past was the apparent ignorance of both laymen and professionals of the problems of the handicapped. With increasing industrialization and with continuing technological progress the community's ability to absorb the handicapped person became progressively impaired. The problem of finding means of livelihood and interaction for those not handicapped, yet poorly educated, heightens the intensity of the problem for the handicapped themselves.

The need to lessen the effects of the debilitating condition becomes more and more the immediate interest of the health professions. The narcissistic rewards accruing to the practitioner were less in this type of activity professionally, economically, and socially, since the problems presented were not considered of sufficient import to warrant an investment of energy beyond meeting immediate needs. The goals appeared to be so restricted and the possibility of achievement at higher levels so remote that the efforts of the practitioner were directed into more satisfying channels.

New insights and techniques which contribute to the understanding of normal processes and growth principles are being derived from the further investigation of the problems of the handicapped. Not only the overtly identifiable disabilities, such as congenital amputations, but also the more subtle chronic diseases, such as asthma or diabetes which result in internal derangement of psychological and social functioning, must be given attention. Because of their concern about their bodily integrity, these patients are often unable to make an adequate response to their environment or to their peers, nor are they able to structure realistic goals commensurate with their intellectual and physical abilities.

With these considerations in mind, the approach to the diagnosis and management of any individual with a handicap or chronic disease must include the following elements. A comprehensive historical survey of the life of the child and an orderly documentation of his growth and development is the basic step. Meticulous attention to genetic and other hereditary phenomena is essential. The total diagnostic approach should go further than the traditional history and physical examination and should reach out towards the more complex areas of the interaction of the child, his family, and his environment. The individual characteristics of these children and the unique personal world within which they dwell require an accurate assessment. Such a survey permits a realistic appraisal so that goals for habilitation can be structured.

Consultation and laboratory studies that do not bear significant relationship to the patient and his problems tend to compound the already difficult and complex situation. Parents are often given a false sense of security in that they feel that the miracles of modern science and medicine, if brought to bear in a strong enough fashion, will invariably solve their

child's problem and their own interrelated concerns. In approaching the handicapped child, we should not create a greater anxiety than already exists in the family unit. The academic need for the orderly collection of data, often an integral part of clinical research, is recognized and must be dealt with in such a way that it does not interfere with the management of the patient.

The Comprehensive Care Program for Children with Handicaps was established in the Department of Pediatrics at Cleveland Metropolitan General Hospital in January 1961. A description of the staff and operational structure of the program is presented.

STAFFING

This program is pediatrically based under the direction of a pediatrician who has the responsibility for maintaining open avenues of communication among the staff, other professional and nonprofessional people in the hospital and with community facilities utilized in enhancing the effectiveness of the program. He provides a stability and continuity of care for the patient in contrast with the usual experiences with changing personnel.

Medical service to the patients is provided by a staff of full-time and part-time pediatricians with special interest in this field. This group of pediatricians is reinforced by the full-time staff of the Department of Pediatrics which includes many subspecialties. The advantage of having a comprehensive program for handicapped children situated in a teaching general hospital is the ready availability of specialists and consultants. The specialties actively participating include: neurology, physical medicine, orthopedics, and surgery (including neurosurgery and urology). Consultants in psychiatry, cardiology, radiology, pathology, and hematology are available.

Children with handicaps frequently present problems in the spheres of intellectual and emotional maldevelopment. Intense family problems arise in relation to the disability adding to the disordered picture. Psychological participation in this program is therefore emphasized. The associate director of the program is a clinical psychologist and is charged with the responsibility for coordinating the efforts of psychological and social service personnel, and maintaining open communication between these areas and the medical staff. A coordinator, who is a nurse with public health and administrative background, supervises administrative procedures, the clerical staff, and patient processing. She contributes to the maintenance of liaison within and without the hospital, thus ensuring consistent communication with other staff and involved agencies. A social service unit, composed of a supervisor, caseworkers, and case aides, forms an integral part of the diagnostic and counselling program and assists in the maintenance of continuity for the patient and his family. A Department of Physical Medicine and Rehabilitation, under the direction of a physiatrist, plays a direct role in the diagnostic appraisal as well as in carrying out a variety of treatment programs. The

nurses in the program not only provide traditional nursing care, but contribute pertinent observations of patients and of family interaction. A unique aspect of this program is the Child Life and Educational Program directed by a trained educator. This service is utilized to ameliorate the effects of long-term hospitalization upon the child, to provide recreational programs, and to further educational goals.

An adaptive equipment shop provides assistive devices, splints, braces, and other specific equipment. This function is under the direct supervision of the program. The chief brace maker participates in certain of our clinics where he can see the patients, confer with the psychiatrists, orthopedists, and pediatricians, and aid in the design of equipment or the modification of appliances.

Several specialized diagnostic laboratories previously unavailable in the hospital are functional components of the program. These include cytogenetic and screening chromatography laboratories. Transportation problems have been alleviated by the use of a station wagon and the employment of a driver to transport patients from their home to the clinic as well as to community facilities.

FINANCING

Financial support has been derived from a variety of sources. A major portion of the support is through the normal financial channels of the hospital. Funds have been made available from the Children's Bureau, the Division of Maternal and Child Health of the Ohio State Health Department, and by the National Foundation. Patient fees for both outpatient and inpatient services are paid in a variety of ways—by the patient's family, private insurance programs, Crippled Children's Service programs, welfare sources, and private agencies concerned with one or another aspect of the program. Proper financing from local, state, and national sources is continuously sought, so that exemplary medical care can be given to all patients regardless of their ability to pay.

The complexities of the program, the interrelationships of various departments, the many individuals involved, plus the cost of this type of care, make it imperative that the hospital administration be an active participant in the program, a circumstance which obtains at Cleveland Metropolitan General Hospital.

REFERRAL AND INTAKE

There are two major sources of patients referred to the Comprehensive Care Program. Children who are born in this hospital or come to our pediatric clinics with problems of unusual chronicity or magnitude are given preference. As the program has matured and developed, referrals have been accepted from private physicians and other clinics. The intake procedure serves as an orientation for the patient and family. The family is given an appointment for the intake interview conducted by the coordinator (assisted by the clinic nurse) who explains the mechanisms of the hospital

and the clinic. Financial and registration procedures are then completed. The nurse is assigned the task of photographing the patient for identification and record. A brief interview with the social worker acquaints the patient with her function and allows a preliminary assessment of the family structure, experiences, and interrelationships. These children often have had contact with other physicians, clinics, hospitals, or agencies. Written permission is obtained from the parents to secure records from these sources. The program coordinator then schedules an appointment for the diagnostic study.

THE DIAGNOSTIC PROCESS

The staff of the diagnostic clinic has at its disposal the information that was obtained in the intake procedure as well as the information that has been requested from other hospitals and physicians. The social worker assigned to the patient usually accompanies him during the history-taking session as an observer. This has saved time and also has given the worker more insight into the total patient-parental situation. During the physical examination, it is often possible for the worker to develop further rapport with the family. The clinical psychologist is then introduced to the family and the patient and makes a preliminary evaluation. A conference is held between the pediatrician, house officer and medical student, social worker, nurse, and psychologist. Plans are made for needed studies and preliminary impressions are recorded. Specialized studies, such as formal psychological physical medicine, and orthopedic evaluations, are scheduled when indicated.

More intensive social investigation is carried out by interviews with the parents and by home visits when necessary to inspect physical surroundings and to elaborate on needed social data. When indicated, referrals are made to the Visiting Nurses Association to obtain other information about the home and the feasibility of carrying out procedures within the home setting.

STAFF CONFERENCE AND COUNSELING

Upon completion of the diagnostic work-up, a formal staff conference is scheduled. It is the function of this conference to arrive at a working diagnosis and outline goals of a treatment program. All staff members contribute to this process. Following this conference, an appointment is scheduled for the parents for interpretive counseling. An initial impression of the nature and scope of disability and the possibilities for treatment is presented. Often this has been the end point of the prior experiences of these parents in their previous attempts to seek care for their child.

It has been increasingly clear to us that the families cannot assimilate all the information and guidance given to them in one session. Therefore, repeated counseling is a necessary feature of the contacts with the patient's family to ensure a full understanding of the recommendations evolved by the team and to enable the staff to assess the family's ability to respond

to the structured program. Often the goals originally proposed for the patient may need modification, either in terms of raising our sights or lowering them, depending upon the total response of the family unit. Unrealistic expectations, impulsive over-responsiveness, or feelings of hopelessness and despondency may be encountered in the course of continued activity with the family, necessitating a dynamic response by the staff rather than a static position.

THE TREATMENT PROGRAM

The foundation of the treatment program is exemplary pediatric care. Particular attention is paid to nutritional inadequacies, oral hygiene and dental health, routine immunizations, and frequent surveys to detect early infectious processes. Superimposed upon the basic pediatric approach is a concentration upon the specific disability of the patient through an integrated effort by the team members. A great deal of energy is expended to ensure that continuous and open communication exists between all professional and nonprofessional personnel involved in the care of the child.

The patient and the family are helped to deal with the role of intellectual potential and of complicating emotional factors by means of ongoing evaluation, counselling, and, if necessary, direct treatment by the psychologist, the social worker, or the psychiatric consultant. The staff is sensitive to the problems the patient faces in achieving an adequate learning experience for social living and problem solving. This attention extends into the community, including the school or any other institution or service that will support the efforts of the patient and family.

When emotional problems of unusual complexity are encountered, assistance is sought from the psychiatric treatment facilities in the community or from other social agencies. A primary contribution by the social work and psychology staff is in the assessment of reality factors in the patient and in the family's functioning which enhance, modify, or inhibit the effectiveness of the total program. Continuing study by reassessments and by re-presentation of material for staff thinking is part of the process whereby goals are constantly reevaluated.

An associated activity is the development of cooperative working relationships with specialized community agencies and facilities. When a decision has been made to refer the child to a community facility for service, the communication process must be initiated concurrently and maintained. Thereafter, the child is seen on relatively infrequent visits in the comprehensive care clinics, since he may be attending the community facility on an almost daily basis. Changes in the child's condition, both positively and negatively, are reported back to the program and, in turn, decisions made by the Comprehensive Care staff are conveyed to the appropriate community facility. Frequently it is desirable to send one of our staff into the field to work with community agency personnel to exchange information, observe the child, and contribute in other ways to the total program.

EDUCATION AND RESEARCH

The Comprehensive Care Program provides a unique setting in which to train a variety of students in the health professions in diagnosis, treatment, and management of children with disabilities. Third and fourth year medical students, interns, and residents are included in the teaching program. Teaching is not confined to those whose primary interest is pediatrics, but is open to all other medical specialties and services which have been described above. A similar relationship exists in the nonmedical professional areas such as psychology, social work, nursing, physical therapy, occupational therapy, and similar areas.

Appropriate to their level of training and professional roles, students learn through the mechanisms of actual participation in the service aspects of the program, seminars, demonstrations, and conferences. Students participate in the care of the patient under the direction of the staff without disturbing the basic need of the patient and family for continuity of care.

The Comprehensive Care Program teaching activities extends into the community. Educational activities are exchanged with a variety of community agencies. The program presents the concepts involved in the needs of the handicapped child through public meetings, lectures, and similar activities. An annual institute, attended by an average of 700 nonmedical professional personnel, has been established to provide basic medical information to workers in the field. Members of our staff participate in community planning activities related to providing for the needs of children.

A variety of clinical and laboratory research projects are carried on by the staff of the Comprehensive Care Program. The wide scope of the patient population, coupled with the broad range of interests and skills of the staff, affords an unusual opportunity to participate in clinical research and laboratory studies in this essentially unexplored area.

CURRENT DEVELOPMENTS

Our experience during the past four years has demonstrated that the majority of handicapped children can be handled on an outpatient basis. The ambulatory approach to the diagnosis and management of these children results in a reduction of hospital costs as well as an avoidance of the detrimental effects of separation from the family. It has become equally apparent that those children who must be closely observed in a neutral environment require an inpatient setting. We have, of necessity, hospitalized these children in our general pediatric wards which are designed for the care of the acutely ill child.

Invariably, the immediate demands of the acutely ill siphon off the energies of both the house and nursing staffs, so that the handicapped children are often relegated to a category of second-class patients. The opportunity to make both qualitative and quantitative observations to arrive at a proper diagnosis is often difficult on an acute ward. We are, therefore, constructing a specialized inpatient unit to house a small number of children for prolonged studies and observation. This unit will be fully equipped with specialized playrooms, classrooms, and observation and recording areas. Both the indoor and outdoor settings that may be utilized by the staff in their observation of the behavior of the child are under construction. Demonstration to parents of the optimal functioning of their child in an ideal setting will be an important function of this unit and will greatly aid in the counseling process.

In keeping with our philosophy of comprehensive care, there will be close relationship with the staff taking care of the patients on an ambulatory basis and those dealing with the children in the inpatient unit. In the majority of cases, the professional personnel will handle patients in both areas, thus avoiding disruption of continuity of care. Facilities for special education, both for the individual child and for groups of children, will be available. A variety of study situations will be offered for staff members to pursue clinical research.

CONCLUSIONS

The term "Comprehensive Care Program" is the identifying symbol of an integrated multidisciplinary effort to meet the varied and complex needs of children with handicaps. We firmly believe that children with chronic disabling conditions can be appropriately handled by a concerned group of individuals with a common purpose. While this program was originally designed to deal primarily with neuromuscular and orthopedic handicapping conditions, our experience has led us to include all varieties of disabilities, thus avoiding the multiplicity of specialty clinics and specialized services. There has been an ever-increasing demand for service in a wide variety of diagnostic categories, including mental retardation. Comprehensive Care, as we use it, means careful attention to diagnosis, management, parental counseling, concern with the total family and, above all, continuity of care.

Impending federal legislation, such as Medicare, projects the establishment of programs of comprehensive care for both handicapped children and children with unmet medical needs. Such developments would appear to have particular relevancy to the experience herein described and suggest future developments in this direction as the experience with this form of medical care continues to grow and develop.

REFERENCES

[Six references not reprinted.]

39 Generic Services for the Mentally Retarded and Their Families

R. C. Scheerenberger

Recent years have witnessed many advances in the field of mental retardation, especially as they relate to the development of specialized community programs and services. Paralleling this development has been the growing realization that specialized programs are not the sole answer to meeting the total needs of the retarded and their families. Economic considerations alone preclude the continual proliferation of specialized programs when such may not be required. Manpower is not available. Furthermore, and of greater consequence, providing the continuum of care required by the retarded cannot be attained by a fragmented system of specialized programs. In other words, existing generic services must be utilized more effectively.

A generic service is defined as any health, education, welfare, rehabilitation, or employment agency in the community which serves a broad spectrum of persons, including the mentally retarded. . . . Excluded are special programs intended solely or primarily for the mentally retarded. Research with respect to community programs for the retarded—generic or specific—is extremely limited. Though there are a number of reports on public attitudes and awareness . . . and mental health clinics for retarded children . . . no study of generic services could be located.

The purpose of this study was to obtain information concerning the availability of generic services for the retarded and their families. Specifically, four objectives for the study were posited: (1) to study accessibility of generic services to the mentally retarded and their families; (2) to study variations of accessibility of generic services to the mentally retarded and their families according to state area, taking into consideration both location and socioeconomic status; (3) to identify problems encountered by professional persons in providing generic services to the retarded and their families; (4) to identify problems encountered by parents in obtaining generic services for their retardates.

METHOD

The sample included representatives from four generic service categories: (1) medical, (2) guidance and counseling, (3) religious, and (4) socio-recreational. In addition, parents of retardates on a waiting list for residential care were interviewed. The sample was selected from three socio-geographic areas in Illinois each having a service population of approximately 500,000 persons: (I) middle-class metropolitan Chicago; (II) poverty area, metropolitan Chicago; and (III) downstate communities. A total of 736 professional persons, agency representatives, and parents were interviewed personally during July and August, 1968. (See Table 1.)

Two questionnaires were developed for the purpose of interviewing professional persons and parents. The Professional Form included the following open-ended items.
1. Do you serve the mentally retarded (children and adults)?
2. How many retardates do you serve in a year?
3. How many persons do you serve per year (total number of clients)?
4. Do you refer your retarded clients to other agencies or practitioners?
5. Do you accept referrals of retardates?
6. Do you work with parents of the retarded? What services do you provide?
7. Do you refer parents to other agencies?
8. What problems have you encountered working with parents?
9. Do you work directly with other children in the family of a retardate? What services do you render to these children?

In addition, representatives from professional agencies or practitioners were asked: "What, in your opinion, is required in order to provide comprehensive community programs for the retarded?"

The Parent Form included four open-ended items:
1. What generic services have you attempted to obtain for your child or adult with respect to: medical and dental; diagnosis and counseling (psychological and social); educational; recreational; religious; vocational training or placement; residential; other?
2. What generic services is your child or adult now receiving?
3. What generic services have you not been able to acquire for your child or adult?
4. What do you feel needs to be done about increasing availability of local generic services and programs?

Each person or agency selected for the study was contacted by letter from the Governor's Interdepartmental Committee on Mental Retardation requesting their participation. The response form enabled the respondent to indicate his willingness or unwillingness to participate. In the latter instance, the respondent could offer an explanation by checking one of the following three statements: (1) Do not serve the retarded, (2) Do not know if the retarded are being served, and (3) Other.

If no response was received within two weeks, a second letter was mailed. If no response was received to either letter after four weeks, the person or agency was contacted by telephone, if possible. Interviews were arranged entirely at the convenience of persons to be interviewed. Results of the interviews were recorded on the appropriate form and returned to the principal investigator for collation and analysis.

RESULTS

Three factors have to be kept in mind when interpreting the results: (1) A "do not serve" response does not mean "will not serve." There were

Table 1. Total Responses Distributed According to Generic Service Category and Nature of Response

Category	Total sample contacted	Number responding		Serve the retarded		Do not serve the retarded		Don't know if served		Unable to participate for other reasons	
		(N)	(%)[a]	(N)	(%)[b]	(N)	(%)[b]	(N)	(%)[b]	(N)	(%)[b]
Generic agencies	504	474	94	124	26	270	57	41	9	39	8
Medical services											
Primary physician	110	108	98	22	20	67	62	8	7	11	11
Dentists	104	98	94	19	19	51	51	15	15	13	14
Community health	25	25	100	3	12	22	88	0	0	0	0
Guidance and counseling	32	32	100	14	44	17	53	1	3	0	0
Religious programs (church)	130	123	95	47	38	58	47	7	6	11	9
Socio-recreational agencies	103	88	85	19	22	55	63	10	11	4	4
Parents	232	143	61	..	..	..	..	..	..	..	..

[a]Percent of total sample.
[b]Percent of responses.

only a few instances, all of which were confined to generic guidance and counseling and socio-recreational agencies, in which an organization did not serve the retarded as a matter of policy. There was no evidence that any private practitioner or church program had ever refused to serve the retarded or their families. (2) The number of retarded served were, for the most part, estimated by the respondent. In spite of the limitations associated with the classification responses, a general indication as to the nature of the retarded population served is still provided. Criteria used by the classifiers are unknown. Consequently, reliability of data is suspected. It was observed, however, that unless a generic agency had a special program for the moderately, severely, or profoundly retarded, a primarily mildly retarded population was served. (3) Beyond consideration of the total number of individual practitioners and agencies serving the retarded, the results are of limited generality. In other words, the number of persons serving the retarded in any generic category proved to be quite small; therefore, responses to questions concerning services, difficulties encountered, and the like, provide only an indication of some of the existing programs and associated problems. Though there was remarkable consistency among responses of individuals and agencies serving the retarded, firm conclusions are dependent upon a much larger sample.

As shown in Table 1, response to the study especially among generic agencies was excellent. A total of 474 (90%) of the 504 persons representing generic agencies responded. There

were no statistically significant differences with regard to either frequency of response among generic agencies or among socio-geographic areas. Of the 474 respondents 124 (26%) indicated that they served the retarded. All know parents with retardates on the waiting list for placement in a state institution residing in the selected socio-geographic areas were to be included in the study; however, only 143 (71%) of the 232 parents could be contacted.

Generic Service Agencies

As shown in Table 1 (column 2), the majority of agencies contacted *did not* serve the mentally retarded. The highest recorded level of participation involved guidance-and-counseling agencies; however, of the fourteen agencies serving the retarded, six received state aid for that specific purpose. Therefore, on a totally voluntary basis, the church was most active in providing for the retarded. Of the 25 community health agencies contacted, only three served the retarded. In each instance, the hospital had an extensive social service or mental health department. In view of the few positive responses, no further reference will be made to community health agencies.

As shown in Table 2 (column 2), there were only four instances where the percent of retardates served in terms of total client population approximated or exceeded the frequently estimated 3% level: pediatricians, mental health clinics, social centers, and YMCA/YWCAs. The 6% level recorded for generic guidance-and-counseling services again was the result of those clinics receiving finan-

Table 2. Summary: Generic Services for the Retarded and Their Families

	Respondents serving MR (N)	MR served— % of total clients	Referral other agencies	Accept referrals of MR	Counseling parents about MR	Counseling sibling about MR
General practitioner	11	0.28	100.0%	64%	81%	18%
Pediatrician	11	2.00	100.0	100	54	37
Dentists	19	0.43	55.0	89	10	0
Guidance and counseling services	12	6.00	90.0	50	50	50
Mental health clinics	6	9.00	80.0	100	50	50
Family agencies	6	1.10	100.0	..	100	100
Religious services	47	0.40	51.0	100	..	..
Catholic	16	0.30	73.0	100	80	15
Jewish	8	0.60	28.0	100	80	18
Protestant	23	0.40	44.0	100	86	12
Socio-recreational services	19	7.00	2.7	0	78	15
Parks	7	2.60	57.0	..	0	0
Social centers	5	7.00	..	..	..	..
Youth centers	3	1.30	100.0	..	..	..
YMCA/YWCA	4	12.00	..	..	..	..

cial aid to serve the retarded. The relatively high incidence of retardates served by social centers and YMCA/YWCAs is attributed to the fact that most of the facilities were located in poverty areas. The estimated retarded population served by those YMCA/YWCAs in nonpoverty areas was below 1%. Statistical analysis was precluded by the limited number of reporting agencies.

As indicated in Table 2 (column 3), most agencies referred retarded persons to other services for assistance. The exception involved generic socio-recreational agencies which did not believe it was within their realm of professional responsibility to become involved with the broad ramifications of retardation.

Reasons for referral varied according to profession. While most general practitioners referred retarded patients to mental health clinics for diagnosis and treatment, the majority of pediatricians referred retarded patients to specialized hospitals and clinics, primarily for further diagnosis. Dentists referred clients to dental specialists when anesthesia was required. The generic guidance-and-counseling services referred clients to a variety of community programs for the retarded. The churches, however, showed variance with regard to both frequency of referral and agencies involved. As will be observed, 73% of the 16 responding Catholic churches indicated that they referred retarded individuals; however, such referrals were primarily to a denominational agency serving the retarded. A similar report was provided by Protestant churches. In contrast, Jewish respondents indicated that they referred retarded members to professional agencies (e.g., mental health clinics) for diagnosis, evaluation, and special programs. In other words, while Catholic and Protestant churches relied on denominational services, Jewish retardates were referred primarily to nonsectarian professional agencies.

As shown in Table 2 (column 4), with the exception of family service and socio-recreational programs, all agencies accepted the retardates on a referral basis. Family service agencies indicated that retardation was considered incidental to a broader family problem.

Most generic agencies provided counseling to parents about mental retardation (Table 2, column 5). Exceptions included dentists and socio-recreational services. Two dentists had attempted to offer counseling to parents concerning retardation, and both indicated that their efforts resulted in parental hostility. All dentists did, however, counsel families with regard to appropriate dental care for their retarded child.

As shown in Table 2 (Column 6), while many agencies and professional persons counseled parents about mental retardation, only a few provided similar counseling to normal siblings. The noteworthy exception was three mental health clinics which offered counseling programs for both siblings and parents.

Table 3 lists primary problems associated with serving the retarded and their families. The two most frequently recorded difficulties associated with meeting the needs of the retarded included communication and finding sufficient time to provide required services. Primary parental problems involved accepting and under-

Table 3. Problems Associated with Serving the Retarded and Their Families

	Physicians			Guidance-counseling, M.H. clinics (N=6)	Religious organizations			Socio-recreational agencies (N=14)	Total (N=101)
Problem category	Ped. (N=11)	G.P. (N=11)	Dentists (N=19)		Catholic (N=15)	Jewish (N=7)	Protestant (N=18)		
With retarded									
Communication	9%	45%	68%	..	..	..	..	..	17%
Management	18	9	26	..	..	..	..	7%	8
Time required to serve	18	9	37	..	7%	14%	6%	..	14
Accompanying handicaps	..	..	26	..	..	..	..	..	5
Acceptance by others	..	..	..	..	7	14	28	..	7
None	18	54	32	100%	70	14	44	93	50
With parents									
Acceptance and understanding	72	72	..	72	20	86	78	7	44
Program support and interest; following recommendations	18	27	47	17	..	..	..	14	16
None	27	45	89	17	66	..	..	79	48

standing mental retardation and following recommendations of professionals. It should be observed, however, that approximately 50% of the respondents indicated that they had not encountered any serious problem in serving either the retarded or their parents.

As shown in Table 4, representatives of generic service agencies felt an acute need for additional community resources, central points of referral and information, and increased professional manpower.

There were no statistically significant differences among the socio-geographic areas with regard to the percent of generic agencies serving the retarded, percent of retarded served, referral to other agencies, acceptance of referrals, parent counseling, sibling counseling, or needed community services. The only indication that a higher percent of retardates was being served in the poverty area was provided by the social centers and YMCA/YWCAs as previously discussed. The absence of any statistically significant differences among socio-geographic areas probably is a result of the small number of reporting agencies.

Parent Response

As stated previously, all known parents of retardates on the waiting list for residential care residing in the selected socio-geographic areas were to be included in the study; however, only 143 (61%) of the 232 parents could be contacted. Of the 143 respondents, 99 (69%) stated that they would be willing to be interviewed, and 44 (31%) indicated that they preferred not to be interviewed for a variety of reasons. Retarded individuals whose parents were interviewed ranged across all chronological age groupings as well as levels of retardation. The majority (80%), however, were moderately, severely, or profoundly retarded.

All parents had received diagnostic and counseling services for the mentally retarded. The two primary resources were hospitals (used by 54% of the parents) and mental health clinics (used by 28% of the parents). Other agencies offering related services included the courts, public schools, day centers, churches, and private practitioners. None of the latter, however, received more than a 10% response. There were no statistically significant differences with regard to socio-geographic area.

All parents had received physician care for their child—95% were receiving such attention at the time of the study. There were no statistically significant differences according to socio-geographic area. None of the parents had ever been denied medical attention for their retarded child by a physician, and only six indicated that they had encountered any difficulty whatsoever with medical personnel. It was observed that 43% of the parents in the poverty area (Area II) relied solely on publicly sponsored medical programs.

As shown in Table 5, of the 86 parents with ambulatory retardates over three years of age, only 42% had received or requested dental attention for their retarded child. Inadequate dental concern was particularly evident among parents in Area II. Differences between Areas I and II were

Table 4. Needed Community Services—Professional and Parental Responses

Recommendations	Physicians (N=22)	Dentists (N=19)	Guidance-counseling services (N=12)	Religious services (N=47)	Socio-recreational agencies (N=19)	Total generic services (N=119)	Parents (N=99)
Better diagnostic treatment facilities	50%	..	..	..	..	9%	..
More community services	50	..	100%	33%	53%	38	73%
Improved residential facilities	23	..	60	40	..	10	43
Central point of referral and more information	18	27%	33	..	..	24	14
Financial assistance to parents	23	..	..	..	20	8	15
Increased professional manpower	8	10	100	..	17	17	3

Table 5. Services Requested and Received for Retarded Persons by Geographical Area

	Area I		Area II		Area III		Total	
	Eligible retardates (N)	Received service (%)	Eligible retardates (N)	Received service (%)	Eligible retardates (N)	Received service (%)	Eligible retardates (N)	Received service (%)
Dental services	30	54	26	24	24	45	86	42
Special education	22	95	14	50	13	100	49	84
Community recreation	22	82	14	11	13	69	49	61
Family recreation	22	18	14	79	13	31	49	39
Religious programs	22	59	14	7	13	77	49	49

statistically significant $(x^2 = 6.19;$ df $= 1$; p $<$ .05). In other words, fewer retardates in Area II were receiving dental care. Again 47% of parents in the poverty area relied solely upon services of publicly sponsored dental clinics. Only one parent indicated that she had been unable to find a dentist to work with her retarded child. This was the only negative comment directed toward dentists.

Of the 99 retardates, 49 (49%) were considered eligible for school participation according to criteria of moderate or mild retardation, six years of age or older. As shown in Table 5, 84% of the 49 school-eligible retardates were enrolled in school or had completed school. Again, there was marked contrast between the number of retardates enrolled in a training program for Area II as compared with Areas I and III—50% of school-eligible retardates from Area II were not and had not been enrolled in a training program.

Based on the same criteria as used with regard to special education, 30 (61%) of the 49 retardates were engaged in some form of recreation outside the home. A wide variety of recreational programs were available and used, including school programs, camps, city parks, youth clubs, and the library. No single category received a plurality of response. There were statistically significant differences between recreational patterns of retardates in the poverty area (Area II) as compared with Areas I and III $(x^2 = 22.44,$ df $= 1,$ p $<$ .05; and $x^2 = 4.45,$ df $= 1,$ p $<$ .05, respectively). As shown in Table 5, most of the retardates in the poverty area

(79%) limited their recreational activities to the home and neighborhood. Differences between Areas I and III were not statistically significant.

Only 16 of the total retarded sample satisfied criteria for participation in vocational training or sheltered workshop program, i.e., moderately or mildly retarded, 16 years of age or older. Only one (11%) of the nine mildly retarded was receiving vocational training, and only 2 (29%) of seven mildly retarded were receiving vocational training. Unavailability of local vocational training programs and sheltered workshops willing to accept the retarded was one of the critical problems confronting parents.

Twenty-four (49%) of the 49 moderately or mildly retarded individuals, six years of age or older, were participating in a church program. The number of retardates attending church in the poverty area was considerably less than that reported in Areas I and III. Differences between Areas I and II as well as Areas II and III were statistically significant $(x^2 = 7.65,$ df $= 1,$ p $<$ .05; and $x^2 = 11.69,$ df $= 1,$ p $<$ .05, respectively). Differences between Areas I and III were not statistically significant.

In addition to the generic programs previously cited, 15% of the parents indicated that other services had been requested and received, including speech and hearing therapy, home training, physical therapy, and foster home placement.

As shown in Table 4, parents were primarily concerned with expansion of community programs (73%), development of local residential services (43%), increased financial assistance for the retarded (15%), and creation of central points of referral (14%). Whereas responses from generic agencies did not reveal statistically significant differences as affected by socio-geographic location, parental responses did. Retarded children in the poverty area were receiving appreciably less attention to their educational, recreational, religious, and dental needs than their peers from middle-class and semi-rural environments. A qualitative difference also was recorded by the interviewers. Parents from the poverty area did not appear to understand fully either mental retardation or its implications with regards to comprehensive community programs. In essence, mental retardation apparently assumes a relatively low priority in their daily lives.

DISCUSSION

Though the small number of respondents serving the retarded precludes positing definitive conclusions, the data were sufficient to warrant a brief discussion of the results with respect to the original purposes of the study. Each of the four objectives will be considered individually.

1. *To study accessibility of generic services to the mentally retarded and their families:* Generic services, in all categories studied, were available to the retarded and/or their parents. There were only a few recorded instances when an agency did not serve the retarded as a matter of policy, and such policies did not always appear consistent with the retardates' needs or abilities to benefit from the program offered. Problems involving generic services include: (a) There are too few of them, especially in poverty areas. (b) Their activities are uncoordinated with those of other generic agencies as well as specialized programs. (c) Services, especially among nonmedical agencies, have low visibility and parents are unaware of their existence. (d) There is an absence of external support and guidance from persons professionally trained in programming for the retarded. (e) Financial considerations preclude the use of generic services by some parents. (f) There is an absence of specialized programs essential to complement generic services. In other words, specialized and generic services must participate in a balanced partnership to meet the needs of the retarded, and their programs must be identifiable, well publicized, readily accessible, and coordinated.

2. *To study the variance of accessibility according to socio-geographic area:* Variance of availability of generic services for the retarded was evidenced by parental comments rather than by the responses of representatives from generic agencies. There was a definite shortage of resources, including both private practitioners and community agencies, in the poverty area. Furthermore, those which did exist apparently were not utilized to the fullest extent by parents because of costs, transportation, language, and/or apathy based on lack of understanding.

3. *To identify problems encountered by professionals:* It was interesting to observe that professionals reported very few problems associated with serving the retarded. Also, difficulties which did arise appeared to be ac-

cepted by professionals as indigenous to their occupational responsibilities. With regard to problems posed by parents, the professionals were in relatively common agreement that the major difficulty involved parental understanding and acceptance of retardation. The only other problem of consequence has been mentioned, i.e., the lack of understanding by parents in poverty areas concerning mental retardation which results in a general apathy towards using and supporting related programs.

4. *To identify problems encountered by parents:* Parent responses indicated little or negative reactions toward private medical personnel, including general practitioners, pediatricians, and dentists. The basic problems they expressed revolved around a lack of community resources, both generic and special, to serve the retarded, especially in the areas of education and training, vocational training and sheltered workshops, and local residential care.

An inchoate need of the parents was, however, *inferred* on the basis of their responses: Parents must have access to a program of guidance and counseling which will assist them in making decisions concerning their retardate at each stage in his life. As evidenced in this study, parents in general did not possess sufficient information about mental retardation and community programs nor did they have access to any agency which could provide the continuity of assistance required.

This finding also raises a question concerning compatibility of parental expectations with professional commitments. It would appear that though professional persons representing a variety of specialties and agencies profess many responsibilities for both the retarded and their parents, such responsibilities are not communicated to parents. For example, parents seem to accept the physician's role with regard to retardation in the same manner as they accept his role in any medical problem. If he provides appropriate medical attention in a pleasant manner, he is viewed as having fulfilled his role most adequately. Apparently, parents do not expect the primary physician to assume the broad responsibilities associated with lifelong planning for the retarded.

Though, as previously stated, the data certainly do not justify conclusions, they do, nevertheless, emphasize the need to implement the following four recommendations: ... (1) Open every generic community agency to the retarded insofar as these agencies' competence and ability permit. (2) Provide basic training in mental retardation for every health worker. (3) Place a mental retardation specialist, either full-time or part-time, in every generic agency of any size or significance. (4) Establish a coordinating mechanism within each community to ensure balanced services.

REFERENCES

[Seven references not reprinted.]

Part VI

SURVEILLANCE

40 Introduction to Part VI

Webster's New Collegiate Dictionary defines *surveillance* as keeping "a close watch over someone" or "supervision." In professional literature it is rarely defined and generally implies a variety of concepts. It almost always refers to something which is done after treatment or a stage of treatment, and it overlaps with the concepts of continuity of care and follow-up services. To some degree the parent is given a role in the surveillance of a child with a handicap. For instance, when medication is prescribed, the parent is advised to "watch out for" various symptoms which may reflect side reactions. Also, since many problems are predictable, the professional may provide anticipatory guidance; he may advise the parent to watch for the emergence of a problem, suggest ways of handling it, and identify the circumstances under which the parent should return the child to the service system. Usually, however, *surveillance* refers to what persons in the service system do to keep track of cases, making periodic observations of progress and checking on the need for further diagnosis and/or treatment.

All of this adds up to a completely unacceptable definition of surveillance both from the perspective of this book and from the perspective of the current service systems. The parent does have the day-to-day care, the day-to-day surveillance of the child, and on the basis of that surveillance, initiates contact with medical, social, recreational, and educational providers. In other words, parents conduct surveillance every day, and the service system does it occasionally.

But the service system provides little surveillance on its own, possibly from lack of interest by some and definitely from lack of funds. Unfortunately no study exists of surveillance contacts initiated by the service system over a long period. From personal experience, communications with service system personnel, and the tone of the literature, this writer is convinced that surveillance by the service system is the exception rather than the rule.

A better definition of surveillance is suggested: *Surveillance is a continuing assessment of the child's progress, of the emergence of new problems, and of the parents' capacity to cope with both progress and problems.* Given such a definition, the service system should specify the standards for its part of surveillance. It has not done so, although articles such as Schild's (Part III) on the continuing casework relationship and Hawley's (1963, not printed) on public health nursing are starts. Second, the service system should help the parents provide their own surveillance. Several of the articles on counseling, group counseling, and information sharing touch on this subject; although the term is infrequently used, these articles really refer to "anticipatory guidance"—telling the parents what to look for and what to do.

All in all, however, the service system has not generated a literature on surveillance. This omission probably reflects too little formal attention to the concept which, not incidentally, covers most of the time the child is alive. The lack of attention to surveillance also helps to explain the second class status to which the term "continuity of care" has been relegated. In the previous section on treatment, continuity of care was seen as part of "comprehensive" care. This displaced "continuity" is a principal desired characteristic of medical care in the early 1960's in the context of massive Federal spending on health care. It refers principally to the capacity of one program to mobilize all the resources which are required to ameliorate a family's multi-faceted problem. Certainly this is desirable, but it is best suited to the treatment of acute, not chronic conditions. It is postulated here that "comprehensive care" and "continuity of care" are related to each other as width is related to length. Comprehensivity is the width of the program—the capacity of one program to respond to a broad array of problems in the family. Continuity is the length—the capacity of a program to carry out, or participate in, a logical sequence of services over a long period of time. By extension, it is postulated that—in reference to chronic conditions—continuity of care is more intimately related to surveillance than to comprehensivity of care.

In the absence of a literature on surveillance, the "Summary" of McKinlay's article (1972) was selected for several reasons. The other readings in this book focus on just one type of consumer, the parent of a handicapped child. There is a broader literature on the utilization of service generally, and McKinlay systematically reviewed 359 works on that subject. In his discussion of strengths and weaknesses of the literature as a whole, he identifies an area that has been neglected, "the current status and utility of the concept of a 'social network' for the understanding of utilization behavior."

It is easy to consider only two classes of problems, those parents feel capable of handling themselves and those which require help from the official service system. In a third class of problems, however, advice, support, information, or guidance from kin or friends may be enough for the parent. Indeed, kin and friends in this "social network" may go beyond supportive services to supplementary services (such as weekday care of the child) or to substitute services (such as total care of the child for a period of time or permanently).

Indeed, parents may use this social network to avoid unnecessary consumption of official services which are stressful, time-consuming, and costly. But the parents' social network may know no more about care of the retarded child than the parents; consequently there is a need for something more expert than the usual social network and less official than the service system. Parents' organizations serve such a function for many; for others, relationships with other parents of retarded children allow the exchange of information and support. Thus a new social network is established when the child's needs are beyond the parents' self-assessed capacities. When even the new social network is inadequate, it serves as a referral system to the official service system. (For example, some retarded children, detected at birth, show up in special-education classes at the appropriate age. From whom did the parents learn about the special-education program and where to apply?)

The social network is not one of the eight basic concepts of the consumer-provider division of labor, but it is a ninth concept with particular relevance to the surveillance period.

41 Some Approaches and Problems in the Study of the Uses of Services—An Overview

John B. McKinlay

This paper represents what the author considers to be a new attempt to provide a much-needed, systematic review of the literature that has appeared in the last two decades concerning utilization behavior. It has endeavored to trace the development of work in this area, highlighting a number of shortcomings as well as promising avenues for future research. Six analytically distinct approaches, or research strategies, have been isolated—the economic, socio-demographic, geographic, social-psychological, socio-cultural and organizational approaches—and selected studies, of widely varying quality, considered in relation to each of them.

There are a number of issues or problem areas arising from the foregoing discussion which the author considers worthy of detailed future attention by researchers. While some of these relate to more general methodological questions, others involve substantive recommendations regarding specific areas of issue in the utilization field. Either these areas have been clearly neglected, or the precise importance of their contribution remains uncertain.

First, with regard to methodology, it would appear timely for researchers, rather than constructing or devising artificially sophisticated research schemes, to be prepared to be a little more flexible in approach and to let an inductive tendency characterize their work. Specifically, there is a need for a number of hypothesis-generating, small-scale, exploratory studies. Of course, the author realizes that such studies are sometimes regarded as "cop outs," avoiding issues relating to quantification, reliability, and replicability, as well as being difficult to fund. On the other hand, there are some well-known precedents for small-scale exploratory studies.

Second, given the present inadequate state of knowledge in some areas of utilization behavior, it would seem useful to replicate a number of earlier studies discussed in this paper. These confirmatory studies would perhaps assist in "unraveling" the apparently conflicting findings that exist in some areas. In particular, much work is needed concerning the relative importance (if any) of what have been termed "social-psychological factors" such as knowledge, attitudes, beliefs, and "triggers" or cues.

There has been a tendency for researchers to attempt to employ routinely collected records or official statistics—with all their limitations—in attempts to understand utilization behavior. As was pointed out earlier, these data inevitably force investigators to leave untouched the very questions that need to be considered. A third need therefore in the future is for survey studies that are explicitly concerned with the prospective investigation of the utilization behavior of identifiable groups in relation to particular services. Only then will answers be forthcoming to the more subtle types of questions that have been raised in the second half of this paper.

Turning now to the more substantive recommendations, it seems that much more baseline, socio-demographic information needs to be acquired. It was suggested earlier that, despite the many socio-demographic studies reported, relatively little is known about utilizers, underutilizers, and especially overutilizers, except at a very superficial level. Particularly useful at this time would be intensive data relating to the possible importance for utilization behavior of such broad factors as area of residence, occupational group (as distinct from social class), occupational and residential stability, household composition, and stage in the life cycle.

A second area that appears worthy of separate and detailed attention relates to the current status and utility of the concept of a "social network" for the understanding of utilization behavior. It is perhaps truistic to point out that family, and its associated kin and friendship networks, are important influences on health and illness behavior, yet there have been remarkably few attempts to specify the nature of such influences. The author considers that the following types of questions deserve particular consideration: Is it possible to detect intrafamily patterns of utilization behavior? Are there certain conditions or states in which the members of the total family play a more important role in defining, consulting, referring, etc., while other conditions involve noticeably fewer members? Does the geographical proximity of the family, related kin, and friends affect the nature of their influence on utilization? Are kin and friends more important determinants of use of health and welfare services than association with different social classes, ethnic groups, or even regions? Does the total family play a more influential role in utilization behavior when only certain age groups are involved or at different points in the family cycle? Is the influence of the family on utilization behavior in any way related to the particular type of agency being utilized? Do the family and its associated networks in any way affect the efficacy of care after a service has been used? Does the age structure of the family and its networks influence the quality and content of the lay advice received?

Earlier, it was suggested that there have been few attempts to specify in specific detail the various processes, stages, and types of decisions made in help seeking. In the author's view, this constitutes a third area that needs separate and detailed discussion. Of particular interest at the present time would be detailed empirical information relating to the number and various types of stages typically passed through in the use of some services; whether different stages involve different types or orders of decisions; and the extent to which different orders or types of contingencies or parameters operate to affect decisions at different stages. It would also be valuable to know whether there are condition-specific careers (e.g. pregnancy, venereal disease, cancer, etc.) and if these differ from the typical help-seeking careers outlined above. It is clear that information regarding the influence of the structure of social networks on utilization behavior would also facilitate a greater understanding of aspects of help-seeking careers. There is no doubt that much of the work to date, reviewed in the foregoing discussion, would be included in the organizational or "Official" perspective—professionals' typifications of clients. There can of course be no doubt regarding the importance of understanding the nature of officials' definitions of clients, of locating their sources, and of considering their subsequent effect on service provision. However, it is equally important that the counter or oppositional typifications of professionals and agencies by clients be examined. Some of the reasons for the present imbalance in research have already been discussed.

A fourth area, therefore, which, in the author's view, deserves the attention of researchers relates to the study of clients themselves, and organizational impedimenta from the clients' perspective. It would be valuable, for example, to know whether, and to what extent, certain client definitions or typifications of agencies are specific to certain types of organization and delivery, or specific to a certain area of activity regardless of organizational type. Useful also in this respect would be information regarding whether and under what circumstances certain definitions are transferred from agency to agency and the subsequent effect on the interpersonal strategies adopted to obtain service. As was pointed out earlier, utilization research in the Seventies will probably become increasingly preoccupied with the effects on behavior of organizational or delivery system variables. One would hope that the current imbalance, which has been alluded to above, will not be perpetuated and that clients themselves in relation to the organizations they utilize will be studied.

In conclusion, it should be reiterated that the author has deliberately not attempted to cover every possible approach—a task clearly beyond the scope of one paper. Instead, an attempt has been made to indicate the range and scope of some approaches and to trace their emergence by touching on a number of their limitations and highlighting new directions of sociological interest. Moreover, the various approaches have been only analytically distinguished for heuristic purposes. Seldom do researchers in the area of utilization behavior adopt only one approach to the exclusion of all others, although one may be given greater emphasis.

Part VII

CONCLUSIONS AND GUIDE TO FURTHER READING

42 Conclusions

All of the sections above and all the selected readings were intended to attain two objectives. First, the narrative components of the text were intended to develop a simplistic mode of conceptualizing the clinical interface between the service system and parents of children with handicapping conditions. Secondly, both the narrative and the selected readings were intended to apply the conceptualization to parents of children with one type of handicapping condition, mental retardation.

At its simplest level, the mode of conceptualization is an eight-concept model. The first concept is *time*, in reflection of the long-term relationship between parents and the service system for the care of the handicapped child. The next four concepts describe the four types of encounters consumers and providers have over time: *detection, diagnosis, treatment* and *surveillance*. The final three concepts focus on the three divisions of labor necessary to carry out the encounters over time: *interdisciplinary, interorganizational* and *consumer-provider* divisions of labor. This book has focused on the consumer-provider division of labor (relationship). Furthermore, the eight-concept model has been limited to the clinical interface of the consumer and provider and did not consider the higher levels of service administration, the role of training programs or the full role of research.

Mental retardation is the handicapping condition which has been used to illustrate the conceptualization. To remain consistent with most handicapping conditions, the focus of the book has been limited to mental retardation of an organic rather than a socio-cultural etiology.

The consumer-provider relationship develops in response to the problems encountered by parents in the care of their retarded children. Although the literature which identifies such problems is quite voluminous, no typology of problems has yet been offered and gained widespread acceptance. It was suggested that any typology which is to be developed might begin with a dichotomy of problems: (i) the problems encountered in the care of the child and (ii) the problems encountered in the consumption of service. From such a dichotomization the service system may evolve the dual role of ameliorating the first set of problems and reducing the extent of the second.

The basic operating unit of the service system is the professional, and the service system's self-definition of role tends to be the sum of the role statements of the participating professions. Role statements in the literature are uniformly concerned about the emotional equilibrium of the parents and are rather uniformly focused on the provision of counseling. The question of dominance characterizes the literature on the general relationship between consumer and provider. Although much of the literature describes a search for an equal partnership (egalitarian) relationship, the tendency of at least some parents to become at least temporarily emotionally disabled inclines many to adopt a stance of benevolent dominance.

Detection is the precipitator of the long-term interaction between consumer and provider. It refers to the first realization that "something may be wrong"—a realization made first by parents in some cases and first by the service system in others. The literature on detection is quite meager and may reflect an under-emphasis by the service system on early casefinding. To the degree that early casefinding is important, the service system has been remiss in its role of studying the consumer-provider division of labor for discovering new cases.

Diagnosis is the logical sequel to detection and has commanded considerable attention in the literature. Although the diagnostic process is quite technical and falls mainly within the purview of the service system, the parent has been studied in roles such as providing reliable histories on the basis of accurately perceived child development. However, the preoccupation of the service system appears to be on the parents' capacity to understand the diagnosis and act on it in an atmosphere of extraordinary stress.

Treatment is the subject of choice in the literature since most of the professionals in the service system are derivatives of treatment-oriented training programs. The various treatment modalities tend to cluster into the areas of supportive, supplementary and substitute services, all with the goal of maximizing the growth potential of the child. Supportive services leave all child care roles to the parent and consist of service inputs for the parents alone. They tend to consist of the provision of counseling, the sharing of information or the teaching of child care or child treatment techniques. Supplementary services absorb some parental functions in child care or treatment in such forms as day care, home-maker services, or direct treatment of the child for problems associated with the retardation. Substitute services consist of the absorption by the service system of all parental functions, and generally do so in the form of institutionalization, foster care or adoption placement. The trend in recent years has been away from substitute services and toward the organization of supportive and supplementary services in the community in comprehensive care programs.

Surveillance is the continuing assessment of the childs' progress or the emergence of new problems, and of the parents' capacity to cope with both the degree of progress and the new problems. The absence of much consideration of surveillance in the literature reflects the limited practice of surveillance by the service system. Consequently, and operationally, surveillance is what the parent does. The social networks parents form over time are probably the critical determinants of the quality of parental surveillance.

ASSESSMENT OF THE LITERATURE

The literature has been treated in two ways throughout this work. First, readings have been selected to provide detail on the concepts of the book. Second, the readings as a whole have been studied as indicating the degree and type of interest the service system has in the various concepts. As we have seen there are relatively few articles on detection and surveillance and many articles on treatment. As in the literature on other handicapping conditions, most authors limit their attention to one condition, even one aspect of one handicapping condition. However, when the initial focus is on the families of the handicapped, especially the parents, two problems come to mind as derivatives of such a limited scope of attention by professionals. .

First, knowledge becomes encapsulated around the isolated condition rather than around the subject of families, so that there is limited transfer of knowledge about parenting one handicapping condition to parenting others. To a degree this may be warranted since the problems of parenting one type of handicapped child may not be qualitatively similar to the problems of parenting another type. On the other hand, for instance, one may argue that it is more logical to cluster families of children with congenitally determined and detected retardation with families of children with other congenital abnormalities than it is to cluster them with families of children whose retardation was not diagnosed until the early school years.

In other words, the focus of the professional is initially on the condition of the child and secondarily on the family. Advertently or inadvertently, such an initial focus maximizes the differences, rather than the similarities.

This tendency of authors to focus narrowly forces their audience to integrate knowledge in two stages. First, the integration of individually generated pieces of knowledge about one aspect of one condition. Second, the integration of knowledge about several aspects of a condition into a broader, cohesive body of knowledge. Although several authors have published works on the first level of integration, very few have attempted the second, so that the literature as a whole resembles a partially assembled jigsaw puzzle. This is attributable to the absence of a broader mode of conceptualization which would guide the second stage of integration. (By extension, integration of knowledge across handicapping conditions is still in a pre-conceptional stage.)

In a natural science such as biology, knowledge is advanced in very small areas and is integrated periodically in specialized fields before it is integrated into the totality of biological knowledge, generally in the form of an introductory text. Training biologists is in the reverse order of knowledge generation; that is, embryonic biologists cut their teeth on overview texts before they proceed to branches of biology and through several levels of specialization. Such a sequence of training is geared to perspective setting, so that those in specialized areas of work know what they are a part of, what they are contributing to.

The service system for parents of handicapped children is analogous to the field of biology. However, its functioning unit is the professional, and all professionals have been trained at the specialist level. There is no broader body of knowledge to which all the helping professions (specialists) relate. Consequently, the sum of the literature they generate does not constitute an integrated whole.

It is postulated here that the proper base for building an integrated body of knowledge is the consumer-provider relationship at the clinical interface level. Ultimately knowledge demonstrates its value there. Ultimately all training programs, all administration, all legislation, and all publicly supported research must be evaluated for their contribution to the service system's part of the consumer-provider division of labor. The consumer-provider relationship is the *sine qua non* of an integrating mode of conceptualization.

Relative to families with handicapped children, this book offers a simplistic eight-concept model built on the consumer-provider relationship. The concepts of the model are not the only ones which may be included and they may not be the best ones. In the absence of a competing model, however, it is suggested that the evaluation of this model should not be an absolute assessment of its worth, but an assessment of the degree to which it lends itself to further refinements by other authors, so that work may proceed on the development of a more balanced, more integrated, more relevant body of knowledge than we have now.

43 *Guide to Further Reading*

BOOKS AND MONOGRAPHS

Many books on mental retardation contain sections on the family. Two are particularly recommended: (1) Bernard Farber. *Mental Retardation: Its Social Context and Social Consequences.* A scholarly treatise on mental retardation from the perspective of the social sciences. It also has a comprehensive and well-referenced chapter on the family. (2) Ray H. Barsch. *The Parent of the Handicapped Child.* One of the few books that reports research findings within and across various handicapping conditions.

Many books of readings emphasize one topic. The following are especially good: (1) Herbert G. Birch. *Brain Damage in Children: The Biological and Social Aspects.* Eight major papers on various dimensions of the subject. Of particular interest is Kelman's article on the family. (2) Richard Koch and James Dobson. *The Mentally Retarded Child and His Family: A Multi-disciplinary Handbook.* Twenty-nine articles resembling those on professional roles in Part III. (3) William Kvaraceus and E. Nelson Hayes. *If Your Child is Handicapped.* Forty-eight articles by parents of children with various handicaps. Eight are specifically concerned with mental retardation. (4) Robert Noland. *Counseling Parents of the Mentally Retarded.* Thirty-one articles on various aspects of the subject. (5) Wolf Wolfensberger and Richard Kurtz. *Management of the Family of the Mentally Retarded.* Like this book it focuses on the clinical interface of consumer and provider. However, it relies solely on excerpts (ninety in all) rather than complete articles.

Of the monographs available, four are particularly interesting: (1) Michael J. Begab. *The Mentally Retarded Child: A Guide to Services of Social Agencies.* Although this 134-page work speaks principally to social workers, it contains a comprehensive chapter on the family. (2) Elizabeth R. Kramm. *Families of Mongoloid Children.* Fifty-six pages; focuses solely on families with one type of retarded child, but gives more information from interviews than is possible in a journal article. (3) Marian M. Holtgrewe. *A Guide for Public Health Nurses Working with Mentally Retarded Children.* This 49-page report considers case-finding and interdisciplinary processes in the context of the public health nurse's role. (4) Una Hayes. *A Developmental Approach to Casefinding* . . . Eighty-five pages with detailed consideration of detection and special emphasis on the role of the nurse.

Barsch, Ray H. *The Parent of the Handicapped Child.* Springfield, Illinois: Charles C Thomas, 1968.

Begab, Michael J. *The Mentally Retarded Child: A Guide to Services of Social Agencies.* Washington, D.C.: U.S. Government Printing Office, 1963.

Birch, Herbert G. (Ed.). *Brain Damage in Children: The Biological and Social Aspects.* Baltimore: Williams and Wilkins Co., 1964.

Farber, Bernard. *Mental Retardation: Its Social Context and Social Consequences.* Boston: Houghton Mifflin Co. 1968.

Goddard, Henry H. *The Kallikak Family: A Study in the Heredity of Feeblemindedness.* New York: Macmillan Co., 1912.

Gottwald, Henry. *Public Awareness About Mental Retardation.* Arlington, Va.: The Council for Exceptional Children, 1970.

Haynes Una. *A Developmental Approach to Casefinding with Special Reference to Cerebral Palsy, Mental Retardation and Related Disorders.* Washington, D.C.: U.S. Government Printing Office, 1969.

Holtgrewe, Marian M. *A Guide for Public Health Nurses Working with Mentally Retarded Children.* Washington, D.C.: U.S. Government Printing Office, 1964.

Kadushin, Alfred. *Child Welfare Services.* New York: Macmillan Co., 1967.

Koch, Richard and James C. Dobson (Eds.). *The Mentally Retarded Child and His Family: A Multidisciplinary Handbook.* New York: Brunner-Mazel, 1971.

Kramm, Elizabeth R. *Families of Mongoloid Children.* Washington, D.C.: U.S. Government Printing Office, 1963.

Kvaraceus, William C. and E. Nelson Hayes (Eds.). *If Your Child is Handicapped.* Boston: Porter Sargent, 1969.

Noland, Robert L. (Ed.). *Counseling Parents of the Mentally Retarded.* Springfield, Ill.: Charles C Thomas, 1970.

Tizard, J. *Community Services for the Mentally Handicapped.* London: Oxford University Press, 1964.

Tizard, J. and Jacqueline C. Grad. *The Mentally Handicapped and Their Families.* London: Oxford University Press, 1961.

Wolfensberger, Wolf, and Richard A. Kurtz (Eds.). *Management of the Family of the Mentally Retarded.* Chicago: Follett Educational Corporation, 1969.

Wolfensberger, Wolf *et al. The Principle of Normalization in Human Services.* Toronto: (Canadian) National Institute on Mental Retardation, 1972.

ARTICLES

Many articles have been published on the subject. Most of the better ones from 1955 are listed below. For the most recent publications, the reader may refer to the *Index Medicus* and to the references in recently published articles.

Abel, Theodora M. "A Study of a Group of Subnormal Girls Successfully Adjusted in Industry and the Community," *The American Journal of Mental Deficiency,* 45 (September 1940), 66–72.

Adams, Margaret E. "Foster Care for Mentally Retarded Children: How Does Child Welfare Meet This Challenge?," *Child Welfare,* 49 (May 1970), 260–269.

Adams, Margaret E. and Ralph W. Colvin. "The Deprivation Hypothesis: Its Application to Mentally Retarded

Children and Their Needs," *Child Welfare*, 48 (March 1969), 136–141.

Allen, John E. and Louis Lelchuck. "A Comprehensive Care Program for Children With Handicaps," *American Journal of Diseases of Children*, 111 (March 1966), 229–235.

Anderson, Alice V. "Orientating Parents to the Clinic for the Retarded," *Children*, 9 (September–October 1962), 178–182.

Anderson, Kathryn A. "The 'Shopping' Behavior of Parents of Mentally Retarded Children: The Professional Person's Role," *Mental Retardation*, 9 (August 1971), 3–5.

Anderson, Kathryn A. and Ann M. Graner. "Mothers of Retarded Children: Satisfaction With Visits to Professional People," *Mental Retardation*, 11 (August 1973), 36–39.

Andrew, Gwen, William Kime, Vernon Stehman, and Robert Jaslow. "Parental Contacts Along the Route to Institutional Commitment of Retarded Children," *American Journal of Mental Deficiency*, 70 (November 1965), 339–407.

Appell, Melville J. "Description and Analysis of an Information, Referral, and Coordination Unit," *Mental Retardation*, 4 (February 1966), 16–20.

Appell, Melville J. and William J. Tisdall. "Factors Differentiating Institutionalized from Noninstitutionalized Referred Retardates," *American Journal of Mental Deficiency*, 73 (November 1968), 424–432.

Appell, Melville J., Clarence M. Williams, and Kenneth N. Fishell. "Changes in Attitudes of Parents of Retarded Children Effected Through Group Counseling," *American Journal of Mental Deficiency*, 68 (May 1964), 807–812.

Arnold, Irene and Lawrence Goodman. "Homemaker Services to Families with Young Retarded Children," *Children*, 13 (July–August 1966), 149–152.

Ash, Philip. "The Reliability of Psychiatric Diagnosis," *Journal of Abnormal and Social Psychology*, 44 (April 1949), 272–276.

Auerbach, Aline B. "Group Education for Parents of the Handicapped," *Children*, 8 (July–August 1961), 135–140.

Baker, Edith U. "Diagnostic and Treatment Services for the Mentally Retarded Child," *Child Welfare*, 39 (September 1960), 8–13.

Barclay, A., L. R. Goulet, M. M. Holtgrewe, and A. R. Sharp. "Parental Evaluations of Clinical Services for Retarded Children," *American Journal of Mental Deficiency*, 67 (September 1962), 232–237.

Barker, D. J. P. "Numbers of Relatives of Severely Subnormal Children," *British Journal of Preventive and Social Medicine*, 20 (October 1966), 162–164.

Baroff, George S. "Some Parent-Teacher Problems in Mental Retardation," *Training School Bulletin*, 60 (May 1963), 38–42.

Barsch, Ray H. "Explanations Offered by Parents and Siblings of Brain-Damaged Children," *Exceptional Children*, 27 (January 1961), 286–291.

_____. "The Handicapped Ranking Scale Among Parents of Handicapped Children," *American Journal of Public Health*, 54 (September 1964), 1560–1567.

Bartman, Richard E. "Placement of Mentally Retarded Children: Home or Institution?" *Minnesota Medicine*, 49 (January 1966), 137–139.

Bass, Medora S. "Attitudes of Parents of Retarded Children Toward Voluntary Sterilization," *Eugenics Quarterly*, 14 (March 1967), 45–53.

Baum, Marian Hooper. "Some Dynamic Factors Affecting Family Adjustment to the Handicapped Child," *Exceptional Children*, 28 (April 1962), 387–392.

Beck, Helen L. "Casework With Parents of Mentally Retarded Children," *American Journal of Ortho-*

psychiatry, 32 (October 1962), 870–877.

_____. "Counseling Parents of Retarded Children," *Children*, 6 (November–December 1959), 225–230.

Begab, Michael J. "Unmet Needs of the Mentally Retarded in the Community," *American Journal of Mental Deficiency*, 62 (January 1958), 712–723.

_____. "Mental Retardation and Family Stress," *Clinical Proceedings–Children's Hospital–D.C.*, 24 (February 1968), 50–65.

Benda, Clemens E., Newell D. Squires, John Ogonik, and Robert Wise. "Personality Factors in Mild Mental Retardation: Part I–Family Background and Sociocultural Patterns," *American Journal of Mental Deficiency*, 68 (July 1963), 24–40.

Benda, Clemens E., Newell D. Squires, John Ogonik, Robert Wise, and Ruth Akin. "The Relationship Between Intellectual Inadequacy and Emotional and Sociocultural Privation," *Comprehensive Psychiatry*, 5 (October 1964), 294–313.

Bierman, Jessie M., Angie Connor, Marilyn Vaage, and Marjorie P. Honzik. "Pediatricians' Assessments of the Intelligence of Two-Year-Olds and Their Mental Test Scores," *Pediatrics*, 34 (November 1964), 680–689.

Birenbaum, Arnold. "The Mentally Retarded Child in the Home and the Family Circle," *Journal of Health and Social Behavior*, 12 (March 1971), 55–65.

Bitter, James A. "Attitude Change by Parents of Trainable Mentally Retarded Children as a Result of Group Discussion," *Exceptional Children*, 30 (December 1964), 173–177.

Blatt, Burton. "Some Persistently Recurring Assumptions Concerning the Mentally Subnormal," *Training School Bulletin*, 57 (August 1960), 48–59.

Blumethal, Monica D. "Experiences of Parents of Retardates and Children With Cystic Fibrosis," *Archives of General Psychiatry*, 21 (August 1969), 160–171.

Boyd, Dan. "The Three Stages in the Growth of a Parent of a Mentally Retarded Child," *American Journal of Mental Deficiency*, 55 (April 1951), 608–611.

Brown, D.F. "Home Placement of a PKU Child With Severe Mental Retardation," *Developmental Medicine and Child Neurology*, 10 (December 1968), 776–780.

Bryant, Keith, and J. Cotter Hirschberg. "Helping the Parents of a Retarded Child: The Role of the Physician," *American Journal of Diseases of Children*, 102 (July 1961), 52–66.

Butterfield, William H. "Modeling and Shaping by Parents to Develop Chewing Behavior in Their Retarded Child," *Journal of Behavior Therapy and Experimental Psychiatry*, 4 (September 1973), 285–287.

Caffey, John. "On the Theory and Practice of Shaking Infants," *American Journal of Diseases of Children*, 124 (August 1972), 161–169.

Caldwell, Bettye M., and Samuel B. Guze. "A Study of the Adjustment of Parents and Siblings of Institutionalized and Non-institutionalized Retarded Children," *American Journal of Mental Deficiency*, 64 (March 1960), 845–861.

Caldwell, Bettye M., Edward J. Manley, and Yael Nissan. "Reactions of Community Agencies and Parents to Services in a Clinic for Retarded Children," *American Journal of Mental Deficiency*, 65 (March 1961), 582–589.

Caldwell, Bettye M., Edward J. Manley, and Barbara J. Seelye. "Factors Associated With Parental Reaction to a Clinic for Retarded Children," *American Journal of Mental Deficiency*, 65 (March 1961), 590–594.

Caplan, Gerald. "Patterns of Parental Response to the Crisis of Premature Birth," *Psychiatry*, 23 (November 1960), 365–374.

Capobianco, R. J., and Stanley Knox.

"IQ Estimates and the Index of Marital Integration," *American Journal of Mental Deficiency*, 68 (May 1964), 718–721.

Casse, Robert M. "The Professional's Responsibility in Aiding Parental Adjustment," *Mental Retardation*, 6 (February 1968), 49–51.

Centerwall, Siegried A., and Willard R. Centerwall. "A Study of Children With Mongolism Reared in the Home Compared to Those Reared Away from the Home," *Pediatrics*, 25 (April 1960), 678–685.

Chambelain, E.R. "Maximising Treatment Susceptibility During the Diagnostic Process," *Slow Learning Child*, 10 (1963), 32–37.

Chazan, Maurice. "The Incidence and Nature of Maladjustment Among Children in Schools for the Educationally Subnormal," *British Journal of Educational Psychology*, 34 (November 1964), 292–304.

Chidester, Leona, and Karl A. Meninger. "Application of Psychoanalytic Methods to the Study of Mental Retardation," *The American Journal of Orthopsychiatry*, 6 (October 1936), 616–625.

Cianci, Vincentz. "Home Training for the Mentally Retarded," *Children*, 2 (May–June 1955), 99–104.

Clarke, Cicily M., and D. Russel Davis. "The Families of Mentally Retarded Children," *Developmental Medicine and Child Neurology*, 5 (February 1963), 279–286.

Cobb, Dorothy, and Robert C. Wilber. "Explorations in Family Care Placement for Retarded Children," *American Journal of Mental Deficiency*, 63 (May 1959), 1089–1093.

Cohen, Jacob. "Survey of a School Program for Family Care of School Age Children," *The American Journal of Mental Deficiency*, 51 (January 1947), 502–509.

Cohen, Pauline C. "The Impact of the Handicapped Child on the Family," *Social Casework*, 43 (March 1962), 137–142.

Cole, W. Edward. "Three Summers: Experiments in Temporary Residential Care of Retardates," *Training School Bulletin*, 67 (August 1970), 131–136.

Coleman, James C. "Group Therapy With Parents of Mentally Deficient Children," *The American Journal of Mental Deficiency*, 57 (April 1953), 700–704.

Collins, James F., Steven P. Maitinsky, and Bert Jablon. "Handicapped Need Total Care," *Hospital*, 46 (June 16, 1972), 52–56.

Condell, James F. "Parental Attitudes Toward Mental Retardation," *American Journal of Mental Deficiency*, 71 (July 1966), 85–92.

Cook, John J. "Dimensional Analysis of Child-Rearing Attitudes of Parents of Handicapped Children," *American Journal of Mental Deficiency*, 68 (November 1963), 354–361.

Cowie, Valerie. "Parental Awareness of Retardation," *Developmental Medicine and Child Neurology*, 9 (August 1967), 494–496.

Craig, Roy Dale. "Sexual Sterilization," *American Journal of Obstetrics and Gynecology*, 74 (August 1957), 328–340.

Creak, E. M. "Problems of Subnormal Children Studied in the Thousand Family Survey," *Lancet*, 2 (August 7, 1965), 282–283.

Cummings, S. Thomas, and Dorothy Stock. "Brief Group Therapy of Mothers of Retarded Children Outside of the Specialty Clinic Setting," *American Journal of Mental Deficiency*, 66 (March 1962), 739–748.

Cummings, S. Thomas, Helen C. Bayley, and Herbert E. Rie. "Effect of the Child's Deficiency on the Mother: A Study of Mothers of Mentally Retarded, Chronically Ill, and Neurotic Children," *American Journal of Orthopsychiatry*, 36 (July 1966), 595–608.

Curfman, Hope G., and Carol B. Arnold. "A Homebound Therapy Program for Severely Retarded Children," *Children,* 14 (March–April 1967), 63–67.

Dalton, Juanita, and Helene Epstein. "Counseling Parents of Mildly Retarded Children," *Social Casework,* 44 (November 1963), 523–530.

D'Arcy, Elizabeth. "Congenital Defects: Mothers' Reactions to First Information," *British Medical Journal,* 3 (September 1968), 796–798.

Davis, Courtland H. "The Retarded Child: What Can the Physician Do?," *Virginia Medical Monthly,* 87 (February 1960), 66–71.

Davis, D. Russell. "Family Processes in Mental Retardation," *American Journal of Psychiatry,* 124 (September 1967), 340–350.

Deisher, Robert W. "Role of Physician in Maintaining Continuity of Care and Guidance," *Journal of Pediatrics,* 50 (February 1957), 231–235.

Dembo, Tamara. "Sensitivity of One Person to Another," *Rehabilitation Literature,* 25 (August 1964), 231–235.

Denenberg, Victor H. "Critical Periods, Stimulus Input, and Emotional Reactivity," *Psychological Review,* 71 (September 1964), 335–351.

Denhoff, Eric. "The Impact of Parents on the Growth of Exceptional Children," *Exceptional Children,* 26 (January 1960), 271–274.

Dingman, H. F., R. K. Eyman, and C. D. Windle. "An Investigation of Some Child-Rearing Attitudes of Mothers With Retarded Children," *American Journal of Mental Deficiency,* 67 (May 1963), 899–908.

Dittmann, Laura L. "Home Training for Retarded Children," *Children,* 4 (May–June 1957), 89–94.

———. "The Family of the Child in an Institution," *American Journal of Mental Deficiency,* 66 (March 1962), 759–765.

Donohue, Daniel T. "Establishment of Day Care Programs for the Mentally Retarded," *Child Welfare,* 50 (November 1971), 519–523.

Downey, Kenneth J. "Parental Interest in the Institutionalized, Severely Mentally Retarded Child," *Social Problems,* 11 (summer 1963), 186–193.

———. "Parents' Reasons for Institutionalizing Severely Mentally Retarded Children," *Journal of Health and Human Behavior,* 6 (fall 1965), 147–155.

Drayer, Carl, and Elfriede G. Schlesinger. "The Informing Interview," *American Journal of Mental Deficiency,* 65 (November 1960), 363–370.

Drillien, C. M., and E. M. Wilkinson. "Mongolism: When Should Parents Be Told?" *British Medical Journal,* 2 (November 21, 1964), 1306–1307.

Durfee, Richard A. "The Misdiagnosis of Mental Retardation," *Journal of Rehabilitation,* 35 (January–February 1969), 22–24.

Dybwad, Gunnar. "Basic Legal Aspects in Providing Medical, Educational, Social, and Vocational Help to the Mentally Retarded," *Journal of Special Education,* (spring 1973), 39–49.

Dybwad, Rosemary F. "The Widening Role of Parent Organizations Around the World," *Mental Retardation,* 1 (December 1963), 258–358.

Ehlers, Walter H. "The Moderately and Severely Retarded Child: Maternal Perceptions of Retardation and Subsequent Seeking and Using Services Rendered by a Community Agency," *American Journal of Mental Deficiency,* 68 (March 1964), 660–668.

Erickson, Marilyn T. "MMPI Comparisons Between Parents of Young Emotionally Disturbed and Organically Retarded Children," *Journal of Consulting and Clinical Psychology,* 32 (November–December 1968), 701–706.

———. "MMPI Profiles of Parents of Young Retarded Children," *American Journal of Mental Deficiency,* 73 (March 1969), 728–732.

Ethun, Carol A. "Physical Management of the Multihandicapped Child," *GP*, 34 (July 1966), 80–86.

Ewert, Josephine C., and Meredith W. Green. "Conditions Associated With the Mother's Estimate of the Ability of Her Retarded Child," *American Journal of Mental Deficiency*, 62 (November 1957), 521–533.

Eyman, Richard K., Harvey F. Dingman, and Georges Sabagh. "Association of Characteristics of Retarded Patients and Their Families With Speed of Institutionalization," *American Journal of Mental Deficiency*, 71 (July 1966), 93–99.

Eyman, R. K., G. O'Connor, G. Tarjan, and R. S. Justice. "Factors Determining Residential Placement of Mentally Retarded Children," *American Journal of Mental Deficiency*, 76 (May 1972), 692–698.

Fabrega, Horacio, and Katerina Haka. "Parents of Mentally Handicapped Children," *Archives of General Psychiatry*, 16 (February 1967), 202–209.

Fackler, Eleanor. "The Crisis of Institutionalizing a Retarded Child," *American Journal of Nursing*, 68 (July 1968), 1508–1512.

"Family Care and Adoption of Retarded Children: An Annotated Bibliography," *Mental Retardation Abstracts*, 1 (January–March 1964), 332–333.

Farber, Bernard. "Perceptions of Crisis and Related Variables in the Impact of a Retarded Child on the Mother," *Journal of Health and Human Behavior*, 1 (summer 1960), 108–118.

Farber, Bernard, and David B. Ryckman. "Effects of Severely Mentally Retarded Children on Family Relationships," *Mental Retardation Abstracts*, 2 (January–March 1965), 1–17.

Felesenthal, Helen. "The Role of the School Psychologist in Counseling Parents of the Mentally Retarded," *Training School Bulletin*, 65 (May 1968), 29–35.

"The Forgotten: VII. A Family," *British Medical Journal*, 2 (April 24, 1971), 215.

Fotheringham, John B. "Retardation, Family Adequacy and Institutionalization," *Canada's Mental Health*, 18 (January–February 1970), 15–18.

Fowle, Carolyn M. "The Effect of the Severely Mentally Retarded Child on His Family," *American Journal of Mental Deficiency*, 73 (November 1968), 468–473.

Fredericks, H. D. Bud, Victor L. Baldwin, John J. McDonnell, Ronald Hofman, and James Harter. "Parents Educate Their Trainable Children," *Mental Retardation*, 9 (June 1971), 24–26.

Fremont, Albert C. "Utilization of Community Services," *Pediatric Clinics of North America*, 15 (November 1968), 989–1003.

Frey, Marybeth P. "ABC's for Parents: Aids to Management of the Slow Child at Home," *Rehabilitation Literature*, 26 (September 1965), 270–272.

Gamble, Clarence J. "Sterilization of the Mentally Deficient Under State Laws," *The American Journal of Mental Deficiency*, 51 (October 1946), 164–169.

Gardner, Richard A. "Psychogenic Problems of Brain-Injured Children and Their Parents," *Journal of the American Academy of Child Psychiatry*, 7 (1968), 471–491.

Gardner, William I. "Social and Emotional Adjustment of Mildly Retarded Children and Adolescents: Critical Review," *Exceptional Children*, 33 (October 1966), 97–105.

Garrett, Beatrice L. "Foster Family Services for Mentally Retarded Children," *Children*, 17 (November–December 1970), 228–233.

Giannini, Margaret J., and Lawrence Goodman. "Counseling Families During the Crisis Reaction to Mongolism," *American Journal of Mental*

Deficiency, 67 (March 1963), 740–747.

Goldberg, Benjamin, and Paul Max. "Postnatal Psychological Causes of Mental Retardation," *Canadian Medical Association Journal,* 87 (September 1962), 507–510.

Golden, Deborah A., and Jessica G. Davis. "Counseling Parents After the Birth of an Infant with Down's Syndrome," *Children Today,* 3 (March–April 1974), 7–11, 36.

Goodman, Lawrence. "Continuing Treatment of Parents With Congenitally Defective Infants," *Social Work,* 9 (January 1964), 92–97.

Gorelick, Molly C., and Malathi Sandhu. "Parent Perception of Retarded Child's Intelligence," *Personnel and Guidance Journal,* 46 (December 1967), 382–384.

Goshen, Charles E. "Mental Retardation and Neurotic Maternal Attitudes," *Archives of General Psychiatry,* 9 (August 1963), 168–174.

Graliker, Betty V., Arthur Parmelee, and Richard Koch. "Attitude Study of Parents of Mentally Retarded Children: II. Initial Reaction to a Diagnosis of Mental Retardation," *Pediatrics,* 24 (November 1959), 819–821.

Gregg, Grace S. "Comprehensive Professional Help for the Retarded Child and His Family," *Hospital and Community Psychiatry,* 19 (April 1968), 122–124.

Hammar, S. L., and K. E. Barnard. "The Mentally Retarded Adolescent," *Pediatrics,* 38 (November 1966), 845–857.

Hammar, S. L., L. S. Wright, and D. L. Jensen. "Sex Education for the Retarded Adolescent," *Clinical Pediatrics,* 6 (November 1967), 621–627.

Hammond, Jack, Manny Sternlicht, and Martin R. Deutsch. "Parental Interest in Institutionalized Children: A Survey," *Hospital and Community Psychiatry,* 20 (November 1969), 337–339.

Harper, Robert A. "The Responsibilities of Parenthood," *Eugenics Quarterly,* 6 (March 1959), 8–13.

Harrelson, Lawrence E., John E. Jordan, and Hartmut Horn. "An Application of Guttman Facet Theory to the Study of Attitudes Toward the Mentally Retarded in Germany," *The Journal of Psychology,* 80 (March 1972), 323–335.

Hawkins, Robert P., Robert F. Peterson, Edda Schweid, and Sidney W. Bijou. "Behavior Therapy in the Home: Amelioration of Problem Parent-Child Relations With the Parent in a Therapeutic Role," *Journal of Experimental Child Psychology,* 4 (September 1966), 99–107.

Hawley, Eleanor F. "The Importance of Extending Public Health Nursing Services to Retarded Children Living at Home," *Mental Retardation,* 1 (August 1963), 243–247.

Hayes, Gene A. "The Integration of the Mentally Retarded and Nonretarded in a Day Camping Program: A Demonstration Project," *Mental Retardation,* 7 (October 1969), 14–16.

Heilman, Ann E. "Parental Adjustment to the Dull Handicapped Child," *American Journal of Mental Deficiency,* 54 (April 1950), 556–562.

Heriot, James T., and Carol A. Schmickel. "Maternal Estimates of IQ in Children Evaluated for Learning Potential," *American Journal of Mental Deficiency,* 71 (May 1967), 920–924.

Hersey, William J. and Karin R. Lapidus. "Restoring the Balance," *Pediatric Clinics of North America,* 20 (February 1973), 221–231.

Hersh, Alexander. "Casework with Parents of Retarded Children," *Social Work,* 6 (April 1961), 61–66.

Hobbs, Mary T. "A Comparison of Institutionalized and Noninstitutionalized Mentally Retarded," *American Journal of Mental Deficiency,* 69 (September 1964), 206–210.

Hoffman, John L. "Mental Retardation, Religious Values, and Psychiatric Universals," *American Journal of Psychiatry,* 121 (March 1965), 885–889.

Hofstatter, Leopold, and Lilli Hofstatter. "Emotional Problems of the Child with Mental Retardation and His Family," *Southern Medical Journal,* 62 (May 1969), 583–587.

Holt, K. S. "The Influence of a Retarded Child Upon Family Limitation," *Journal of Mental Deficiency Research,* 2 (June 1958), 28–34.

Holt, K. S. "The Home Care of Severely Retarded Children," *Pediatrics,* 22 (October 1958), 744–755.

Honzik, Marjorie P. "A Sex Difference in the Age of Onset of the Parent-Child Resemblance in Intelligence," *Journal of Educational Psychology,* 54 (September–October 1963), 231–237.

Howell, Sarah Esselstyn. "Psychiatric Aspects of Habilitation," *Pediatric Clinics of North America,* 20 (February 1973), 203–219.

Hurley, John R. "Parental Acceptance-Rejection and Children's Intelligence," *Merrill-Palmer Quarterly,* 11 (January 1965), 19–31.

Hutchison, Alexander. "The Mentally-Handicapped Child: The Process of Acceptance by the Family," *Royal Society of Health Journal,* 85 (May–June 1965), 149–152.

Illingsworth, R. S. "Counseling the Parents of the Mentally Handicapped Child," *Clinical Pediatrics,* 6 (June 1967), 340–348.

Jamison, Colleen B., Arthur A. Attwell, and David H. Fils. "Parents vs. Teacher Behavior Ratings of TMR Pupils," *American Journal of Mental Deficiency,* 75 (May 1971), 746–751.

Jamison, John W. "The Impact of Mental Retardation on the Family and Some Directions of Help," *Journal of the National Medical Association,* 57 (March 1965), 136–138.

Jeffree, D. M. and Asher Cashdan. "The Home Background of the Se-

verely Subnormal Child: A Second Study," *British Journal of Medical Psychology,* 44 (March 1971), 27–33.

———. "Severely Subnormal Children and Their Parents: An Experiment in Language Improvement," *British Journal of Educational Psychology,* 41 (June 1971), 184–194.

Jensen, Reynold A. "Clinical Management of the Mentally Retarded Child and the Parents," *American Journal of Psychiatry,* 106 (May 1950), 830–833.

Jew, Wing. "Helping Handicapped Infants and Their Families," *Children Today,* 3 (May–June 1974), 7–10.

Jordan, Thomas E. "Research on the Handicapped Child and the Family," *Merrill-Palmer Quarterly,* 8 (October 1962), 243–260.

Jubenville, Charles P. "A State Program of Day Care Centers for Severely Retarded," *American Journal of Mental Deficiency,* 66 (May 1962), 829–837.

Justice, R. S., Gail O'Connor, and Neil Warren. "Problems Reported by Parents of Mentally Retarded Children—Who Helps?," *American Journal of Mental Deficiency,* 75 (May 1971), 685–691.

Justice, Robert S., Janice Bradley, and Gail O'Connor. "Foster Family Care for the Retarded: Management Concerns of the Caretaker," *Mental Retardation,* 9 (August 1971), 12–15.

Kanner, Leo. "Parents' Feelings About Retarded Children," *American Journal of Mental Deficiency,* 57 (January 1953), 375–383.

Kaplan, Frances, and Joseph J. Colombatto. "Head Start Program for Siblings of Mentally Retarded Children," *Mental Retardation,* 4 (December 1966), 30–32.

Kaplan, Frances, and Elizabeth Fox. "Siblings of the Retardate: An Adolescent Group Experience," *Community Mental Health Journal,* 4 (December 1968), 499–508.

Kaplan, Sidney, and Mary Jane Williams. "Confrontation Counseling: A New Dimension in Group Counseling," *American Journal of Orthopsychiatry*, 42 (January 1972), 114–118.

Keirn, William C. "Shopping Parents: Patient Problem or Professional Problem?," *Mental Retardation*, 9 (August 1971), 6–7.

Kenney, Eleanore T. "Mother-Retarded Child Relationships," *American Journal of Mental Deficiency*, 71 (January 1967), 631–636.

Keogh, Barbara, and Camille Legeay. "Recoil from the Diagnosis of Mental Retardation," *American Journal of Nursing*, 66 (April 1966), 778–780.

Kershner, John R. "Intellectual and Social Development in Relation to Family Functioning: A Longitudinal Comparison of Home vs. Institutional Effects," *American Journal of Mental Deficiency*, 75 (November 1970), 276–284.

Kirman, Brian H. "Advisory Service for Parents of Mentally Handicapped Children," *British Medical Journal*, 54 (January 1, 1966), 41–44.

Klaber, M. Michael. "Parental Visits to Institutionalized Children," *Mental Retardation*, 6 (December 1968), 39–41.

Klebanoff, Lewis B. "Parental Attitudes of Mothers of Schizophrenic, Brain-Injured and Retarded, and Normal Children," *American Journal of Orthopsychiatry*, 29 (July 1959), 445–454.

Knobloch, Hilda, and Benjamin Pasamanick. "Predicting Intellectual Potential in Infancy," *American Journal of Diseases of Children*, 106 (July 1963), 43–51.

Koch, Richard, Betty V. Graliker, Russell Sands, and Arthur H. Parmelee. "Attitude Studies of Parents With Mentally Retarded Children," *Pediatrics*, 23 (March 1959), 582–584.

Koch, Richard A., Nancy Ragsdale, Betty Graliker, Sylvia Schild, and Karol Fishler. "A Longitudinal Study of 143 Mentally Retarded Children (1955-1961)," *Training School Bulletin*, 61 (May 1963), 4–11.

Koegler, S. J. "The Management of the Retarded Child in Practice," *Canadian Medical Association Journal*, 89 (November 16, 1963), 1009–1014.

Kogan, Kate L., Herbert C. Wimberger, and Ruth A. Bobbitt. "Analysis of Mother-Child Interaction in Young Mental Retardates," *Child Development*, 40 (September 1969), 799–812.

Kohut, Susanne A. "The Abnormal Child: His Impact on the Family," *Physical Therapy*, 46 (February 1966), 160–167.

Krevelen, V. "The Problem of Communicating the Diagnosis to the Parents," *Acta Paedopsychiatrica*, 32 (February 1965), 33–34.

Kysar, John E. "The Two Camps in Child Psychiatry: A Report from a Psychiatrist-Father of an Autistic and Retarded Child," *American Journal of Psychiatry*, 125 (July 1968), 103–109.

Leeson, Joyce. "A Study of Six Young Mentally Handicapped Children ant Their Families," *The Medical Officer*, 104 (November 18, 1960), 311–314.

Legeay, Camille and Barbara Keogh. "Impact of Mental Retardation on Family Life," *American Journal of Nursing*, 66 (May 1966), 1062–1065.

Lei, Tzuen-Jen, Edgar W. Butler, and Georges Sabagh. "Family Sociocultural Background and the Behavioral Retardation of Children," *Journal of Health and Social Behavior*, 13 (September 1972), 318–326.

Levine, Samuel. "Sex-Role Identification and Parental Perceptions of Social Competence," *American Journal of Mental Deficiency*, 70 (May 1966), 822–824.

Levy, Joseph H. "A Study of Parent Groups for Handicapped Children,"

Exceptional Children, 19 (October 1952), 19–26.

Lewis, Juliet. "Effects of Group Procedures with Parents of MR Children," *Mental Retardation,* 10 (December 1972), 14–15.

Liberthson, Eva. "Helping Families Live with and for the Mentally Retarded Child," *Journal of Rehabilitation,* 34 (November–December 1968), 24–26.

Lund, Alton. "The Role of the N.A.R.C. in Advancing Horizons for the Retarded," *American Journal of Mental Deficiency,* 63 (1959), 1071–1077.

Lyle, J. G. "Environmentally Produced Retardation—Institution and Preinstitution Influences," *Journal of Abnormal and Social Psychology,* 69 (March 1964), 329–332.

Mamula, Richard A. "Developing a Training Program for Family Caretakers," *Mental Retardation,* 8 (April 1970), 30–35.

———. "The Use of Developmental Plans for Mentally Retarded Children in Foster Family Care," *Children,* 18 (March–April 1971), 65–68.

Mandelbaum, Arthur. "The Group Process in Helping Parents of Retarded Children," *Children,* 14 (November–December 1967), 227–232.

Mandelbaum, Arthur, and Mary Ella Wheeler. "The Meaning of a Defective Child to Parents," *Social Casework,* 41 (July 1960), 360–367.

Mann, Philip H., James D. Beaber, and Milton D. Jacobson. "The Effect of Group Counseling on Educable Mentally Retarded Boys' Self Concepts," *Exceptional Children,* 35 (January 1969), 359–366.

Marshall, Nancy R., and Steven G. Goldstein. "Effects of Three Consultation Procedures on Maternal Understanding of Diagnostic Information," *American Journal of Mental Deficiency,* 74 (January 1970), 479–482.

Matheny, Adam P., and Joel Vernick.

"Parents of the Mentally Retarded Child: Emotionally Overwhelmed or Informationally Deprived," *The Journal of Pediatrics,* 74 (June 1969), 953–959.

McCarty, Katharine A., and Margery M. Chisholm. "Group Education with Mothers of Retarded Children," *Nursing Clinics of North America,* 1 (December 1966), 703–713.

McIntire, Matilda S. "Counseling the Parents of Mentally Retarded Children," *GP,* 32 (November 1965), 124–127.

McKeown, Thomas, and J. R. Teruel. "An Assessment of the Feasibility of Discharge of Patients in Hospitals for the Subnormal," *British Journal of Preventive and Social Medicine,* 24 (May 1970), 116–119.

McKibbin, Elsie H. "An Interdisciplinary Program for Retarded Children and Their Families," *American Journal of Occupational Therapy,* 26 (April 1972), 125–129.

McKinlay, John B. "Some Approaches and Problems in the Study of the Use of Services—An Overview," *Journal of Health and Social Behavior,* 12 (June 1972), 115–152.

Meile, Richard L. "Referral Network: Brokers and Providers," *American Journal of Mental Deficiency,* 78, (January 1974), 404–408.

Mellette, R. Ramsey. "Prevention of Adverse Emotional Attitudes in Families of Chronically Handicapped Children," *Southern Medical Journal,* 57 (March 1964), 267–269.

Menolascino, Frank J. "Emotional Disturbance and Mental Retardation," *American Journal of Mental Deficiency,* 70 (September 1965), 248–256.

———. "Psychiatric Aspects of Mental Retardation in Children Under Eight," *American Journal of Orthopsychiatry,* 35 (October 1965), 852–861.

———. "Parents of the Mentally Retarded: An Operational Approach to Diagnosis and Management," *Journal* of the American Academy of Child Psychology, 7 (October 1968), 589–602.

Mercer, Jane R. "Social System Perspective and Clinical Perspective: Frames of Reference for Understanding Career Patterns of Persons Labelled as Mentally Retarded," Social Problems, 13 (summer 1965), 18–34.

———. "Patterns of Family Crisis Related to Reacceptance of the Retardate," American Journal of Mental Deficiency, 71 (July 1966), 19–32.

Meyerowitz, Joseph H. "Self-Derogations in Young Retardates and Special Class Placement," Child Development, 33 (June 1962), 443–451.

———. "Parental Awareness of Retardation," American Journal of Mental Deficiency, 71 (January 1967), 637–643.

Meyers, C. E., E. G. Sitkei, and C. A. Watts. "Attitudes Toward Special Education and the Handicapped in Two Community Groups," American Journal of Mental Deficiency, 71 (July 1966), 78–84.

Michaels, Joseph, and Helen Schucman. "Observations on the Psychodynamics of Parents of Retarded Children," American Journal of Mental Deficiency, 66 (January 1962), 568–573.

Mickelson, Phyllis. "The Feeble-Minded Parent: A Study of 90 Family Cases," The American Journal of Mental Deficiency, 51 (April 1947), 644–653.

Miller, Lee G. "Toward a Greater Understanding of the Parents of the Mentally Retarded Child," The Journal of Pediatrics, 73 (November 1968), 699–705.

Milligan, G. E. "Counseling Parents of the Mentally Retarded," Mental Retardation Abstracts, 2 (July–September 1965), 259–264.

Minde, Klaus K., J. D. Hackett, D. Killon, and S. Silver. "How They Grow Up: 41 Physically Handicapped Children and Their Families," American Journal of Psychiatry, 128 (June 12, 1972), 1554–1560.

Molony, Helen. "Parental Reactions to Mental Retardation," The Medical Journal of Australia, 1 (April 24, 1971), 914–917.

Mullen, Frances A. "The Teacher Works With the Parent of the Exceptional Child," Education, 80 (February 1960), 329–332.

Murphy, Ann, and Lois Pounds. "Repeat Evaluations of Retarded Children," American Journal of Orthopsychiatry, 42 (January 1972), 103–109.

Murray, Mrs. Max A. "Needs of Parents of Mentally Retarded Children," American Journal of Mental Deficiency, 63 (May 1959), 1078–1088.

Nadal, Robert M. "A Counseling Program for Parents of Severely Retarded Preschool Children," Social Casework, 42 (March 1961), 78–83.

Noble, Mary Anne. "Nursing's Concern for the Mentally Retarded Is Overdue," Nursing Forum, 9 (1970), 192–201.

Oberman, J. William. "The Physician and Parents of the Retarded Child," Children, 10 (May–June 1963), 109–113.

Olshansky, Simon. "Chronic Sorrow: A Response to Having a Mentally Defective Child," Social Casework, 43 (April 1962), 190–193.

———. "Parent Responses to a Mentally Defective Child," Mental Retardation, 4 (August 1966), 21–23.

O'Neill, Jane. "Siblings of the Retarded. II. Individual Counseling," Children, 12 (November–December, 1965), 226–229.

Oppenheimer, Sonya. "Early Identification of Mildly Retarded Children," American Journal of Orthopsychiatry, 35 (August 1966), 845–851.

O'Regan, Gerard W. "Foster Family Care for Children with Mental Retardation," Children Today, 3 (January–February 1974), 20–24, 36.

Parmelee, Arthur H. "The Doctor and the Handicapped Child," *Children*, 9 (September–October 1962), 189–193.

Parsons, Mabel H. "A Home Economist in Service to Families With Mental Retardation," *Children*, 7 (September–October 1960), 185–190.

Peck, John R., and Will Beth Stephens. "A Study of the Relationship Between the Attitudes and Behavior of Parents and That of Their Mentally Defective Child," *American Journal of Mental Deficiency*, 64 (March 1960), 839–844.

––––––. "Marriage of Young Adult Male Retardates," *American Journal of Mental Deficiency*, 69 (May 1965), 818–827.

Peffer, Peter A. "A Physician Discovers a Retarded Child . . . What Should He Do?" *Delaware Medical Journal*, 37 (November 1965), 259–260.

Perrin, Jane C. S., Edna L. Rusch, Janet L. Pray, Gregg F. Wright, and Glen S. Bartlett. "Evaluation of a Ten-Year Experience in a Comprehensive Care Program for Handicapped Children," *Pediatrics*, 50 (November 1972), 793–800.

Pinkerton, Philip. "Parental Acceptance of the Handicapped Child," *Developmental Medicine and Child Neurology*, 12 (April 1970), 207–212.

––––––. "Pitfalls in Interpretive Procedure within the Diagnostic Clinic," *Developmental Medicine and Child Neurology*, 12 (August 1970), 516–517.

Popenoe, Paul. "Eugenic Sterilization in California," *New England Journal of Medicine*, 201 (October 31, 1929), 880–882.

Poznanski, Elva. "Psychiatric Difficulties in Siblings of Handicapped Children," *Clinical Pediatrics*, 8 (April 1969), 232–234.

Prichard, W. I. "Sterilization of the Mentally Deficient in Virginia," *The American Journal of Mental Deficiency*, 53 (April 1949), 542–546.

Raech, Harry. "A Parent Discusses Initial Counseling," *Mental Retardation*, 4 (April 1966), 25–26.

Rajokovich, Marilyn. "Meeting the Needs of Parents With a Mentally Retarded Child," *Journal of Psychiatric Nursing and Mental Health Services*, 7 (September–October 1969), 207–211.

Ramsey, Glenn V. "Review of Group Methods with Parents of the Mentally Retarded," *American Journal of Mental Deficiency*, 71 (March 1967), 857–863.

Rankin, Joseph E. "A Group Therapy Experiment with Mothers of Mentally Deficient Children," *American Journal of Mental Deficiency*, 62 (July 1957), 49–55.

Renton, David. "The Outlook for the Mentally Retarded: (a) Parents' Choice," *Royal Society for Health*, 90 (November–December 1970), 302–305.

Rheingold, Harriet L. "Interpreting Mental Retardation to Parents," *Journal of Consulting Psychology*, 9 (May 1945), 142–148.

Ricci, Carol Stanislavski. "Analysis of Child-Rearing Attitudes of Mothers of Retarded, Emotionally Disturbed, and Normal Children," *American Journal of Mental Deficiency*, 74 (May 1970), 756–761.

Richardson, William P. "Interagency Coordination: A Basic Need in Serving Handicapped Children," *Rehabilitation Literature*, 27 (July 1966), 194–196.

Robbins, Lillian Cukier. "The Accuracy of Parental Recall of Aspects of Child Development and of Child Rearing Practices," *Journal of Abnormal and Social Psychology*, 66 (May–June 1963), 261–270.

Rodriquez, Joseph, and Thomas P. Lombardi. "Legal Implications of Parental Prerogatives for Special Class Placements of the MR," *Mental*

Retardation, 11 (October 1973), 29 –31.

Roos, Philip. "Psychological Counseling With Parents of Retarded Children," *Mental Retardation,* 1 (December 1963), 345–350.

Rosen, Leonard. "Selected Aspects in the Development of the Mother's Understanding of Her Mentally Retarded Child," *American Journal of Mental Deficiency,* 59 (January 1955), 522–528.

Rosen, Shirley R., Samuel Hirschenfang, and Joseph Benton. "Aftermath of Severe Multiple Deprivation in a Young Child: Clinical Implications," *Perceptual and Motor Skills,* 24 (February 1967), 219–226.

Routh, Donald K. "MMPI Responses of Mothers and Fathers as a Function of Mental Retardation of the Child," *American Journal of Mental Deficiency,* 75 (November 1970), 376–377.

Rybak, W. S., and B. Todd. "Together We Learn: Reaching the Parents of the Mentally Retarded," *Clinical Pediatrics,* 7 (December 1968), 705–706.

Ryckman, David B., and Robert A. Henderson. "The Meaning of a Retarded Child for His Parents: A Focus for Counselors," *Mental Retardation,* 3 (August 1965), 4–7.

Sabagh, Georges, Richard K. Eyman, and Donald N. Cogburn. "The Speed of Hospitalization: A Study of a Preadmission Waiting List Cohort in a Hospital for the Retarded," *Social Problems,* 14 (fall 1966), 119–128.

Scheerenberger, R. C. "Generic Services for the Mentally Retarded and Their Families," *Mental Retardation,* 8 (December 1970), 10–16.

Scher, Bernhard. "Help to Parents: An Integral Part of Service to the Retarded Child," *American Journal of Mental Deficiency,* 60 (July 1955), 169–171.

Schild, Sylvia. "Counseling with Parents of Retarded Children Living at Home," *Social Work,* 9 (January 1964), 86–91.

Schonell, Fred J., and B. H. Watts. "A First Survey of the Effects of a Subnormal Child on the Family Unit," *American Journal of Mental Deficiency,* 61 (July 1956), 210–219.

Schonell, Fred J., and Meg Rorke. "A Second Survey of the Effects of a Subnormal Child on the Family Unit," *American Journal of Mental Deficiency,* 64 (March 1960), 862–868.

Schreiber, Meyer, and Mary Feeley. "Siblings of the Retarded: I. A Guided Group Experience," *Children,* 12 (November–December 1965), 221–225.

Schucman, Helen. "Further Observations on the Psychodynamics of Parents of Retarded Children," *Training School Bulletin,* 60 (August 1963), 70–74.

Schulman, Jerome L., and Shiela Stern. "Parents' Estimates of the Intelligence of Retarded Children," *American Journal of Mental Deficiency,* 63 (January 1959), 696–698.

Shellhaas, Max D., and Kazuo Nihira. "Factor Analysis of Reasons Retardates Are Referred to an Institution," *American Journal of Mental Deficiency,* 74 (September 1969), 171–179.

Shelton, James T. "Treatment of the Mentally Retarded: The Role of the Local Physician," *California Medicine,* 101 (July 1964), 19–22.

Siegel, Bess, Kathleen Sheridan, and Edward P. Sheridan. "Group Psychotherapy: Its Effects on Mothers Who Rate Social Performance of Retardates," *American Journal of Psychiatry,* 127 (March 1971), 1215–1217.

Silverstein, A. B., and Harvey F. Dingman. "General Response Tendencies and Parental Attitudes in the Mothers of Mentally Retarded Children," *Psychological Reports,* 16 (June 1965), 1141–1144.

Skelton, Mora. "Areas of Parental Concern about Retarded Children," *Mental Retardation,* 10 (February 1972), 38–41.

Slobody, Lawrence, Margaret J. Gianinni, H. R. Kelman, John B. Scanlon, and H. Michal-Smith. "An Interdisciplinary Personnel Training Program in a Specialized Clinic for Retarded Children," *American Journal of Mental Deficiency*, 62 (March 1958), 866–869.

Smith, Ira A., Gerald Rubin, Concetta M. DiLeonardo, and Karen Griswold. "A Parental Involvement Program for Institutionalized Retarded Children in Need of Behavior Training," *Training School Bulletin*, 69 (November 1972), 115–120.

Snodgrass, Joel S. "Counseling Parents of the Mentally Retarded," *Mental Retardation Abstracts*, 2 (July–September 1965), 265–270.

Solnit, Albert J. and Mary H. Stark. "Mourning and the Birth of a Defective Child," *Psychoanalytic Study of the Child*, 16 (1961), 523–537.

Solomons, Gerald. "What Do You Tell the Parents of a Retarded Child?," *Clinical Pediatrics*, 4 (April 1965), 227–232.

Stafford, Richard L., and Roger J. Meyer. "Diagnosis and Counseling for the Mentally Retarded Child," *Clinical Pediatrics*, 7 (March 1968), 153–155.

Stayton, Samuel E., Carolyn A. Sitkowski, Donelda J. Stayton, and Stephen D. Weiss. "The Influence of Home Experience Upon the Retardate's Social Behavior in the Institution," *American Journal of Mental Deficiency*, 72 (May 1968), 866–870.

Stephens, Wyatt E. "Interpreting Mental Retardation to Parents in a Multi-Discipline Diagnostic Clinic," *Mental Retardation*, 7 (December 1969), 57–59.

Sternlicht, Manny. "Parent Counseling in an Experimental Rehabilitation Center," *Journal of Rehabilitation*, 35 (September–October 1969), 15–16.

Stevenson, Karl. "The Reactions of Parents to Their Retarded Children," *North Carolina Medical Journal*, 29 (April 1968), 150–160.

Stone, Marguerite. "Parental Attitudes to Retardation," *American Journal of Mental Deficiency*, 53 (October 1948), 363–372.

Stone, Nellie D. "Family Factors in Willingness to Place the Mongoloid Child," *American Journal of Mental Deficiency*, 72 (July 1967), 16–20.

Stone, Nellie D., and Joseph J. Parnicky. "Factors in Child Placement: Parental Response to Congenital Defect," *Social Work*, 11 (April 1966), 35–43.

Strazzulla, Millicent. "Nursery School Training for Retarded Children," *American Journal of Mental Deficiency*, 61 (July 1956), 141–151.

Stubblefield, Harold W. "The Ministry and Mental Retardation," *Journal of Religion and Health*, 3 (January 1964), 136–147.

———. "Religion, Parents, and Mental Retardation," *Mental Retardation*, 3 (August 1965), 8–11.

Talkington, Larry, and Barbara Simon. "A Comparison of Broken Home and Stable Home Retardates on Selected Variables," *Training School Bulletin*, 67 (August 1970), 131–136.

Tallman, Irving. "Spousal Role Differentiation and the Socialization of Severely Retarded Children," *Journal of Marriage and the Family*, 27 (February 1965), 37–42.

Taylor, Fred M. "Attitudes Toward Mentally Retarded Children," *Postgraduate Medicine*, 36 (July 1964), 62–66.

Taylor, Fred M., and Frank A. Borreca. "On Mentally Retarded Children: A Philosophy of Concern," *Linacre Quarterly*, 29 (May 1962), 53–65.

Terdal, Leif, and Joan Buell. "Parent Education in Managing Retarded Children with Behavior Deficits and Inappropriate Behaviors," *Mental Retardation*, 7 (June 1969), 10–13.

Thomas, Elizabeth C., and Kaoru Yamamoto. "School-Related Perceptions in Handicapped Children," *The Journal of Psychology*, 77 (January 1971), 101–117.

Thurston, John R. "A Procedure for Evaluating Parental Attitudes Toward the Handicapped," *American Journal of Mental Deficiency*, 64 (July 1959), 148–155.

———. "Counseling the Parents of the Severely Handicapped," *Exceptional Children*, 26 (March 1960), 351–354.

———. "Attitudes and Emotional Reactions of Parents of Institutionalized Cerebral Palsied, Retarded Patients," *American Journal of Mental Deficiency*, 65 (September 1960), 227–235.

Tips, Robert L., and Henry T. Lynch. "The Impact of Genetic Counseling Upon the Family Milieu," *JAMA*, 184 (April 20, 1962), 183–186.

Tisza, Veronica B. "Management of the Parents of the Chronically Ill Child," *American Journal of Orthopsychiatry*, 32 (1962), 53–59.

Turner, Edward T. "Attitudes of Parents of Deficient Children Toward Their Child's Sexual Behavior," *The Journal of School Health*, 40 (December 1970), 548–550.

Voysey, Margaret. "Impression Management by Parents with Disabled Children," *Journal of Health and Social Behavior*, 13 (March 1972), 80–89.

Wahler, Robert G., Gary H. Winkel, Robert F. Peterson, and Delmont C. Morrison. "Mothers as Behavior Therapists for Their Own Children," *Behavior Research and Therapy*, 3 (September 1965), 113–134.

Warner, Frank, Thomas Golden, and Maureen Henteleff. "Health Insurance: A Dilemma for Parents of the Mentally Retarded," *Exceptional Children*, 39 (September 1972), 57–58.

Waskowitz, Charlotte H. "The Parents of Retarded Children Speak for Themselves," *Journal of Pediatrics*, 54 (March 1959), 319–329.

Watts, Evadean M. "Family Therapy:

Its Use in Mental Retardation," *Mental Retardation*, 7 (October 1969), 41–44.

Weber, Beth. "A Parent of a Retarded Child Gives Her Idea of Services Needed," *Child Welfare*, 53 (February 1974), 98–101.

Weinrott, Mark R. "A Training Program in Behavior Modification for Siblings of the Retarded," *American Journal of Orthopsychiatry*, 44 (April 1974), 362–375.

Wenar, Charles, and Jane B. Coulter. "A Reliability Study of Developmental Histories," *Child Development*, 33 (June 1962), 453–462.

Werner, Emmy E., Marjorie P. Honzik, and Ruth S. Smith. "Prediction of Intelligence and Achievement at Ten Years from Twenty Months Pediatric and Psychological Examinations," *Child Development*, 39 (December 1968), 1063–1075.

Wildman, Peggy Riggs. "A Parent Education Program for Parents of Mentally Retarded Children," *Mental Retardation*, 3 (December 1965), 17–19.

Willie, Blanche M. "The Role of the Social Worker," *American Journal of Mental Deficiency*, 66 (1961), 464–471.

Wolfensberger, Wolf. "Embarrassment in the Diagnostic Process," *Mental Retardation*, 3 (June 1965), 29–31.

Wolfensberger, Wolf. "The Principle of Normalization and Its Implications for Psychiatric Services," *American Journal of Psychiatry*, 127 (September 1970), 291–297.

Wolking, William D., George H. Dunteman, and John P. Bailey. "Multivariate Analysis of Parents' MMPIs Based on the Psychiatric Diagnoses of Their Children," *Journal of Consulting Psychology*, 31 (November–December 1967), 521–524.

Woodward, Katherine F., Norma Jaffee, and Dorothy Brown. "Psychiatric Program for Very Young Retarded Children," *American Journal of Diseases of Children*, 108 (September 1964), 221–229.

Worchel, Tillie L., and Philip Worchel. "The Parental Concept of the Mentally Retarded Child," *American Journal of Mental Deficiency*, 65 (May 1961), 782–788.

Yarrow, Leon J. "Maternal Deprivation: Toward an Empirical and Conceptual Re-evaluation," *Psychological Bulletin*, 58 (November 1961), 459–490.

Yates, Mary L., and Ruth Lederer. "Small, Short-Term Group Meetings with Parents of Children with Mongolism," *American Journal of Mental Deficiency*, 65 (January 1961), 467–472.

Zigler, Edward, David Balla, and Earl C. Butterfield. "A Longitudinal Investigation of the Relationship Between Preinstitutional Social Deprivation and Social Motivation in Institutionalized Retardates," *Journal of Personality and Social Psychology*, 10 (December 1968), 437–445.

Zook, Linn, and Charles Unkovic. "Areas of Concern for the Counselor in a Diagnostic Clinic for Mentally Retarded Children," *Mental Retardation*, 6 (June 1968), 19–24.

Zuckerberg, Harvey D., and Gordon R. Snow. "What Do Parents Expect from the Physician?" *Pediatric Clinics of North America*, 15 (November 1968), 861–870.

Zuk, G. H. "Autistic Distortions in Parents of Retarded Children," *Journal of Consulting Psychology*, 23 (March–April 1959), 171–176.

——. "The Religious Factor and the Role of Guilt in Parental Acceptance of the Retarded Child," *American Journal of Mental Deficiency*, 64 (July 1959), 139–147.

——. "The Cultural Dilemma and Spiritual Crisis of the Family With a Handicapped Child," *Exceptional Children*, 28 (April 1962), 405–408.

Zuk, G. H., Ralph L. Miller, John B. Bartman, and Frederick Kling. "Maternal Acceptance of Retarded Children: A Questionnaire Study of Attitudes and Religious Background," *Child Development*, 32 (September 1961), 525–540.

Index